SURVIVORS

1945

Group

Meridian Books

Published 1988 by Meridian Books for the Birmingham Jewish History Research Group.

British Library Cataloguing in Publication Data

Josephs, Zoë
    Survivors : Jewish Refugees in Birmingham
    1933-1945.
    1. West Midlands (Metropolitan county).
    Birmingham. Jewish refugees, 1933-1945
    I. Title
    942.4'96'004924

    ISBN 1-869922-02-6

Typeset from AppleWorks discs by Minstrel, Dane Road, Sale, Cheshire.

Printed in Great Britain by A. Wheaton & Co. Ltd., Exeter.

Meridian Books, 40 Hadzor Road, Oldbury, Warley, West Midlands B68 9LA.

Contents

Foreword

by
David Cope-Thompson
Chairman
Central British Fund for World Jewish Relief

My Council are very glad to be associated with this remarkable book *Survivors*. We believe that this is a unique record of this important period. It illustrates the dilemma of the refugees of the Nazi era, the reaction of the Jewish and the general community, and the problems faced not only by those uprooted but also by their hosts.

Zoé Josephs' account presents a microcosm of this period in the United Kingdom. On going through our archives which are still in existence, we see the Central British Fund (with occasional name changes) as instrumental in pleas to various deprtments of HM Government for permission to give asylum to fleeing refugees from the Spring of 1933 onwards. The Registration Cards (and, in some instances, the case histories) of those who applied, with dates of arrival and other details, are part of CBF's archival material. Although we have copies of 4/500,000 registration slips, many applicants, unhappily, were not able to come to the United Kingdom for a variety of reasons, the principal one being, of course, the inability to escape the ever increasing anti-Jewish laws passed by the Nazi government. Nevertheless, after the infamous Kristallnacht, November 9/10 1938 permission was sought and received from HM Government to bring over 10,000 unaccompanied children. Nine hundred of these youngsters came to the Birmingham area. Over 9,000 came to the United Kingdom up to the outbreak of World War II, not all Jewish but it is suggested that over 90% were Jewish. During the pre-war period, in addition to the children, approximately 70,000 persons found refuge in the United Kingdom.

The participation of Jewish helpers in the non-sectarian Refugee Children's Movement, chaired by Lord Gorrel, was outstanding. Lord Gorrel, in his autobiography *One Man ... Many Parts*, writes of the passing of a special Act of Parliament which made him legal guardian of all these children.

He also writes "The Committee, and in particular Mrs Neville Blond and Mrs Hahn-Warburg, on whom fell the brunt of the labour, and Mrs Hardisty, our really splendid general secretary, can at last look back upon those years as ones in which thousands of young lives were rescued from the certainties of degradation and death. That was our only, our real, reward"*.

The CBF Council not only appreciates the historic value of this book but also sees it as recognition of a remarkable lady - Ruth Wolf MBE (neé Simmons). From the very beginning of this rescue operation Ruth Wolf has competently and compassionately carried on her work for Jewish refugees in the Midlands. CBF World Jewish Relief pays tribute to her, and is infinitely indebted to her outstanding efforts.

David Cope-Thompson
Chairman
CBF World Jewish Relief
February 1988

* *One Man ... Many Parts*, Ronald Gorrel Barnes, Lord Gorrel, Odhams Press 1956, p304.

Preface

A group of people who had emigrated from Central Europe as a result of Nazi persecution, and had settled in Birmingham, decided in March 1984, that after some fifty years, it was time to tell the story of their experiences. Eighty-nine volunteers came forward, several of whom have unfortunately not lived to see the completion of the project. Of the eighty-nine, seventeen were from Berlin, forty-two from the provincial towns of Germany (including six from East Prussia), fifteen from Austria, six from Czechoslovakia, three from Poland, five from Hungary and one from Galicia. A few of those questioned had been born in Poland or Russia but had moved westwards at a very early age and were counted among the countries where they had spent most of their lives before emigration to Britain.

Some of the evidence is documentary, but the majority is preserved in taped recordings, much of it the work of Doreen and Peter Price of the West Midlands Oral History Group in association with the Local History Department of the Birmingham Museum and Art Gallery. The tape recordings will be deposited in the Birmingham Sound Archives at the Museum. Besides the former refugees, some local people contributed to the narrative from their own viewpoint.

The Birmingham Jewish History Research Group undertook to co-ordinate the material, and produce from it *Survivors*, this being the third volume of *Birmingham Jewry*. As before we must thank Bill Williams of Manchester and I.A. Shapiro of the Shakespeare Institute of the University of Birmingham for their invaluable help.

Professor John Grenville, Professor of Modern History at the University of Birmingham and Elizabeth Lesser provided the historical introduction to the chapter on 'The Background'. R.E. Levy wrote the chapters on 'Bunce Court School' and 'The Refugees and the Birmingham Jewish Community': he was also responsible for the index. Sonja Shindler wrote the chapter on 'Restitution and Compensation'. Elli Faerber contributed the section on Elpis Lodge in 'The Hostels', and Herta Linden helped with the 'Conclusion'. The remaining chapters were written by Zoë Josephs.

We thank our typists Dorothy Gillman, Miriam Clark, Audrey Hawkins, Geraldine Thompson, Carol Ash and Gladys Levy for their patience. Lilian Bishop of the Rushgrove Agency, London NW7 undertook the word processing. Elli Faerber not only helped with the typing but stepped in at the last moment to complete some extra word processing. The photographs were processed by the Manchester Jewish Museum, the Dead-Right Design Co. (c/o Manchester Jewish Museum), Stanley Busby, Adrienne Bloom and the Local History Department of the Birmingham City Museum. We thank the Keeper of the Local History Department, Stephen Price for his kind help. The illustrations on pages 5, 19, 21, 31, 40, 56 and 208 are reproduced by kind permission of the Wiener Library, London. The photograph of Magda Bloom on page 180 was taken by Simon Livingstone Studios.

Survivors is first and foremost an example of team-work. It is impossible to thank all the people involved individually, but mention must be made of the following: Walter Stranz, Professor E.S. Kirby and Mrs Ruth Kirby, Helen Libman, Minnie Lesser, Eva Mitchell and Joan Stiebel of the Central British Fund, Harry Levine for his splendid scrapbook, Ernest Wolf, Harry Josephs, the late Leonard Corfan and the late David Goodkin.

My personal thanks must also go to Elizabeth Lesser, who has been at hand at all times to give friendly advice and assistance from the conception of the Birmingham Jewry series now thirteen years ago. I should also like to put on record my gratitude to Patrick Baird and his staff in the Local Studies Department of the Central Library for their unfailing courtesy and help in making available the necessary records.

Leafing through *Survivors*, the initials CBF seem to shine out through this dark period we have attempted to describe. We thank the council of the Central British Fund for World Jewish Relief for its generosity in sponsoring the publication of our book as a tribute to Ruth Simmons. Finally we thank Ruth herself, for tirelessly delving into her vast collection of documents and most of all for her wisdom, born of such long experience in this great humanitarian undertaking.

We apologise for the poor quality of some of the photographs, but would remind our readers that many are taken from snapshots over forty years old, all the more poignant in that they are, for their owners, the sole reminders of happier days.

Zoë Josephs
February 1988

Survivors is the third volume in the series *Birmingham Jewry*. Volume I (*Birmingham Jewry: 1749-1914*) and Volume II (*Birmingham Jewry: More Aspects 1740-1930*) were published by
The Birmingham Jewish History Research Group
c/o 10 Lenwade Road, Oldbury, Warley, West Midlands B68 9JU.

1

Number Two, Duchess Road

During the summer of 1907, Bernard Simmons, a Birmingham manufacturing jeweller, set out on a Continental walking tour with a friend, a young man from Frankfurt-on-Main, who had been living in Birmingham for some time. This friend eventually returned to his native land and, nearly forty years later, perished in Auschwitz.

Bernard Simmons' family had lived in England for at least three generations; his grandfather, who was apprenticed to a japanner in London in 1798, had served at Trafalgar. Thereafter, from 1810, for nearly fifty years, he was Rabbi at Penzance.

Bernard's friend introduced him to his family, and while in Frankfurt, he met Johanna Selig, whom he subsequently married. Her father had recently died, but her mother continued to run the family business, a trousseau shop. Hanna (Johanna) arrived in England with immense quantities of monogrammed and embroidered table and bed linen, some of it still in use seventy years later.

Hanna and Bernard Simmons' married life at 2 Duchess Road, Edgbaston, with their three children, was happy and uneventful. Hanna's original German nationality may well have presented problems during the First World War, but her children heard nothing of this. Meanwhile the Simmons' family business gradually changed to a manufactory of metal small-wares.

Bernard was a wiry, athletic person, an oarsman, boxer, rider, gymnast and swimmer. He was still swimming across the Edgbaston Reservoir in his seventies, breaking the ice when necessary, and with satisfaction. He cycled from his home to his factory in Vyse Street in the jewellery quarter twice daily and back, until he was eighty-six.

Over the years, most of Hanna's relatives had married and left Germany, some for America. Only her mother had remained and Hanna visited her at least once a year until she died in 1932. Ruth, Hanna's eldest child, retained a vivid impression of her mother's final return. She was profoundly shaken. "I shall never return to Germany", she vowed, "terrible things are happening there. I am determined to devote the rest of my life to getting my family, my friends and everyone I can out of that country". And that is precisely what she did.

She confided her apprehensions to Dr Abraham Cohen, Chief Minister of Singers Hill Synagogue, a scholar and a formidable personality. At first neither he, nor anyone else, took her seriously. But very soon life at 2 Duchess Road began to change. The spare rooms in the big Victorian house now seemed providential. Often they were occupied by people staying sometimes a night or two, sometimes longer. Some were on their way to the United States, South America, South Africa or Australia, anywhere where they could start a new life. But meanwhile, they had to wait in Duchess Road until their quota position enabled them to obtain a visa. After a few months, events occurred that induced Dr Cohen to acknowledge Hanna's percipience. In March 1933, he wrote to the *Birmingham Post*: "A bloodless pogrom is taking place in Germany. Doctors may not be on the staff of a hospital, students are driven from the universities, judges and lawyers may not appear in the courts, musicians and actors are barred from concert halls and theatres, shopkeepers may not open their stores. The Jews must starve or commit suicide or emigrate." [1]

The horror of this sudden attack is amply borne out by many surviving refugees still living in Birmingham. But paradoxically those who were most shaken often fared best. At this stage the official Nazi policy was to encourage Jewish emigration. The problem for would-be emigrants was to find a country that would accept them. Those fortunate enough to find a refuge in those early days were often allowed to take their belongings, including machinery and even capital, with them. Experienced business people, craftsmen and technicians, were able to settle without too much disruption in a strange land.

Hanna and Bernard Simmons, 1938.

The Simmons children, meanwhile, were enjoying the excitement of so many visitors, charming and interesting people, who enlivened and enriched their circle of friends. The younger visitors were quickly integrated into the English way of life, joining Hanna's children in cycling, youth hostelling, and enjoying themselves at theatres, films and dances. But this agreeable period did not last long. Soon, every corner of the old house was filled with people, some sleeping on camp beds and some on sofas. Each week, Hanna fried vast quantities of fish for the traditional Friday night Sabbath meal, at which up to twenty guests regularly sat around the table. Many were distressed and fearful for relatives still in Germany, where the plight of the young men was especially serious, for at any moment they were liable to be herded into labour camps and in most cases, although no visas were required until 1938, the British Government insisted on a guarantee of one hundred pounds before they could enter the country. This depended on the immigration officers' discretion.

A young English girl, who was privileged to hand round tea at week-end gatherings, remembered the large and crowded sitting room of 2 Duchess Road. "Mr Simmons would be deep in his old brown corduroy armchair, puffing away at his pipe, behind a newspaper. Mrs Simmons was always to be found in a corner of the sofa, knitting socks or tackling a pile of family darning. One after another the guests would come up to sit beside her, seeking advice on accommodation, work permits, guarantees, travel visas; above all, help in their anguish for families left in danger. Yet, laughter would keep breaking in, more often than not because of language difficulties. The very respectable wife of a professional gentleman, who had found work at a factory bench, generously larded her conversation with "bloody". Another, who had recently left London, talked of her life in the "WC". And silence fell suddenly on a tea-party when a young man described the harbour of his home town on the Baltic Sea as "full of buggers". Only later it transpired that the German word for "dredger" was "bagger", mispronounced "bugger"

Bernard throughout was invaluable in finding the refugees work, or machinery for starting up factories, but he had no German and was naturally quiet and reserved. Hanna was eager and outgoing, possessed of an enviable ability to enjoy the moment. Her daughter recalled a New Year's Eve party only a few weeks before her death. "Mother was singing and laughing in the centre of a group of young men. They were *schunkeling*" (the boisterous German equivalent of Auld Lang Syne). She loved the company of young people, and would join their theatre parties, climbing to the gallery and applauding enthusiastically, despite the gruelling stairs and the hard benches. Yet she possessed immense reserves of understanding and practical compassion. Hanna and Bernard were a devoted and complementary couple, bound together in their dedication to the task of rescue, and in providing a still centre where the refugees could meet and be certain of sympathy. Hanna realised the dreadful urgency of her efforts, which she could not have sustained without the active support and encouragement of her husband.

Meanwhile Hitler proceeded with his plans. It seems unthinkable that nothing could stop him. An undergraduate remembered going home from University one evening in March 1936 on the Bristol Road tram. "On the opposite bench a man opened his *Birmingham Mail*. I could read the headlines, 'Hitler marches into the Ruhr'. Surely this meant war! I was terribly scared, almost listening for air-raid sirens. But the faces around me betrayed only indifference and nothing happened."

3

10% of takings of Cinemas and other places of entertainment tonight goes to Baldwin's Fund for Jewish Refugees.

We CANNOT ask you to -

BOYCOTT THIS

SHOW! AS THE LAW DOES NOT PERMIT

BUT WE CAN AND DO ASK -

WHY SUPPORT A FUND TO GIVE RELIEF TO ALIENS WHEN POVERTY AND UNEMPLOYMENT ARE RIFE IN BRITAIN? .   .   .   .

We have been asked in the past four years to support Abyssinians, Basques, Chinese, Czechs, Austrians, Spaniards, and now Jews.

MOSLEY SAYS -

NOT A PENNY FOR ALIENS WHILE BRITONS STARVE. .

Our own MINERS, TEXTILE WORKERS, AGRICULTURAL WORKERS & OTHERS are desparately in need of RESCUE from UNEMPLOYMENT & SEMI-STARVATION

CHARITY BEGINS AT HOME

JOIN BRITISH UNION, AND PUT BRITAIN FIRST

Apply to :
BRITISH UNION 16, Great Smith St., Westminster, S.W.1

Published by F Hill 16, Great Smith Street, Westminster, S.W.1.
Printed by A. E. Baker & Co. (Printers) Ltd. T.U. N.W.6.   1,000

Notice posted by the British Union of Fascists, 1937.

The ugly face of Fascism was now showing itself, albeit hesitantly, in the Birmingham Bull Ring, where Sir Oswald Mosley and his Blackshirts were holding meetings. "No expense spared, chaps, plenty to drink and a thoroughly good time to be had by all."[2] Fortunately, even with these blandishments, Birmingham folk remained largely indifferent.

Intermittent warfare was however being waged in the correspondence columns of the *Birmingham Post* throughout the nineteen thirties, in an endless controversy over the Nazi menace. Many people thought the Germans were misunderstood. "If only the Hitler Jugend (Youth Movement) could visit England we would realise what splendid young men they really are—the finest, most virile stock of the Continent."[3] "The women have given up smoking and few use lipstick and paint ... a very wholesome thing."[4] The Link, a new Anglo-German Society, was formed to promote Anglo-German friendship. Many people argued in Hitler's favour that he would attack Communism and should be allowed to do so. Others observed that it was preferable to make friends with the Germans rather than push them into the arms of another highly industrialised nation, the Japanese. The Jewish problem was exaggerated and would pass. In any case, it was only the Jews in the Communist party who were to be execrated. Respectable Jews could go about their business in complete security.[5] All these claims were forcefully demolished by Dr Cohen, who knew Hitler's book *Mein Kampf* and could quote from it with devastating effect.

Hanna redoubled her efforts to open the eyes of an often reluctant Community. "The fate of every individual was important to her. No time, no effort, no sacrifice was spared if there were a possibility of offering help. How happy she was when she saved someone from Hitler's clutches, and how sad when success evaded her."[6]

Many people were generous with money, but hospitality was a different matter. Some of the more anglicised members of the Jewish Community resented the invasion, fearing it might jeopardise their own hard-won acceptance.

The *Birmingham Jewish Recorder*, founded in 1936, scarcely mentioned the refugees until October 1938, when Dr Cohen issued the first of many pleas in an editorial message. "A boy of sixteen has been accepted as a pupil by a local technical school. But he is still in Vienna and unable to leave because there is no home for him." In December 1938, "At least take them out of the atmosphere of despair, which has driven thousands to suicide", and on the eve of war in August 1939, "If they cannot offer hospitality, they must be heartless, if they refuse to contribute and enable these children to be cared for in a hostel."

Meanwhile in the British press, fears were expressed that the refugees would "take all the jobs". The stringent application of the work permits, and the opportunities that German-Jewish expertise were opening up, were equally ignored. Oscar Deutsch, the Birmingham cinema-chain pioneer, at the height of building up his Odeon Cinema empire in 1937, had to explain that he was only training the newcomers on his staff to work in another country.[7] Some pointed to the apparent prosperity of the German ladies in their heavy fur coats, (for the older ladies, Persian lamb was almost a uniform) and to their handsome, if ponderous, furniture. Few realised this often represented their capital, the only possession they were then allowed

Ruth Simmons, 1967.

to take out of the country, and even this was to continue only for a little longer. Even Hanna herself did not escape criticism. "She will kill Bernard with her refugees" pronounced one patrician lady. Ironically it was Hanna who was shortly to succumb to a fatal virus infection, while Bernard lived on for another sixteen years.

In the autumn of 1938, Ruth Simmons went to Paris to pursue what was to have been a career in dress design. In November, a seventeen-year-old Jewish youth, Herschel Grynspan, who was living in Paris, heard that his parents, who were of Polish origin, had been deported from their home in Germany across the eastern frontier. Crazed with anxiety, he shot and killed one of the secretaries of the German Embassy, Ernst von Rath. This immediately set in train the Kristallnacht (the Night of Broken Glass) so-called from the thousands of plate-glass shop windows smashed by Nazis and their followers. Six hundred synagogues in Germany were set on fire and 30,000 Jews flung into concentration camps.

Little of this penetrated Ruth's couture house in Faubourg St. Honoré, but at a synagogue in Paris she met people even more desperate than those she had left behind in Duchess Road. They had escaped across the frontier with nothing but their lives. Several times she was implored to cross the German frontier with her British passport and retrieve money or jewellery. "I felt like a sponge sucking up all the miseries of Europe", she recalled, and returned home, more determined than ever to identify herself with her mother's cause.

The annexation of Austria, and the farce of Munich, had already taken place. Czechoslovakia was to be swallowed up in the spring of 1939. The urgency of the situation resulted in a clamour for exit permits. People who had previously refused to apply, queued for days at legations and consulates for entry visas to any country that was willing to take them.

The Children's Transports were now set in motion, resulting in the resettlement of 10,000 unaccompanied youngsters. Ruth was later to become Regional Secretary of the Refugee Children's Movement. Hundreds of women from all walks of life had to be found a means of earning a livelihood. Little but nursing or domestic work was open to them. Some fortunate girls were welcomed into British homes where they were treated as daughters, others were exploited for a niggardly wage of 12s. 6d. (63p) per week. "How can I ever forget the chill of scrubbing those long tiled halls?" recalled one of these maids, "or the loneliness of days spent by myself in those big, dark houses. I just longed for my Sunday off when I could go to Duchess Road."

During that winter, it became clear that 2 Duchess Road could no longer accommodate the numbers that then sought comfort. The Communal Hall of Singers Hill Synagogue (now the Joseph Cohen Hall) was offered by the Community and a Birmingham Jewish Refugee Club was founded in May 1939. But 2 Duchess Road remained a haven for the newcomers. When early the following year, Hanna died, Ruth took up the challenge. "I fried the fish the following Friday", she said, "and we continued without a break."

Going through her mother's papers, Ruth was horrified by what even she had not realised. So many people who knew or claimed to know Hanna's family had deluged her with appeals for help. She could refuse no one.

"I must have gone to school with your mother", became a family catch-phrase. The emotional strain of receiving these pleas in such impossible numbers must have been almost insupportable. But for one of such generosity of spirit, put in that situation, she had no choice. "She was our mother", said one refugee simply. "She was good at twisting arms", Ruth recalled. "I like to think I have inherited something of that myself."

Nothing could have been more true. Ruth continued her mother's task, long after the war and the successful settlement of the majority of the refugees who had sought sanctuary in this country.

References

1. *Birmingham Post* 28 March 1933
2. *Jewish Chronicle* 4 June 1933
3. *Birmingham Post* 6 October 1937
4. ibid. 18 September 1933
5. ibid. 5 April 1933
6. From the memorial service on the first anniversary of Hanna Simmons' death.
7. *Jewish Chronicle* 23 April 1937

2
The Background

Antisemitism had long been endemic in Europe, but reached a virulence in Germany after the First World War not seen in any country that prided itself on its culture. The Jews became convenient scapegoats, blamed for the trauma of losing the 1914-1918 war, for the harsh peace treaty and penal reparations, for the hyper-inflation of the early 1920s, even for the 1929 Wall Street crash and large scale unemployment.

Hitler built much of his following on anti-semitism and anti-Communism during the decade previous to his becoming Chancellor on 30 January 1933. The burning down of the Reichstag (Parliament) building the following month, promptly blamed by the Nazis on the Communists, was utilised by Hitler to secure the necessary votes from a terrorised Reichstag to give him dictatorial powers under the Enabling Law.

Public and private institutions were brought under Nazi control or closed down; those who openly opposed the new regime lost their jobs, hundreds were arrested and beaten up by the Nazis. The campaign against the Jews began with the national boycott of Jewish businesses on 1 April 1933. The law of the 7 April ousted "non-Aryans" from the Civil Service (with some exceptions as a result of President Hindenburg's intervention), and steadily the professions were "purified"[1]. These measures not only affected the majority of Jews but also Christians who had in their families one Jewish grandparent. Less than two years after Hindenburg's death in 1934 the concessions made to him were struck out.

Many in the Jewish community established for centuries in Germany and apparently integrated thoroughly into society (for many families their Judaism had become a minor part of their lives), believed Hitler's policies could not be other than temporary. Others like the Reform Rabbi of Berlin, and President of the Council of German Jews, the renowned Leo Baeck, recognised that an era of integration and understanding had come to an end. In 1933 began the exodus of Jews from Nazi Germany; they were the far sighted. It was easier for the better-off, because host countries, still struggling through the depression years, would normally only admit those with capital or with a definite position to go to, and the German Government had not yet instituted measures against emigrants which took away practically all they possessed. Zionism which had up to 1933 only enjoyed minority support now attracted many, especially the younger generation, to seek a new beginning in Palestine. British restrictions soon stemmed the inflow for fear of Arab reactions. The Nuremberg Laws (September 1935) forbade marriage or any form of sexual relationship between Jews and Aryans; the Citizen Law reduced Jews to the status of second-class citizens. Some Jews over-optimistic, thought that this "settled" their status; other recognised Nazi intentions as akin to an ever-tightening screw. More and more Jews became virtually unemployable; the numbers of would-be emigrants grew, but now host countries were tightening their immigration controls, fearing a flood of impoverished Jews, as most of the assets of the emigrants were confiscated by the Nazis.

The Olympic Games of 1936 saw a temporary and deceiving halt to open persecution. The Games over, the screw was tightened again; Jews had to sell their businesses to Aryans.

The Anschluss of March 1938 when Austria was taken over by Germany, created a huge wave of refugees stripped of almost everything they possessed. In the following September, when the Munich Agreement of 30 September 1938 handed a sizeable part of Czechoslovakia to Germany, a further Jewish community was in danger: for the Jews in Germany all illusions were finally shattered by the Government-inspired pogrom of 9/10 November (the Kristallnacht) when the synagogues were burnt and thousands of Jewish men were hounded into concentration camps. This was the real turning point. Now nearly all the remaining Jews in Germany wished to get out fearing for their lives. The Jewish organisations in Germany revealed a remarkable courage, and inspired self-help and efficient organisation. Efforts to save first and foremost the young were redoubled at the very time when other countries were closing their doors to Jewish immigrants. By a great effort of co-ordination from abroad and with Jewish organisations in Germany, friendly public opinion was aroused to pressurise governments to respond with more generosity, efforts particularly successful in Britain. Christians and Jews collaborated to meet the moral challenge between November 1938 and the outbreak of war in September 1939.

With the declaration of hostilities the borders of all the belligerents closed. Small numbers were still able to emigrate through neutral countries, but the bulk of the Jewish population in continental Europe fell into the grasp of conquering German armies[2].

From the outset Hitler had determined to purge first Germany, and then the rest of Europe, of its Jewish population. The pace and intensity of the Nazi persecution varied as did individual experiences. The build-up of pressure however resulted in a steady stream of emigration even before November 1938.

In the following sections of this chapter the experiences of people from various regions are compared.

BERLIN

According to the people interviewed, Berlin, the capital, and Hamburg, the main port with its numerous international connections, stood rather apart from the rest of Germany. The general population tended to be left wing in politics and sceptical about the Nazi ideology. The sophisticated revue entertainment, for which Berlin was famous, lent itself superbly to the satirical treatment of Nazi attitudes. Both cities contained large Jewish communities, which before 1933 had been powerful in business, academic and artistic circles.

Many Berliners ignored the "Boycott Day" of 1 April 1933 and took no notice of the uniformed SA men stationed outside Jewish stores to warn off would-be shoppers.

As late as 1936, at the time of the Olympic Games, Kurt Rose came home to Berlin on holiday from his English school. He was riding on a tram with a blonde friend from England when somebody called out to her, "What are you doing with that Jew-boy?" "I'm one hundred per cent Jewish and proud of it", she retorted. Everybody on the tram clapped.

But the atmosphere was soon to change. Heinz Shire also returned from his school in England in 1937 and 1938. "We felt enclosed, we couldn't open our mouths and people seemed to follow us." He narrowly escaped being put in a concentration camp. People began moving from larger houses into smaller ones. Many took to sharing their houses or flats with relatives or friends, partly because of income reduced by restrictions in business or professions, but often for the comfort of being together in adversity and so feeling more secure. During the war the Nazis were thus helped to herd the Jews together in certain houses so facilitating "the final solution".

Typical of many Berliners was the family of Henry Warner. They had originated in Breslau, where his father was area manager of the Deutsche Bank. After leaving school, Henry Warner was apprenticed to a bank in Berlin. "We were very, very German. We went to Synagogue occasionally, and held a *Seder* at Passover (ceremonial meal celebrating the departure from Egypt), but not much else. We were sure the highly civilised German people would not put up with Hitler for long, and when we woke up—it was too late." German Jews were reluctant to abandon their German rights, but the attempt to be both Jewish and German came to an abrupt end with the Kristallnacht in November 1938. During the years 1933-1938 Jewish scholars and students were driven from the universities, children from the schools, lawyers, doctors and dentists from their practices.

For some the horror of the first impact was something from which they never recovered. Dr Hilde Eisner was never able to get over the shock of finding her surgery sealed against her. Ruth Price, though only nine years old, remembered the windows of Berlin shops being smashed and smeared with "*Jude*" and the Star of David at the time of the Kristallnacht. Looting went unpunished. The more percipient had already left the country while emigration was still relatively easy. "See you on the Thames", was a regular form of farewell.

Gerhard Salinger was a Berlin businessman who emigrated early. He recalled a happy childhood before the First World War in Posen where his family had a summer residence in the surrounding woods. After serving with the German army and being decorated with the Iron Cross at Cambrai in 1917, he returned to qualify as a mechanical engineer and became head of the department of a factory making sanitary equipment and technical instruments. Here he was responsible for one thousand workers. "In 1933, many people in our trade knew Germany was already turning out weapons. We were sworn to secrecy on pain of being shot." Despite a comfortable life-style and a circle of distinguished friends, which included his relative the great mathematician and physicist, Albert Einstein, Gerhard Salinger realised there was no future for him in Germany. His ambition to become a patents attorney came to nothing and he was excluded from the Association of Mechanical Engineers. During an exploratory visit to London in 1936 he was strongly advised to try Birmingham. Here he obtained an introduction to a manufacturer of technical instruments, who agreed to employ him. "But it took four anxious months before the Home Office work permit came through. On my first day at the factory the boss gathered all the workers together and introduced me. 'He's a German, but he's a refugee and he hates Hitler as much as we all do'. From that moment I had no trouble."

Oddly, his German employers treated him generously. They offered him a patent to try to sell, and gave him £20 as a parting gift. "But it took months to get it, they were so short of foreign currency."

Heinz Eisner, brother of Dr Hilde Eisner, determined to leave Berlin with his wife after Boycott Day, but they did not arrive in England until December 1936. Heinz had inherited his parents' factory for turning and pressing ebonite, a predecessor of plastics. They were able to bring two machines with them, and helped by a single workman, they set up a small plastics factory in Acocks Green, Birmingham. At this comparatively early date, they were able to bring their household goods also and even some jewellery, although, as Anneliese Eisner remarked, "there was not much left by the time we had paid to get away. A duty officer watched as we packed, but he was a decent fellow and sometimes looked the other way." The Eisners were greatly helped by the firm of N.C. Joseph, canners, in Stratford-upon-Avon, and by Elliotts, a local plastics and glass firm, which employed many refugees.

Those who delayed leaving Germany, or could find no country willing to take them, felt the net gradually but inexorably closing in on them. For a time people struggled with the regulations. Herta Linden's mother had a knitwear shop; when it became impossible to run this, she took on an agency in coal and linen. Kurt Rose, back again on holiday in Berlin in 1937, became suddenly aware of the deteriorating situation when he saw the former head of a famous electrical firm trying to sell tea and coffee to his mother in her flat.

Gerhardt and Berthold Kornhauser also tried at first to adapt to the Nazi regime. The family, which came from Cracow in Poland, had settled in Berlin in 1912 and the brothers were born there. After an education at the famous Rabbi Munk's Jewish school and a *gymnasium* (grammar school), Berthold Kornhauser commenced work in a men's outfitters. In 1935 he was dismissed, classed as a Polish subject, and deprived of his work permit. He was nevertheless still allowed to work on his own account, if this meant creating jobs for others, this being at the time the policy of the German government. Although only twenty years old, he took two rooms, bought some machines on hire purchase and employed ten girls making raincoats. His task became more difficult as the Jewish firms he had been supplying closed down, although he still managed to keep going with the help of a non-Jewish sub-contractor friend who got orders for him from German firms.

Following the Kristallnacht, as a Polish national, Berthold Kornhauser, got wind of his impending arrest. He made over his business, the machines and the staff, to his sub-contractor for what money he could get, and with the proceeds bought a ticket for England. "Everybody was trying to get out of Germany and luckily my brother and I had obtained visitors' visas just five days before. There was not much checking. The Germans seemed glad to be rid of us." Within a week he was in England.

The obligatory yellow star worn by Jews during the third Reich.

Henry Warner had also been able for a time to find employment in engineering in Germany. After the Kristallnacht he, like many other male Jews, was flung into the concentration camp of Sachsenhausen. His widowed mother wrote feverishly to every possible English organisation, and it was her son's good fortune that the Federation of University Women realised the urgency of his predicament. A visa was quickly forthcoming and within three weeks of his release from the camp he was in England. He was well aware of his luck. "There was a terrible atmosphere of panic in Berlin. My friends were queuing every day at the consulates and legations, trying to get to Shanghai, Montevideo, Uruguay, anywhere! I had been released from Sachsenhausen on a faked Shanghai visa. Many South American officials were selling illegal visas and huge sums of Jewish money were being passed over for means of escape from Germany."

Deutſches Reich

J

Kennkarte

Cover of Ruth Price's passport.

Ruth Price, thirteen years old at the time of the Kristallnacht, spoke of the humiliation of applying for a J (Jude) passport. "Hours of waiting, no seats, proving that one did not owe a penny anywhere." She had been well aware of the situation from the beginning, the slogans on the walls, the disturbances in the street, but most of all, she feared passing the SS men.

Yet everywhere there were strange anomalies. A Berlin businessman recorded how he was able to travel to and from Belgium almost to the outbreak of war. On his last trip, a friend sent him a telegram ''don't come back''. He took the advice and went to Brazil.

The fate of the Jewish hospital in Berlin is also surprising. It was under Gestapo supervision but some of the old and chronically sick Jews remained in the wards until the end of the war. It continued to the end to employ Jewish doctors and nurses who had survived through marriage (before 1933) to Aryans[3]. One of the patients, a cousin of a refugee interviewed, had thrown herself under a train when she was betrayed to the Nazis. She was not killed but seriously injured, and remained in the Jewish Hospital until the Russians arrived. A very small Jewish hospital also survived in Hamburg.

PROVINCIAL GERMANY

The industrial towns of the Rhineland and the Catholic South were very nationalistic and were quick to embrace the Nazi ideology. In some of the smaller towns and villages the new ideas took some time to penetrate and in others old friends were protective towards their Jews.

The experience of Ernst Aris exemplifies the slow encroachment of Nazism in some of the remoter areas. He lived in the medieval walled town of Preussisch-Holland in East Prussia and was able to continue at the *Volkschule* (Primary School) until he left with the Children's Transports early in 1939.

The experience of Gerda Mindelsohn, who came from a village some distance from Wurzburg, was a complete contrast. ''We were isolated by an almost total lack of transport, but we were happy and contented. Of the hundred or so families, thirty-five were Jewish, the rest Catholic or Protestant. All were equally *frum* (pious), but apart from religion our lives were much the same. We attended each other's funerals and the town crier called out the times of services in the synagogue and churches impartially. 'The Nazis don't concern us', said the village people.

''On the morning of the Kristallnacht I met a boy from school at the well. 'Something is going to happen to you. Your synagogue will be burnt down', he warned me. I went home and told my parents. No one would believe me. When it happened my little sister, who saw it go up in flames, had to go into hospital with shock.'' In Kommern, a tiny village in the Eiffel, the Nazis smashed windows and ransacked houses. ''My mother was engaged to be married'' said Helen Libman. ''They threw her wedding-dress out of an upstairs window into the water below.''

Emmi Simson and her husband were wardens of a Jewish Youth Hostel in the Rheinland. ''Soon after the Kristallnacht we saw two cars coming up our long drive, filled with SS men. As they approached they began shouting and one man carried an axe. Every book and paper was thrown out of the window and set alight. They ransacked the place of blankets, gramophones, cameras and typewriters. When an SS officer approached my baby's cot I was terrified. I had heard dreadful tales of cruelty. But he only asked, 'Is it a boy or a girl?' They took my husband away; a fortnight later he returned, exhausted, his head shaven. He would never speak of his experiences.''

Emmy Golding (neé Kaufmann) at Kommern, 1987.

Jewish Youth Hostel run by Emmi Simson and her husband in the Rheinland, 1938.

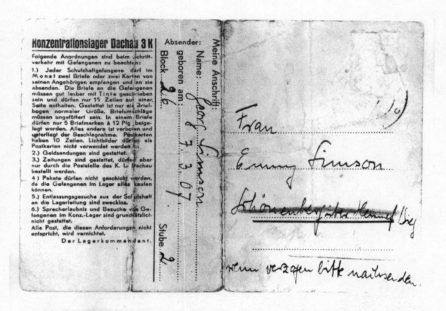

Postcard written by Emmi Simson's husband from the concentration camp at Dachau, 1939.

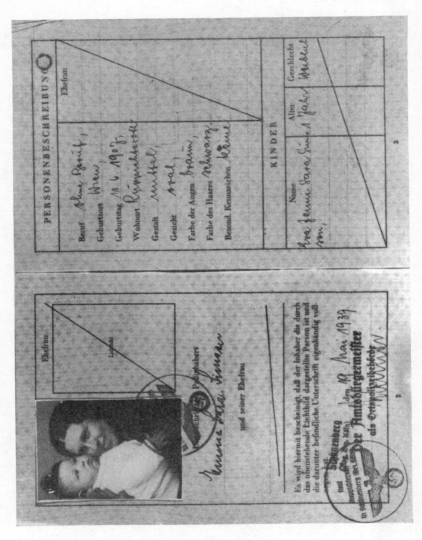

Passport of Emmi Simson with her baby, 1939.

Emmi Simson's husband had been trained to go abroad as an agriculturalist, and they were chosen to take part in a Rothschild scheme in Argentina. But meanwhile they obtained a visa for England and left just before war was declared. Emmi Simson's parents were among the few who were able to get away after the outbreak of war, and settled in Brazil.

Landau Synagogue on fire during the Kristallnacht, 1938.

Charlotte Singer retains terrible memories of the Kristallnacht in a little town on the border between Germany and Czechoslovakia. "I was awakened by the clatter of china—I thought the dog had upset the breakfast table. But there was more and more clatter and the shouts of a large crowd ...

"I did not know that this clatter was taking place at this hour in nearly every Jewish home in Germany. A man stood in my room, a patient of my husband's, the son of a plumber who had done many jobs for us. Wielding a hatchet the furniture was broken in a few seconds, my writing table overturned, ink dripping on to the carpet. 'To set fire to the place would be best' he called to somebody outside ... A brick came sailing through the window pane and hit my leg ... Another evil-looking crowd, women among them, wrecked the kitchen ... Outside, the synagogue was burning ..."

Ruth S. came from a small town in Thuringia, near Leipzig, and although she experienced a certain amount of hostility at school, she was able to remain there until 28 October 1938 when she was eight years old. On that day, she was called out of class by a policeman. He escorted her home, where she found her mother packing. "I don't know where you are going but it won't be for long, just lock the door and give me the key", the policeman explained. With the other Jewish families of the place they were locked in a train and sent to a centre on the Polish frontier where 75,000 other Jews were assembled. "Here we stayed until June 1939 when we were allowed into Poland.

"War was on the horizon and somehow it became possible to send one child in each family to England. First we went to Warsaw. It really looked like a place preparing for war. The railway station was closed and guarded by soldiers with fixed bayonets, but they opened the heavy gates for us. We travelled to Gydnia and came on the last boat before war to England."

Renate Jacobs from the city of Breslau was able to continue her education until 1938. She attended a Roman Catholic school chosen by her parents because the headmistress was known to be friendly to the Jews. She was good at sports and brought credit to her school at athletic events, receiving for her prowess certificates which were headed with swastikas. But she was never asked to the homes of ther schoolmates. "One day I felt quite proud because one of them came round to my house. I taught her to ride my bicycle. This was really unusual. My parents moved from a large house to a flat and then to a smaller flat so that we would be less conspicuous. They decided my brother and I should go to school in England. While we were away in 1938, the Gestapo came to visit my father in his office. They only wanted to check something, but it gave him such a shock he disappeared over the frontier to Bratislava. He didn't want to abandon his business, a long-established family grain and seed firm, but when at last the Nazis decided to take it over, they did it cleverly. First one tax, then another tax, then a little more. People's suspicions were lulled in between, but in this case the Gestapo gave him a push, and did him a good turn in making up his mind for him."

Pressure of a more sinister kind was exerted on Mr 'X' of Dresden, an "Aryan". He was an engineer working on ships' turbines. The Gestapo took him away several times and tried to persuade him to stay and work for them. "They wanted him to divorce me", said Mrs 'X', his Jewish wife. "They were more successful with my brother-in-law, also an engineer who worked for Siemens. He did divorce my sister, who fortunately was saved from committing suicide and eventually remarried and went to the United States."

The Nazis burn the books, 1933

Irma Lindenstein, 1919.

People whose families had turned to Christianity in a previous generation suddenly found themselves regarded as "non-Aryan" because they had a Jewish grandparent. Walter Stranz related how his father, a Berlin lawyer, had been arbitrarily arrested: "I remember my mother going to one of my father's clients who had the *Goldenes Parteiabzeichen* (gold party badge) which meant he was an early member of the Nazi party. He said he would write to the Party about my father because, as he said, we regularly went to church so we were more Christian than he was. Father was shortly released."

Irma Lindenstein's family originated in Wurttemberg where one member had been "Court Jew" to the King, entrusted with all his financial affairs. Her grandfather had been Rabbi of the little town of Burchau-am-Sedersee where the synagogue was distinguished by a clock, given to the community by the King of Wurttemberg in return for services rendered. About 1860, the family moved to Frankfurt where they set up a poultry and egg business, supplying it from their own farm. Here they installed one of the first plants for processing geese. At a time when feather beds were universally used, geese and their feathers were of great economic importance, and they developed a profitable trade with Russia. "Sometimes three waggon loads would trundle into the courtyard at a time."

Irma Lindenstein was born in 1893 in one of the old patrician houses on the walls of Frankfurt. "The shop was downstairs and we lived on the two floors above. The garden was part of the moat. Steps led down to lawns and terraces with old cherry trees and gooseberry and currant bushes. There were peaches trained against the walls, and two ramshackle summer houses where we played during the long summer days. When Hitler came in 1933, the business was taken over — in any case, we no longer had permits to obtain supplies." Irma meanwhile had married an orthopaedic surgeon, Louis Lindenstein of Nuremberg, one of the key cities of Nazism with its Parteitag — the Führer's annual celebration of flag-waving, marching and strident speeches. Louis Lindenstein soon found it difficult to make a living but the family did not emigrate until 1939.

Henry Freeland came from Coburg in Northern Bavaria, where the Duke, a descendant of Queen Victoria, was notoriously anti-semitic. He welcomed Hitler in 1923 and the Swastika flag flew in Coburg before most people in Germany had heard of the dictator. Henry Freeland, as the only Jewish boy in his school, had suffered, and was anxious to get away. In 1933 he obtained a visa for France. His father had a flourishing department store, which he looked forward to handing over eventually to his son. Optimistically, he bought him a return ticket. It was difficult for a foreigner to obtain a work permit in Paris, and he and a friend decided to try for England. "It all depended on the immigration officer whether you were accepted or rejected." Henry Freeland was lucky. His friend was sent back. He managed to get to Yugoslavia, but after the war it proved impossible to trace him.

Of all the immigrants to Birmingham in the 1930s, Dr Kossi Strauss, in co-operation with his partner, Eric Weiss, was perhaps the greatest benefactor to his adopted city. Together they founded the firm of Foseco which rendered outstanding help in the war effort and later gave employment to thousands. Kossi Strauss's forebears came, like Henry Freeland, from Coburg, where they were cattle-dealers; a popular trade in this largely agricultural country, where Jews were not allowed to own land. His father Emanuel was a teacher in the state schools. In Catholic Bavaria education was based on religion, and where there were ten Jewish children in a town or village, a Jewish school was provided. Emanuel Strauss moved to Weiden in Southern Bavaria, where he had obtained a post as a schoolmaster, doubling up as minister, cantor and *Shochet* (ritual slaughterer) to the small Jewish community.

Kossi Strauss attended his father's school. "He was very strict and I had to call him *Herr Oberlehrer*." He graduated through this school to the *Realschule* (Technical High School) in Wurzburg. Like Henry Freeland, he experienced the virulent anti-semitism in Bavarian schools in the 1920s. Added to this, Julius Streicher, the vicious editor of the Nazi paper, "Der Sturmer", toured Bavaria and blared forth his nationalistic tirades Sunday after Sunday.

In 1923 Kossi Strauss enrolled at the University of Munich as a student of organic chemistry. Only a week after his arrival on 8 October, Hitler was billed to speak in the famous Bierkeller. "I just went out of curiosity", said Kossi Strauss. "I didn't look Jewish or it would have been dangerous. I saw a very ordinary looking young man in a trench coat, but he could speak and was very convincing. He announced that the Bavarian Government had abdicated and that he himself would take over. There was uproar, and when he couldn't make himself heard, he pulled out a revolver and fired at the ceiling."

During the night the Bavarian Government underwent a change of heart, brought in troops and prepared to face an armed revolt. Kossi Strauss was at the University at 9 o'clock in the morning for a physics lecture, but the room gradually emptied as the students, most of whom supported Hitler, slipped away to join the demonstration. A mass march headed by Hitler and General Ludendorff, the leader of Germany in the First World War, followed by thousands of storm troopers and students, was converging on the Feldherrnhalle, a monument to former generals. As they entered the narrow street, soldiers and police on the roof of the Feldherrnhalle opened fire and nine Nazis were killed. The demonstration broke up in disarray. Hitler was not caught until three days later. He was interned in a fortress, where he spent several months in comfort and wrote his famous book *Mein Kampf*.

Kossi Strauss graduated in 1927, and obtained a doctorate in engineering. He took a research post at the University of Karlsruhe, and had some patents granted in his name. At the end of the year he was offered the position of Chief Industrial Chemist in Halle, a firm making compounds for the foundry industry. Two years later, owing to a bank failure[4], the firm was declared bankrupt and the director, Dr Ludwig Weiss, committed suicide. Kossi Strauss had known Dr Weiss's nephew Eric from childhood, and met him again at the funeral. From Kossi's experience and from reading *Mein Kampf,* it was not difficult to see trouble ahead, and the young men made plans to start a similar firm in England. For a time, Kossi Strauss returned to Karlsruhe, where he had the laboratory facilities necessary for research work for the new firm. Eric Weiss, meanwhile, established himself in Birmingham, where he was joined in 1933 by Kossi Strauss.

AUSTRIA

Despite a strong pro-Nazi movement, Austria was an independent country, a member of the League of Nations. In 1934 an internal attempt at a Nazi takeover had been put down. It was doubtful how long Austria would be able to maintain any independence, especially as the Führer himself was an Austrian.

In spite of this the parents of two undergraduates of the University of Birmingham raised no objection to their children's travelling to Austria in the summer of 1936 for the statutory study of the German language required by the syllabus. David Goodkin was "exchanged" with a student from the University of Innsbruck, while the present writer went as "au pair" girl to a wealthy Jewish family in Vienna. Both were conscious of an unpleasant atmosphere, but it was only on the periphery of their experience. David Goodkin's exchange student was an avowed Nazi. On the other hand, his landlady discussed the German-Jewish dilemma with him openly and sympathetically. It was only on their way home through Germany that both these English students felt something of the chill of Nazism. In the writer's case, the police entered the railway carriage as the train steamed out of the border town Passau into Germany, and roughly snatched the Austrian newspapers from the passengers. She had arranged to meet her former German teacher when the train stopped at Cologne. This lady had spent most of her working life at a Jewish boarding school in England and had recently returned to her native city. She had altered in the short time since leaving England, her face was thin and drawn, and her reluctance to talk of her sad new life was obvious.

David Goodkin's experience was more frightening. He had been persuaded to travel by coach through Germany to see the new autobahn. On the way he had to spend the night in a small village. In the early hours came a knock on the door, the police entered and demanded to search his luggage. His *tephillin* [5] (phylacteries) were in his rucksack, but on seeing his British passport they made no comment and departed.

Austria had for a long time suffered from serious unemployment problems, and the Germans had been in the habit of inviting the Austrian unemployed to work in their armaments factories. When, with the Anschluss in March 1938, Hitler marched into Austria the ground for Nazi ideology had been well prepared by the fierce anti-semitism which had always been a feature of Austrian life. With the arrival of the German troops across the border in March 1938, a rash of swastikas and brown uniforms broke out overnight. "Even my schoolmates appeared in uniform", recalled one lady, "although one or two rang to say 'we're still friends'." But the German Wehrmacht were to be seen in Vienna, holding the ardent Austrian Nazis back from vicious attacks on the Jews. The police were too frightened to interfere and, in some cases, joined in.

Hetty Leyton watched the arrival of the German Führer from a window near the Vienna West Bahnhof. "Hitler drove down the Mariahilferstrasse to a tremendous reception. Planes flew overhead the whole time and there was a terrific force of troops. No question of any resistance, although we felt it impossible that England or some country wouldn't come to our help."

Margaret Rubinstein came from a comfortably-off family who owned a store. She had married a prosperous bookseller. "It was all very sudden.

Gina Gerson (née Bauer), 1938

Dr.Alfred Schwarz
Wien VI.
Gumpendorferstrasse 72

MEDICAL CERTIFICATE

Place : VIENNA
Date: ......*4/5.*....1938

I hereby certify that I have examined
..*Regina Bauer,*....*14 years of age*..................
and find ..*her.*.. not to be mentally or physically defective in any
way, that ..*she.*.. is not afflicted with tuberculosis in any form
or with an infectious, loathsome or contagious disease, that
..*she.*.. is not suffering from favus, leprosy, framboesia or yaws,
trachoma, syphilis or scabies.

..*T. V. d. Graaf*..............

Medical adviser to the
British Consulate.

Mentally defective includes:

Idiots
Imbeciles
Feebleminded persons
Insane persons
Epileptics
Persons having previously had attacks of insanity
Persons of constitutional psychopathic inferiority
Persons suffering from chronic alcoholism.

I also certify that ....
has never been in a mental hospital nor in prison.

Vienna, ...1938

Gina Gerson's medical certificate issued prior to her emigration, 1938/9.

(a)

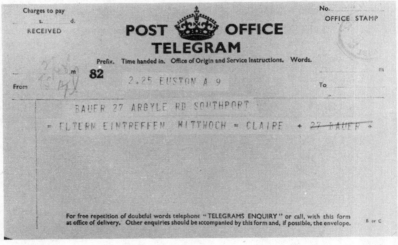

(b)

The hopes of Gina Gerson's parents were shattered by the outbreak of war.

    (a) "27 June 1939. Guarantee found Klara".
    (b) "3 July 1939. Permit for father just sent kisses Klarile".
    (c) "31 August 1939. Meet parents Wednesday Claire".

By Wednesday 6 September the war had started and the gates had closed.
    (d) 10 January 1956. A message arrived in Vienna saying that Aron and Berta Bauer had been deported 5 June 1942 to Izbica and there were no records of their return.

POST ✠ OFFICE TELEGRAM

Prefix.   Time handed in.   Office of Origin and Service Instructions.   Words.

m   **98**

From

98 11.2 EUSTON A 12

No.

OFFICE STAMP

To

BAUER 27 ARGYLE RD SOUTHPORT =

PERMIT FUER PAPA SOEBEN ABGESANDT KUESSE KLARILE +

For free repetition of doubtful words telephone "TELEGRA   or call, with this form
at office of delivery. Other enquiries should be accompanied b   possible, the envelope.

(c)

Israelitische Kultusgemeinde Wien
I, Schottenring 25

Wien,   10. Jänner 1956

DUPLIKAT.

Auf Grund unserer Aufzeichnungen bestätigen wir, daß

Herr   A r o n   B a u e r , geb. am 28.4.1877   und

Frau   B e r t a   B a u e r , geb. am 6.6.1889

Letzte Adresse: Wien 2., Schmelzgasse 7

am   5. Juni 1942   nach   I Z B I C A   deportiert wurde und

in unserer Rückkehrerkartei nicht aufscheint.

ISRAEL. KULTUSGEMEINDE WIEN
BEVÖLKERUNGSWESEN

(d)

29

That day the air was thick ... we had to tell our family servant to go." The Rubinsteins, too, were lucky enough to get a guarantee for England.

The experiences of Stella Kornhauser and Gina Gerson were in some ways similar. Stella Kornhauser was fourteen when her former "best friend" at school passed her suddenly in the street without recognition. Worse, the caretaker of her father's patisserie shop whom they had thought completely loyal, appeared suddenly in a brown uniform, daubed a swastika in tar on the pavement and forced her mother to get down on her knees and scrub the paving stones.

Stella Kornhauser, who had lived in Baden, outside Vienna, had not had to leave school immediately. Gina Gerson, on the other hand, who lived in the capital, was forced to enter a Jewish school straight after the Anschluss. After the Kristallnacht the family were locked out of their flat "for their own protection" and had to find shelter with friends. Her half-sister was a Latvian by marriage, but divorced. "At that time the Nazis still respected foreign nationals, they all wore their flags. She managed to get out on a domestic permit and once in London arranged for Gina Gerson to come as a "trainee".

Stella Kornhauser's father, anxious to get his two daughters to safety, arranged a marriage of convenience for Stella's elder sister to a young man who had turned up from Palestine. They were to separate on arrival in Palestine. But the young man turned out to be a confidence trickster and her father lost his money. He made a second attempt, this time at illegal immigration for the two girls into Palestine. But the ominous question "can the little one swim?" made him lose his nerve. An advertisement in *The Times* finally resulted in a domestic permit and in September 1938 Stella Kornhauser was on her way to London as a cook. "When you get across the German border at Aachen say the *Shema*[6] and send us a telegram", were her mother's final instructions. But at Aachen all the Jewish passengers were told to get out, and were locked in a hut in the station. "We were terrified. Then everyone else was allowed back on the train. For some reason I was held back, but I did get on the next one."

Gina Gerson's journey to London was even more alarming. In January 1939, just after her fourteenth birthday, she travelled to England alone, without the protection of any organisation. Like Stella Kornhauser, she was ordered to dismount at Aachen with the rest of the Jewish passengers. "I was taken to a little wooden building where a large woman stripped and searched me. Two men were reading my diary in which I had described how my uncle committed suicide when the Nazis came, by throwing himself from the window of his flat. They squashed my chocolates, slashed the lining of my new winter gloves and cut up my manicure set — a parting birthday present. I was very fair and looked Aryan. Perhaps they thought, as a child, I was being used to smuggle something"

Meanwhile, she had missed all her connections. At Brussels, a Jewish porter tried to comfort the distraught child in Yiddish. His was the first kindly face she had seen since she left home.

In neither case was the arrival of these two girls in England very propitious. "It was my first time on a boat and it was pretty rough", recalled Gina Gerson. "I was very sick. When I got on the train I saw my compartment was upholstered. I was used to wooden seats in the third class, and was frightened they'd throw me off the train. At Victoria I was twelve hours late. I must have sat down on my suitcase and gone to sleep, because my sister passed me several times without recognising me. She was frantic. We went back to her room by underground and I was terrified again. I thought the railwaymen in their black uniforms were SS (Schutz Staffel) men'."

Because of the delay, nobody met Stella Kornhauser in London. She was forced to find her own way to her job in Dorset Square. "It was a beautiful house, but I was in a real 'Upstairs, Downstairs' situation, where I wasn't allowed to use the front stairs. I cried for two days and two nights."

After the Anschluss of Austria in the Spring of 1938, some people managed to make their way across the frontier into Czechoslovakia. It must have seemed a haven to them, as it did to Charlotte Singer and her husband, who lived in the border town of Neisse. "We had a frontier-pass and all our week-ends were spent across the border in Czechoslovakia. We could swim, go shopping and enter an hotel without spotting the ubiquitous sign, 'Jews are not wanted here'. More important, we could mail letters without having them opened by the censor."

Es wird den Einwohnern von Luxemburg-Stadt und Land hiermit zur Kenntniss gebracht, dass in Zukunft in das Reglement für Gastwirtschaften, Variétès und Kinos folgender Passus eingefügt wird:

Juden u. Schweinen

ist das Betreten des Lokales strengstens

verboten !

HUNDEN ist der Zutritt gestattet.

"The attention of residents in Luxemburg and the surrounding countryside is herewith directed to the following passage which in future will be inserted into the regulations for public houses, music halls and cinemas:
Jews and Pigs are strictly forbidden to enter these places.
Dogs are allowed entry."

But Charlotte Singer and her friends were soon to lose their frontier passes, just as the safety of the fleeing Austrian Jews was short-lived. In October 1938, after a summer of intense Nazi agitation on behalf of the German-speaking inhabitants of the Sudetenland, Britain and France obliged the

Czechs to cede this frontier province to Germany at the Munich Agreement; the price of what Neville Chamberlain, the British Prime Minister, called "peace in our time". Another great wave of refugees resulted, some fleeing to the Polish frontier, whence they were firmly returned into the arms of the Gestapo. There was an outcry in Britain. Many felt this country bore responsibility for the plight of these terrified people. Large sums of money were collected and three hundred and fifty visas granted immediately for those in acute danger. But in November the horrors of the Kristallnacht were let loose, and the following March Hitler marched into Prague. The rest of Czechoslovakia was occupied.

CZECHOSLOVAKIA

Six of the people interviewed came from Czechoslovakia. Of these, two had vivid memories of nightmare car journeys under cover of darkness. Lia Lesser and Gerda Solomon were both eight years old when they reached Prague from their village homes and found safety through the Refugee Children's Movement in England. But Gerda Solomon could recall a previous journey from her village to the town of Teplitz. "I was woken in the night. My father had to be back in his factory by morning. He didn't want anyone to know where we were. But it was no use and we had to return. He was arrested and sent to Sachsenhausen. I remember the door bell ringing on a Sunday morning, two Gestapo men came in ... he was in bed. They wouldn't leave him for a moment, even in the bathroom. They said he would be back in the evening. Well, evening came and, needless to say, he didn't return. We didn't know where he was, alive or dead.

"One day we received a card with his signature and we realised he was in Sachsenhausen. After about nine months he was released, they said because he had fought in the Austrian army against England in the First World War ... we were playing in the garden, we saw a man come up—my mother was with us—none of us recognised him."

Paul David was twenty when he came to England. Both he and his father were jewellers in Gablonz, a jewellery centre. His father had connections with the firm of Empson in Birmingham. They offered Paul work, and in July 1939, a few weeks before the outbreak of war, he made his escape.

"I remember only one incident in Czechoslovakia, when the Nazis decided to collect all the Jews in one place. We were taken by car, I think to Breslau. We drove all through the night and were put in a sort of no-man's-land. It was terrible for my parents. I was young and didn't feel the hardship so badly. Then suddenly the project, whatever it was, was abandoned and we were sent back. I remember my mother falling on her knees and kissing the Gestapo officer's hand.

"After I arrived in Birmingham, my parents sent me letters begging me to help them, but I knew no-one who could act as guarantor. My father died soon after I left. He had gone to live in Warsaw with my sister. It was the worst place to be. My mother was on a farm until 1945, but somebody gave her away and she died in Theresienstadt."

Ilse Reinstein came from a small town near the Moravian border of Czechoslovakia with Poland. When Hitler marched into Prague, where she was in her final year at the German grammar school, she was already engaged to be married. Her fiancé had left the country shortly before and by the end of March he was in Britain.

Despite the Nazi occupation, Ilse Reinstein matriculated in June 1939. Her fiancé meanwhile had sent her a visa for her to come to England as a domestic. She returned to her family in Moravia where her uncle had been an official in the railways, and managed to get herself smuggled on to a cattle truck for the thirty-minute journey across the border to Poland. There was a heart-stopping moment half-way when the train came to an unscheduled halt. "Somebody started tapping on the wheels and I heard queries as to whether the train should be allowed to proceed." But go on it did, and within a week Ilse Reinstein was on a transport of refugees to England. "We were locked into a carriage for Gdynia on the Baltic, and there loaded into a little herring boat. We ate herrings three times a day. The worst moment was going through the Kiel Canal—Germans on either side of us." But after three days they chugged under Tower Bridge where her fiancé awaited her and they were married.

Both were soon engaged in work of national importance, he making gauges for aeroplanes, she in a geriatric hospital. Nevertheless, they were interned on the Isle of Man. "The poor refugees worked for the rich. I did knitting and my husband opened a Chinese laundry. He was good at ironing."

After the war there was an outcry for teachers. "Anybody with any sort of educational qualifications was welcome." She taught infants and juniors, secondary and grammar school pupils. Her husband taught mathematics at Sowerby Bridge, Yorkshire, and later took a degree. In 1957 they moved to Birmingham where he became a mathematics master at Lordswood Boys' Technical School. Ilse Reinstein then studied for a teaching certificate at the Teacher Training College in Westbourne Road, Edgbaston. She obtained a post at Lordswood Girls' School where she remained until her retirement in 1985.

HUNGARY

"We were dancing in the garden", recalled Lola Maté, a teacher who lived with her architect husband and two children in the small Hungarian town of Nagykanizsa, ten miles from the Yugoslav border.

"Early in 1944 the war seemed virtually over. On the Russian front the Germans were in retreat. Hungary remained Germany's last ally but nothing could happen to us. The Nazis had neither the time nor the power to do us any harm.

"Yet, on 18 March 1944, we woke up to the sound of massed aeroplanes circling overhead. Within an hour it was announced on the radio that Hungary had been taken over by the Germans."

Anti-semitism was deeply rooted in Hungary. At the universities, Jewish students had daily to run the gauntlet of semi-official spite and there was a strict *Numerus Clausus*[8] of three per cent. Lola Maté herself was only allowed to teach in the Jewish school. "But we never felt threatened by the Nazis. We had no idea of the scale of what was happening in Germany, had never heard of concentration camps. How could we have been such idiots? Because we saw ourselves as loyal Hungarians and we were blinded by our patriotism."

This loyalty persisted, despite the order in October 1943 that Jews must give up any form of transport they possessed. The family car, a motor-cycle Lola Maté's husband used for work, and their four bicycles, had to be handed in. "The children kept kissing the saddles of their bikes all the way to the police station." "Why do we have to give them up?" asked the little girl. "Because there's a war on and they need them", answered her mother. "But children's bikes? The policemen will give them to their own children", replied her daughter, wise beyond her years.

Lola Maté took the precaution of buying stout boots and rucksacks for her family in case of a sudden need to escape, "but from the war, never from the Germans".

"The very day of the occupation my husband's brother came from Budapest. 'Every Jew in Hungary will be killed', he announced. 'We must get over the border with our families and join the Yugoslav partisans'. My husband listened in incredulous fury. 'We have done nothing. We are respected members of the community. Never let me hear you speak like that again'. 'I hope you won't be sorry', said my brother-in-law as he left for Budapest.

"A terrible sadness now overcame the Jewish Community. Nobody ever smiled. Posters started to appear. We must wear the yellow star. We must leave our homes and go to the synagogues and the Jewish school, which had been designated as ghettoes. This order came very suddenly. It happened to be wash-day and I had to leave my bed-linen soaking. My husband's foreman came to the school fence and offered to take the children into safe-keeping. 'But everyone will know the children have gone, and it could only be with you. You will be shot. But please, go to my house and hang up the washing'.

"The foreman returned an hour later. My washing had already been stolen. My husband had been born in that house and I had lived there twelve years. What sort of neighbours did we have?

"After a few days we were marched to the station and packed into cattle-trucks."

Lola Maté's account of her imprisonment in Germany is told in the chapter on 'The Survivors'.

Peter Hegedus was saved by the presence of mind of a neighbour. "I was born in Budapest in 1941. The Nazis came for my parents in 1944 but I was left at home with my grandmother because I had scarlet fever. Later they came for us, and a neighbour saw me in my pram, ready to go. She snatched me out, and put in a bundle instead. My grandmother and all the other Jews were taken to the banks of the Danube and machine-gunned into the river".

Peter was cared for by the Red Cross until his parents returned from Germany, after the war.

In 1956, at the age of 15, he was imprisoned for lobbing hand-grenades at the invading Russian tanks as they rumbled through the streets of Budapest. Early in the following year he escaped, swimming an icy canal to the safety of Austria. Here he stowed away in a 'plane-load of Hungarian miners, who had volunteered to work for the British National Coal Board. His age was discovered on arrival at a miners' hostel in Nuneaton, and Ruth Simmons, who had worked so long with refugees, received an urgent 'phone-call to come to his rescue.

Peter Hegedus joined Ruth's own family and remained for five years, studying for a degree in civil engineering. He is now vice-president of an American consultancy and engineering company with world wide ramifications.

References and notes

1. Sharf A. *The British Press and Jews under Nazi Rule* (1964) 22.
   The early 1933 exclusions were largely for state employees, which included teachers, judges and public notaries. There were some substantial exceptions at first, especially for those who had served in World War I.
2. Sharf A. *ibid.* (1964) 156.
3. Bentwich N. *They Found Refuge* (1956) 178.
4. The collapse of the Dresdener Bank was related to the collapse of the stockmarket in the USA in 1929.
5. Tephillin. (Heb. phylacteries). Small boxes used in prayer containing passages from the Bible.
6. Shema. A prayer proclaiming the unity of God, considered to represent the essence of all Judaism.
7. SS (Schutz Staffel) were the elite group of Nazis who wore black uniforms. They were the most committed and were always armed. SA Brownshirts (Sturm Abteilung)—mass movement of people who supported the Nazis.
8. *Numerus Clausus*. A fixed number or percentage of entrants to an academic institution.

CLUBS FOR REFUGEES

In the top photograph Czechs and Austrians are seen enjoying a sing-song at the Seventy Club at Carrs Lane Congregational Church. The lower picture was taken at the club held in the Jewish Communal Hall, Ellis Street.

Czechs and Austrians at Birmingham refugees clubs (*Birmingham Mail* 23 February 1940)

3

The Reaction in Britain

Until the Anschluss any decision regarding the entry of foreigners into Great Britain lay normally with the immigration officers. It was for them to decide whether a prospective immigrant could support himself or herself, or had guaranteed means of support from relatives or friends. In the late 1920s and early 1930s, Britain was suffering from very serious depression with mass unemployment. No foreigner therefore might take work without special permission from the Ministry of Labour and from the Home Office, and in no case could he or she be given work which could be done by a British subject. "In every case the interests of this country must predominate over all other considerations."[1]

Early in 1933 Otto Schiff, President of the Jews' Temporary Shelter in the East End (always the first port of call for the needy immigrant), Neville Laski, President of the Board of Deputies and Leonard Montefiore, President of the Anglo-Jewish Association, gave an undertaking to the Home Office that the Jewish Community of Great Britain would assume responsibility for Jewish refugees coming into this country.[2] Immense sums of money had to be raised and the rescue was organised entirely on voluntary aid.

The Central British Fund for Jewish Relief and Rehabilitation (CBF) was set up in London early in 1933. This incorporated the Jewish Refugees Committee and many other organisations. Among the local committees was the Birmingham Council for Refugees. The President was the Lord Mayor, and the voluntary helpers included several prominent business men. Hilde Hunt was the secretary, and Ruth Simmons undertook the welfare work, with particular emphasis on the younger people. There was besides a Jewish Refugees Committee, which was much involved with a hostel set up in Wheeley's Road, Edgbaston, for boys and girls without families in this country. All these bodies had to deal in the main with professional and business people, who had lived for many years in Central Europe and were overwhelmed to find themselves rejected as German, Austrian or Czechoslovak citizens. In this they contrasted sharply with the previous wave of refugees from persecution in Poland and Russia, who had been forced into a crippling existence within the Pale of Settlement[3], differed all too visibly in speech, dress and mannerisms from the host community, and who for the most part were miserably poor.

A helping hand was soon extended to the professional people leaving Germany by the rapid formation of the Society for the Protection of Science and Learning.[4] Within two years, two hundred scholars had found permanent or temporary posts in British universities.

Many far-sighted businessmen, with their expertise, were able to establish themselves in this country without too much difficulty. Some were able to bring their machinery, and in the early days, even a proportion of their capital. It was confidentially reported that "the Home Office were not at all dissatisfied with the present position (November 1933) as regards the numbers and quality of refugees from Germany ..., but we certainly don't want present numbers increased and it is our policy to do nothing to encourage further immigration."[5]

The Nazi policy intensified in September 1935 with the passing of the Nuremberg Laws. "There was a rash of posters everywhere", said Anneliese Eisner. A code of restrictions on Jewish life had been formulated. "We felt shut out everywhere. We couldn't go any more to places of amusement, or swimming pools. It was building up steadily."

The numbers attempting to leave Germany increased startlingly and the difficulties escalated. Refugees were now permitted to bring only a modicum of German currency with them, and in any case many were almost penniless after paying the crippling *Reichsfluchtsteuer* (flight-tax) to escape. Some were lucky enough to be able to send "lifts", large wooden containers filled with furniture and household goods, but these were often broken into, or lost *en route*. Other people were stripped of all their personal possessions. After the Kristallnacht of November 1938, the remaining Jews were fined collectively one billion Reichsmarks (£83 million).[6]

Now even the most reluctant to leave realised their lives were in imminent danger. The British Consulates were swamped with applications for visas (one thousand a day, said the Home Office).[7]

It was in order to rescue as many as possible of these destitute and terrified people that many more committees were now set up. CBF was the supreme body for administering help to refugees. The various religious denominations had their own committees. There was a Christian Council of Refugees, a Church of England Committee, a Catholic Committee and an Emergency Committee of the Society of Friends. A Medical Committee supported the cause of the doctors and a Business Advisory Committee helped the smaller industrialists. Hitler's invasion of the Sudetenland in October 1938 resulted in the setting up of a British Council for Czech Refugees.[8]

Many of these bodies functioned from Woburn House in Bloomsbury. It was soon impossible to contain the lengthening queues and Bloomsbury House Hotel was acquired so that all the offices could be under one roof. Here, in Bloomsbury House, the Central Office for Refugees became a meeting place for the exchange of information and future planning.

After 1938 visas became obligatory and applicants had to show evidence of definite means of support. However, thanks to the good relationship between the Central Office of Refugees and the Home Office, the visa system was modified for certain categories. The ten thousand children who came with the Refugee Children's Movement were admitted almost without formalities.[9] Nurses were always welcome due to the shortage in this country. Doctors and dentists were permitted in small numbers. Women and sometimes married couples came on domestic permits. It was stipulated that a position must have been offered before they could come, but there was a shortage of domestic servants in Britain, and the British Press and German-Jewish newspapers were full of advertisements. Elderly people, guaranteed by a relative or by an institution, and younger people between eighteen and thirty-five years of age designated as "trainees" destined for re-emigration, were also admitted. There were "visitors' visas" for those coming to examine specific work opportunities and "transit visas" for those who intended to move on to other countries within two years. A large number hoped to enter the United States, which insisted throughout the period on a strict application of the quota system. Many of these would-be transmigrants were overtaken by the war and could not leave. Afterwards many chose to remain.

In July 1938, President Roosevelt called a conference at Evian in France in an attempt to settle the refugee problem internationally. The representatives all sympathised, but did little to help.[10]

With war approaching, the situation was at last realised for what it was, a desperate crisis, demanding desperate measures. The fiendish tactics of the Nazis were now open for all to see, and it was impossible any longer to treat the terror as an internal affair of German politics. The situation was endlessly debated by the League of Nations and by the British Parliament. Every corner of the earth was scoured for a space where the Jews might settle; every suggestion for one reason or another failed. There was even an abortive attempt to consider a scheme, put forward by Dr Hjalmar Schacht, President of the Reichsbank, whereby Jews, to the great advantage of the German economy, might be permitted to use a modicum of their own money to build up new lives abroad.[11]

The White Paper of 1938 on Palestine which severely limited immigration for the next five years, dashed the hopes of many who had clung to a vision of refuge in the Holy Land.[12] Many defied the law and set out in over-crowded and unseaworthy boats, journeys which many times led to tragedy.[13] Others, despite dire warnings, went to Shanghai, the only place where visas were not required. "They would rather die as free men in Shanghai than as slaves in Dachau", observed the British Passport Control Office in Berlin.[14]

With the exception of Palestine, Britain, in the pre-war period, took a larger proportion of refugees than any other country.[15] Moreover, in many cases cited by the Birmingham Refugee Committee, the Home Office showed great sympathy and understanding. But in many instances, the feeling in government circles, the Foreign and Colonial Offices, and a section of the press was not favourable to the refugees.[16] Fears were expressed on the dangers inherent in "opening the floodgates", which would give rise to anti-semitism, unemployment and housing problems. Sometimes there seemed to be a complete lack of humanitarian feeling and even when Ministers, including the Prime Minister, recommended helpful action, the proposals were watered down by unsympathetic elements in the Civil Service, so that they had little effect.[17]

The Baldwin Appeal.
The Times, 10 February 1939.

At the time of the Munich Conference in September 1938, Chamberlain and his "appeasement policy" had many supporters, and there were known sympathisers with Germany in high places. But after the Munich Agreement, which virtually sentenced Czechoslovak Jewry to death, attitudes began slowly to change, although what was then done was too little and too late. "A grant of £4,000,000 for aid to Czech refugees was made, perhaps as a gesture of contrition by the Government."[18]

Gradually a more understanding approach to the refugee problem became noticeable. With re-armament there was less unemployment and the spectre of an invasion of penniless refugees became less menacing. The Baldwin Appeal had been set up in the December after the Kristallnacht and had collected £250,000 in less than two months.[19] Individuals and institutions offered help as the plight of the children touched people's hearts. "Parcels were flooding in from all over the place", recalled a helper at the Dovercourt camp where the young refugees were first received. "Firms sent radios, cases of fruit, clothing. The most touching were from old people in poor circumstances. One kind old lady gathered up bits of different wools and made a pair of multi-coloured mitts. 'They might keep a pair of small hands warm in the cold winter', she wrote."[20]

At the outbreak of war, all public charities were directed to the Red Cross and similar facets of the war effort. There were over 60,000 people registered with the Jewish Refugees' Committee, 10,000 had been brought over by the Refugee Children's Movement, and there were 6,000 from Czechoslovakia. The voluntary organisations were almost without funds.

40

By December 1939, the government agreed to help finance the refugees at the rate of eight shillings (40p) each weekly, the figure to be matched by the refugee committees.[21]

An anti-alien epidemic swept Great Britain in May 1940 with the fall of France and the threat of invasion. Every foreigner was under suspicion of being an enemy agent. The refugees were interned wholesale and the alarm reached panic proportions, which the government did little to control. The situation was exacerbated by the hysteria whipped up in some newspapers.[22]

As the danger of invasion receded, the scare gradually passed. Restrictions on the employment of aliens were lifted to enable them to take part in the war effort. They became self-supporting and integrated more and more with the host community. The need for assistance on a massive scale dwindled and gradually disappeared.

On 14 December 1942 a declaration was made by Anthony Eden in the House of Commons detailing the bestial Nazi policy of cold-blooded extermination. A wave of sympathy swept over the House and the nation, and it was resolved that help must be given to the victims, and the perpetrators of such barbarities be brought to justice. The following April the United Kingdom and the United States of America came together for the purpose at the Bermuda Conference, but little was achieved and those like Eleanor Rathbone MP, Josiah Wedgwood MP, and the Archbishops of York and Canterbury, who fought for the refugees' cause, were dismissed as "extremists and enthusiasts and their efforts as sentimental".[23] Generally speaking, officialdom, with the shining exception of Sir Winston Churchill, lacked the imaginative understanding to compass the appalling truth.[24]

References and notes

1. Sherman, A.J. *Island Refuge*. 30-33.
2. Bentwich, N. *They found Refuge*. 16.
3. Pale of Settlement. From 1791 the Jews were confined by the Tsars to the westernmost provinces of the Russian Empire.
4. Bentwich, N. ibid. 16-19.
5. Sherman, A.J. op. cit. 42.
6. Sherman, A.J. ibid. 24.
   Sharf, A. *The British Press and the Jews under Nazi Rule* (1964)57. In November 1938 a wealth tax of 25% was levied on all Jews, and in addition when emigrating, another tax was payable for fleeing the country.
7. Sherman, A.J. ibid. 175.
8. Bentwich, N. op. cit. 43-45.
9. Bentwich, N. ibid. 66. ex. inf. Miss Joan Stiebel.
10. Wasserstein, B. *Britain and the Jews of Europe, 1939-1945* (1971) 8-9.
11. Sherman, A.J. op. cit. 198-201.
12. Wasserstein, B. op. cit. 16, 51,52.
13. Wasserstein, B. ibid. 54-80.
14. Sherman, A.J. op. cit. 210.
15. Wasserstein, B. op. cit. 9.
16. Sherman, A.J. op. cit. 182.
16. Wasserstein, B. op. cit. 50, 69, 77, 87, 88, 90, and passim.
17. Wasserstein, B. op. cit. 307-320, 344.
18. Wasserstein, B. op. cit. 10.

19. Wasserstein, B. op. cit. 10.
20. Ex inf. Susan Heimler (now Golombok) Glasgow.
21. Sherman, A.J. op. cit. 258.
22. Wasserstein, B. op. cit. 87-90.
23. *Birmingham Post*. 23 March, 1938.
24. Gilbert, Martin. *The Holocaust* (1986) 54, 450-451.

SIE SIND GAESTE GROSSBRITANNIENS.

Hoeflichkeit und gutes Betragen werden Ihnen ueberall herzliche Aufnahme und Sympathie zesichern.

Sprechen Sie nicht laut auf der Strasse, besonders nicht am Abend.

Nehmen Sie Ruecksicht auf die Bequemlichkeit anderer Leute und vermeiden Sie, deren Eigentum und Moebel zu beschaedigen.

Vergessen Sie nie, dass England's Urteil ueber die deutschen Fluechtlinge von IHREM Verhalten abhaengt.

Card issued to refugees from Germany by the Board of Deputies of British Jews "You are the guest of Great Britain. Politeness and good behaviour will more than anything else ensure you a hearty welcome and sympathy.

Do not speak loudly in the street especially in the evening.

Look after the comfort of other people and avoid damaging their property or furniture.

Never forget that England's opinion of her German refugees depends on your behaviour."

4

The Birmingham Jewish Refugee Club

The entry of German troops into Czechoslovakia in the Spring of 1939 finally destroyed the last vestiges of hope from the Munich Agreement of the previous autumn. The outlook for the Jews and the other minorities in Germany darkened rapidly. War was now inevitable and there was a rush to leave before the final closing of the gates. In Birmingham the number of new arrivals increased rapidly and Hanna Simmons' home became quite inadequate for their needs.

She became pre-occupied with finding a warm and welcoming centre where the weary travellers could meet, relax, discuss their situation and receive understanding help to meet their problems. The result was a Birmingham Jewish Refugee Club, which first met at the invitation of the Birmingham Jewish Working Men's Club in Bromsgrove Street on 7 May 1939.

It was organised on formal lines with officers, a committee and a constitution, and there were several efficient organisers, for many of the local refugees were professional people.[1] Bernard Borkon was a dentist, Walter Seelig a high-ranking lawyer, and Eric Haas was a psycho-analyst. A few prominent members of Singers Hill Synagogue, who were Hanna Simmons' personal friends and sympathisers, joined these refugees on the Committee with Hanna herself as Chairman. English Jews were not encouraged. If their names appeared more than three times in the visitors' book, they were to be told "tactfully" that the Society was for the benefit of the refugees.[2] They were, however, to be allowed by special invitation, or if (like Dr Cohen, the Chief Minister) they were in a position to give advice or encouragement, or if they had specific skills. Within a few weeks the Club was offered the Communal Hall in the Singers Hill Synagogue. A very young and inexperienced teacher ran an English class on the stage with the curtain down. "It was chaos. You heard every kind of dialect and accent, Rhineland, Bavarian, Austrian, Hamburg. We read the leader of the *Birmingham Post* in turn, and tried to translate as best we could".

Donations to the Refugee Club came from the Working Men's Club and other sympathisers. Hanna Simmons, practical as ever, begged crockery from local wholesalers. By today's standards subscriptions seem ludicrously small at threepence a week, and one penny for a cup of tea and three biscuits.[3] But the newcomers had few pennies to spare, some of them

The Committee of the Birmingham Jewish Refugee Club.
Left to right—(unknown), Bernard Borkon, Henry Freeland, Ernest Wolf, Ruth Simmons, Martin Deutschkron, Sam Echt, Frank Linden.

were entirely without resources. One girl admitted being too embarrassed to attend because she could not afford the penny for refreshments.

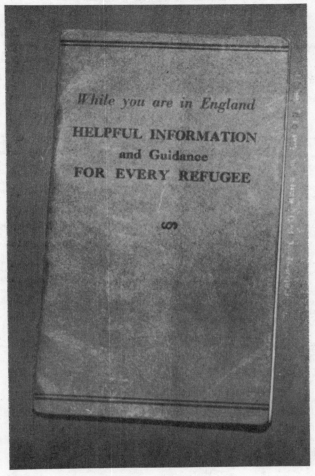

The booklet *While you are in England* issued c. 1938 to refugees by the Board of Deputies of British Jews.

A circular was sent out to all the refugees welcoming them to the Club, giving them information about their strange new environment and advising them to keep a low profile.[4] This had already been impressed upon every newcomer, who had been handed on arrival a small booklet entitled *While you are in England*. It was issued by the Board of Deputies and stressed the importance of adapting to English manners, customs and loyalties as quickly as possible. "The Englishman attaches very great importance to modesty, understatement and quietness in dress and manner. He values good manners more than the incidence of wealth. You will find he says 'thank you' for the slightest service, even for the penny 'bus ticket for which he has paid.

WORK WHICH IS ALLOWED
and
WORK WHICH IS NOT ALLOWED

THE British Government is very sympathetic to the tragedy of Refugees from Greater Germany and other countries. But you must please realise that the maintenance of the Refugees while they remain in Britain must be borne by the Jewish Community and not by the British taxpayer.

This being the case, the Home Office cannot allow anything which will be to the detriment of British employers and workpeople, or take work away from them while there are still a very large number of British men and women out of employment.

It must not be said that the Refugees are taking work away from British workers.

WORK NOT ALLOWED

You must not accept any employment, paid or unpaid, or engage in any business or profession, without written permission from the Aliens Department of the Home Office (*Address: Stanley House, Marsham Street, Westminster, London, S.W.1*). You may not be a "volunteer" without such permission, because this may be taking away the possibility of paid work from a British clerk or mechanic or domestic servant.

Page 18

ERLAUBTE UND
UNERLAUBTE ARBEIT

DIE britische Regierung hat grosses Mitgefühl mit der tragischen Lage der Flüchtlinge aus dem Deutschen Reich und anderen Ländern. Sie müssen jedoch einsehen, dass der Unterhalt der Flüchtlinge während ihres Aufenthalts in Gross-Britannien von der jüdischen Gemeinde und nicht von den britischen Steuerzahlern getragen werden muss.

Daher kann das Home Office (Innenministerium) nichts erlauben, was britischen Unternehmern und Arbeitern schaden könnte, oder was ihnen Arbeit entziehen würde, so lange noch eine sehr grosse Anzahl britischer Männer und Frauen arbeitslos sind.

Auf keiner Fall darf es heissen, dass die Flüchtlinge britischen Arbeitern die Arbeit wegnehmen.

UNERLAUBTE ARBEIT

Sie dürfen keinerlei Stellung—weder bezahlte, noch unbezahlte—annehmen, noch dürfen Sie sich an einem Geschäft beteiligen oder irgendeinen Beruf ausüben, ohne die schriftliche Erlaubnis der Ausländerabteilung des Innenministeriums einzuholen (Adresse: Aliens Department of the Home Office, Stanley House, Marsham Street, Westminster, London, S.W.1). Sie dürfen ohne solche Erlaubnis auch keine Volontärstellung annehmen, da Sie dadurch

Seite 19

Two pages from *While you are in England.*

"Above all the refugees must set about learning English at once. Avoid talking German in public places and do not talk in a loud voice". Hanna Simmons was said to have heard a couple speaking German together on a 'bus. As she moved to get out, she handed them her card hissing "Don't speak German, but come to tea on Sunday".

These efforts at rapid anglicisation were not achieved without cost. The refugees or their forbears had already attempted assimilation with the Germans, now they must do the same with the English. Amid all these confusing instructions, the need for a meeting place like the Refugee Club was obvious, not least to combat loneliness. The minutes of the Club carry a pathetic note in the announcement of a wedding, when it was suggested that such an event be widely circularised, "so that the *Shul* (Synagogue) should not seem so empty".[5] On this occasion, a party was hastily arranged, all the refugees were invited, and on a sunny day the long garden of Duchess Road was packed with guests who, for a few hours, tried to forget their anxieties and join in the celebration.

One of the first acts of the Jewish Refugee Club was the setting up of a section of the Birmingham Hospital Saturday Fund to protect members in case of illness or disability.[6] The grateful refugees were only too ready to repay their hosts by entering enthusiastically into such English activities as flag days for life-boats, hospitals, and non-Jewish refugees, besides donating to the Blood Transfusion Service, yet even here they were warned to "exercise restraint".

Wedding of Selma and Kurt Elias in the garden of 2 Duchess Road, 7 May 1939. Included in the group are: Hanna Simmons, Revd Wolf Lewi (Cantor of Singers Hill Synagogue), Bernard Borkon, Bernard Simmons, Trude Platt and Fritz Stahl. (The last two later left for the USA.)

The Committee immediately made efforts to provide diversions to help the refugees settle as happily as possible into their new surroundings. A ramble into Warwickshire was arranged. Heinz Eisner, one of the few refugees to own a car, met the party to refresh them with lemonade and ice-cream.[7] "Miss Fox's Babes" from a local ballet school gave the refugees a display, and the refugees in their turn were invited to perform at a concert in Water Orton. But the declaration of war on 3 September 1939 was soon to cut short all these activities.

All the refugees were now obliged to appear before a Tribunal, set up by the Home Office, to distinguish genuine refugees from other aliens. The Refugee Committee prepared case papers, undertook interpreting, and gave support to those due to appear before the Tribunal, and later to those with problems of internment (see appendix to this chapter).

Besides standing by the refugees, the Committee's task was to remind the public of the distinction made by the Tribunals between refugees from Nazi oppression (though of German and Austrian nationality) and other aliens. Particularly traumatic was the plight of the parentless young people who had come on the Children's Transports. On reaching the age of sixteen, they were required to appear before the Tribunals, reminding them all too vividly of the unhappy experiences they had already endured in Germany.[8]

The refugees were understandably jittery and a circular was sent out begging them to keep calm. As with all such gatherings, the Club was temporarily closed down, but by mid-October, the Police gave permission for its re-opening, provided the Communal Hall was blacked out. First aid boxes were purchased and an Air Raid Precautions worker was to be in attendance. When Sergeant Rowley of the Aliens' Department, a most understanding and sympathetic member of the Police Force, visited the Club to give advice, it was considered necessary for at least one member of the Committee to be in attendance, so that the Sergeant should not be worried unduly.

The members now hurled themselves into the war effort. A War Charities' Fund was set up and they were urged to make "real sacrifices" for the Red Cross. At a *Chanukah* (the Jewish Festival of Lights) party in December, a raffle was held to buy wool to make gifts for the Lady Mayoress's Depot for Soldiers' Comforts. Within a month, eighteen Balaclava helmets, six scarves, six pairs of socks and a pair of mittens had been despatched.[9]

As winter came and the war seemed to settle to a stalemate, the Club once more got into its stride. The irrepressible Henry Freeland was appointed Entertainments Officer. For many years to come he was to be the mainstay, with his accordion, of communal children's parties and the like. Every Thursday he sat at the piano which his wife, Helen, had managed to get out of Germany, creating a cheerful atmosphere for the meeting. He arranged sing-songs, competitions, keep-fit classes and English lessons. Serious subjects, such as religion and Zionism, were restricted to ten-minute talks. A dance band was formed from the members, and a concert party which offered its services to other societies.

In the midst of these distractions, Hanna Simmons' death in March 1940 was saddening, but the Club, now well established, continued as usual. However, the false calm of the "phoney war" was soon to end. Rationing was first mentioned that Spring, when members were asked to bring small contributions of tea.

In April, Norway and Denmark had come under German occupation. In May, the Low Countries capitulated. The Maginot Line was turned, Northern France was overrun. By early June, the evacuation of the British Forces from Dunkirk was complete, and shortly the Germans were in Paris.

The Battle of Britain was now in progress, and many people thought the invasion of Britain imminent. Churchill vowed to fight the Germans "on the beaches ... in the fields, in the streets". Rumours were rife.

A Birmingham soldier, on leave from the South Coast, swore that his friend had seen the Channel thick with the bodies of German soldiers. "You could have walked over dry-foot." Dr Hyman Hamilton, a well-known member of the Jewish Community, who had come ten years previously from South Wales to practise in Smethwick, went into hospital for an operation on his knee. When he emerged, limping, it was confidently put around that he was an Italian spy, shot in the leg trying to escape!

Small wonder the refugees from Hitler's Germany were viewed with misgiving. The lives of one family were made wretched by a neighbour who accused them of signalling to the enemy from their back garden.

On 22 May 1940, the United Kingdom Emergency Powers (Defence) Act had come into force. All aliens, whether friendly or enemy, could now be interned immediately. Without further warning, on 5 July, most male refugees between the ages of sixteen and sixty were interned, first being collected locally at Thorpe Street barracks. "I shall never forget Ruth Simmons", said Henry Freeland. "She came down in Red Cross uniform to the barracks and tried to explain we were not enemy aliens but friends." It was useless. The country was nervous and "intern the lot" was the order of the day. Many were sent from Birmingham to a holiday camp at Seaton on the South Devon coast. The weather was glorious and there was a swimming pool, but the threat of invasion was hardly conducive to a holiday atmosphere.

The internment took place on a Thursday. The women met as usual at the Club. Henry Freeland had made his wife, Helen, promise to take his place on stage to lead the singsong he had arranged. "I kept my promise", said Helen, "but we were all crying." The Club became more difficult to run without the menfolk, but the need increased. The women, most of them in domestic service or nursing, and not always happy in their unaccustomed tasks, badly needed somewhere to exchange news and experiences. The Club was now for many their only refuge and the women busied themselves with schemes for sending letters and parcels to their menfolk.

Help was given to those applying for release on compassionate grounds. As ever, language remained a problem. One optimistic hernia sufferer pleaded the necessity for an "operation for rapture"!

In August, the tempo of war stepped up with the first serious air-raids of the Blitz. The Communal Hall did not give sufficient protection and it was felt unwise to flood the local air-raid shelters with refugees. Eventually, new premises were found at Kyrle Hall, Gosta Green, further from the centre of Birmingham. [10] It became too dangerous to venture out at night, so meetings were held on Sunday afternoons.

The nerves of many people who had already been through so much were almost shattered by the constant air-raids. "Dr Cohen was our great source of comfort", recalled one member. "His strong faith reassured us. One afternoon there was a long and noisy alert. The ack-ack guns thundered almost continuously. We didn't think he could possibly come. Imagine our astonishment when the door opened and in he walked. It was against wartime regulations, but he had come through the streets to be with us."

Numbers now rapidly increased. Coastal areas were categorised as "protected", and this caused an influx of refugees into the Midlands. Despite the Blitz, three hundred people attended the 1940 *Chanukah* party. The Refugee Children's Movement was bringing many young people to Birmingham, all clamouring for entertainment. Another dance band had to be brought together, and a host and hostess appointed for each meeting to help people mix easily. A Revue, "Youth Calling" [11], went into rehearsal. Chess, draughts, dominoes and darts were introduced and, after some hesitation as to its propriety on Sundays, card-playing.

The more serious minded deplored the lack of "cultural activity" and another committee went to work. An Intelligence Test Competition figured as a rather formidable item on the programme. Volunteer lecturers from the University were recruited. Mr I.A. Shapiro from the English Department spoke on Bernard Shaw, and a Dr Lesser came from Oxford to lecture on Thomas Mann. [12] Among the refugees there was no lack of ability to discuss their own predicament. Some of these meetings appear to have been thrown open to the Community. At a seminar on "Jews Fighting Hitler", Dr Cohen spoke for British Jews, a Dr Meyer of the BBC dealt with the "Fighting Refugees" and Bernard Borkon with "Persecuted Jews". The Minutes noted, regretfully, that there were only refugees in the audience. Advice on Income Tax problems proved more popular. But it was music which provided the greatest solace. Even in the midst of war, there was a magical summer evening in July 1942, at the Birmingham Botanical Gardens, when the Rose Quartet [13] from Vienna played Mozart, Haydn and Beethoven. Arnold Rose at 78 was still the leader and some of the difficulties of the time may be gauged from a letter to the organisers, asking for a written invitation to each member, so that travelling passes might be obtained. Opera singers from Prague and Vienna gave a performance of Mozart's *Marriage of Figaro*, so that "young people could have a chance of hearing a masterpiece ... they had not heard before ... , and older Continental people could remember the work they used to hear in happier times". [14] The Lantern Company from the Little Theatre of Vienna, played a comedy by Franz Molnar, and put on a Viennese cabaret, entirely in German. These were the highlights, but there were besides many concerts and recitals by local performers and the refugees themselves.

BIRMINGHAM JEWISH REFUGEE CLUB

SEDER SERVICE
ON
THURSDAY, APRIL 14th, 7-30 p.m. prompt.
(Doors open 7 p.m.
At the JEWISH CENTRE, Station Street

Admission 5/-   Bring Your Hagadah

Ticket for *Seder* service, 1949.
Hagadah (Hebrew) — the order of service for the festival of the redemption of the Jews from Egypt. This is read at the *Seder*.

One happy outcome of the Club was the Communal *Seder* (Passover) Service, started in 1942. [15] Tickets cost 2s.6d. (13p) and fifty free seats were set aside for children and members of the Forces. Every Spring, as Passover came around, with its poignant memories of family gatherings, the refugees would come together in the Communal Hall to celebrate their own Exodus. "There would be two hundred or more", recalled Ruth Simmons. "In 1947, my own wedding had to be put off for a week until the Seder was over", and indeed it looked like a wedding with long tables decorated with daffodils and tulips. Before each place was a small plate, set out with bright green bitter herbs, scarlet radishes and portions of *charoset*, the "mortar" with which the Israelite slaves built the treasure cities of Pithom and Rameses in Egypt. This was symbolised by a fragrant concoction of apples and nuts, spices and wine. Dr Chaim Pearl, by then second Minister at Singers Hill, recounted the story of the departure from Egypt, and explained the significance of the symbols. The hard-boiled eggs in salt water were eaten and the festive meal of fish (which was off the ration) set on the table. This was *gefillte fish*[16] eked out still further by potato salad. Grace was said, and as the obligatory four cups of wine went round, the mood became expansive. Many thought sadly of dear ones left behind in the nightmare on the Continent, but there was also much laughter, especially among the younger ones, who enjoyed the rare opportunity for dressing up. The old folk tunes, which concluded the service, rang out vigorously. Cantor Wolf Lewi of Singers Hill Synagogue then conducted the impromptu choir with enthusiasm. He himself had come from Germany, and these were the refugees' own freedom songs.

The Club had been forced to move yet again early in that year, as Kyrle Hall had been requisitioned by the Government. The Liberal Synagogue was approached, but made the difficult proviso that no lectures should be delivered in German. Eventually, a home was found with the International Centre in Suffolk Street, where the Club continued to flourish for another year. Useful sums were raised for such worthy causes as Mrs Churchill's Aid for Russia Fund, the Lord Mayor's Christmas Tree Fund and the Fund for Jewish Prisoners of War in Palestine. There was co-operation with other refugee organisations, including the Austrians, the Czechs and the Association of Christian Refugees in Birmingham.

Nevertheless, early in 1943, the Minutes of the Club came to a sudden end. "It just packed up" confirmed Helen Freeland. Committee members were frequently resigning, pleading pressure of war work. Some of the internees were drifting back, only to disappear again into the Pioneer Corps. Others had settled successfully, married and had homes of their own.

There remained the International Centre as a meeting place, and the refugees themselves set up a Youth Club, which met at the Liberal Synagogue. The Communal *Seder*s continued for many years, finally being taken up by the Liberal (now Progressive) Synagogue.

It took a long time for many of the refugees to regain their self-confidence after the terrible ordeal they had experienced on the Continent. To this day, they look back affectionately at the Birmingham Jewish Refugee Club for the support it gave them. "It was no ordinary club, where people go only to dance and enjoy themselves. The people that it gathered together all had a common fate which united them — homelessness. For a few hours the Club was to replace that home to some extent."

Appendix

The Tribunals

Ilse Lewen graphically described the ordeal. "Just after the war started, everyone was sent to the main police station off Steelhouse Lane, and we were all interviewed, one at a time, but all asked the same questions."

"Why did you come to England?"

"Because my sister was here."

"What do you like about England?"

To which everyone replied in their limited English:

"I like your lovely green fields."

"You were then either an enemy alien, in which case you were interned, or a friendly enemy alien, and given a little grey book, which told you all about the curfew. My sister lived just outside Birmingham in Smethwick. If I wanted to spend a night with her, I had to tell the Birmingham police, then the Smethwick police. Next morning I had to tell the Smethwick police that I was going back, and then the Birmingham police that I *was* back."

According to the people interviewed, the distinction between enemy aliens and 'friendly' enemy aliens was difficult to understand. The Tribunal's decisions were, presumably, based on guidelines from the Home Office.

References and notes
1. Club Minutes 7 May 1939; ibid. 11 May 1939
2. ibid. 16 July 1939
3. ibid. 18 May 1939
4. ibid. 16 July 1939
5. ibid. 1 June 1939
6. ibid. 16 July 1939
7. ibid. 8 June 1939
8. Wasserstein B. *Britain and the Jews of Europe* 1939-1945 (1979) 84-86
9. Club Minutes 14 January 1940
10. ibid. 7 March 1942
11. ibid. 7 March 1942
12. ibid. 15 June 1942
13. ibid. 15 June 1942
14. Programme Note *Marriage of Figaro* by Mozart, 18 June 1944
15. Club Minutes 13 March 1942
16. *Gefillte Fish*. Yiddish. Balls of chopped fish, flavoured with spices.

5

The Refugee Children's Movement

The Refugee Children's Movement was founded in November 1938 as a direct result of the Kristallnacht. An Inter-Aid Committee for children from Germany had existed in England since 1936, but events now demanded a drastic speeding-up of the cumbersome visa system. Provided a child's maintenance could be guaranteed, either by organisations or by individuals, and the guarantors were able to provide financial backing for eventual re-emigration, children were allowed to enter this country on a simple travel document.[1]

From 1936 Jewish children in Germany, if they were to be educated at all, were forced to enter the few Jewish schools. Until then they had to endure the humiliation accorded to them in non-Jewish schools by their fellow pupils, and often by the teachers as well. Frank Linden recalled returning to school after one of the Jewish festivals. The desks belonging to Jewish boys were all pushed to one side of the room and they were no longer allowed to mix with the others. After the Kristallnacht every male Jew between the ages of sixteen and sixty went in fear of being arrested and sent to a concentration camp. Orphanages were burnt down and as parents disappeared "bands of homeless children, some of them no more than infants", roamed the countryside. In particular they were to be found in the woods around Berlin, "cold and often starving"[2]. Panic reigned, and the consulates were besieged as parents made every effort to ensure some sort of future for their children, even at the cost of sending them to unknown people in a strange land.

In the House of Commons, in November 1938, Home Secretary Sir Samuel Hoare made an eloquent plea to his fellow countrymen. "Here is a chance of taking the younger generation of a great people ... The chance of mitigating to some extent the terrible sufferings of their parents and friends"[3]. No further justification is needed than the poignant farewell letter written by a father to his sons, secure in the Buckinghamshire countryside. "We derive our courage mainly from the thought of knowing you are in safe surroundings and on the right way to becoming useful and good human beings".

Once the true horror of the Nazi methods penetrated abroad, offers of hospitality, from individual guarantors and from institutions, began to flood in. At first the Movement tried to match each child to a suitable

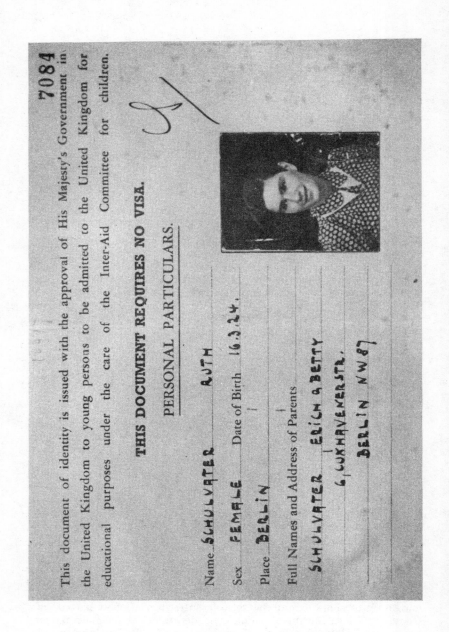

This document of identity is issued with the approval of His Majesty's Government in the United Kingdom to young persons to be admitted to the United Kingdom for educational purposes under the care of the Inter-Aid Committee for children.

7084

THIS DOCUMENT REQUIRES NO VISA.

PERSONAL PARTICULARS.

Name SCHULVATER RUTH

Sex FEMALE Date of Birth 16.3.24.

Place BERLIN

Full Names and Address of Parents

SCHULVATER ERICH & BETTY

6, CUXHAVENERSTR,

BERLIN NW87

Special permit issued to children travelling with the Refugee Children's Movement.

religious and cultural background, but as the crisis deepened, most parents ceased to worry where the children went, so long as they were safe.

Some people found the hardship of separation too much, and held back, waiting until it was too late, for better days ahead. One grandmother, unable to bear the parting, snatched her grandchild down from the train as it was getting up steam. But despite all the obstacles, by the outbreak of war, nearly 10,000 children had been rescued and settled in homes and hostels in this country[4]. Until the war began, the Movement had been organised from Bloomsbury House in London.

Then, in view of the possibility that communications might be cut by enemy action, the country was divided into twelve regional Civil Defence areas. The Movement, therefore set up twelve regional committees to correspond with these areas, and in 1942 Ruth Simmons was appointed Secretary to the Midland area. Although she had been acting unofficially in this capacity for some time, it was a daunting task. But the challenge was met and eventually the majority of the children brought here by the Movement settled down and integrated successfully into life in Birmingham and the Midland region. Unfortunately the outbreak of war and subsequent evacuation meant a further upheaval for many, just as they were becoming settled with their foster-parents. Now they had to move on again, sometimes in school groups. Some hosts found it difficult to understand why they had been asked to receive German-speaking children, often distressed and occasionally with behavioural problems. The Blitz made the situation doubly difficult. Ruth Simmons, tracking down refugee children in Coventry after the attack of November 1940 found herself coldly received by people who had had their homes shattered by the German Luftwaffe.

As well as the trauma of being wrenched suddenly from warm and loving homes, most of the children had experienced, to some extent, the fear of the Nazi terror. On the Kristallnacht, Heinz Finke's home was raided, and everyone, children, parents and grandmother, marched to the police station. He watched the synagogues blaze and groups of Jews being brought out, among them a rabbi improbably carrying a typewriter. "Everybody except Father was released but he was kept in 'protective' custody." One girl out with her mother recalled a Nazi lout spitting at them. To her astonishment, her mother, normally a retiring person, spat back. Others witnessed elderly Jews on their knees scrubbing pavements, and children had stones thrown at them on the way to school. A Viennese girl remembered being locked out of the family flat. "We had to give up the keys and mother asked where we could go, that cold November night. She was given an address, but later we heard all those who sheltered there were deported. We lost our furniture, everything. There was a large teddy bear on the sofa; the Gestapo man told me he had earmarked it for his own child."

Ruth Price, a schoolgirl of fourteen from Berlin, and two friends went for a walk in the country. They were arrested on the station platform as they awaited their train and were taken to Gestapo Headquarters where they were severely warned of "unlawful assembly". This brave girl had been a member of the Bund, a Zionist Youth Group. For months she spent many hours at a small railway station, guiding prisoners who had been released from concentration camps, to the Jüdische Gemeinde[5]. Here these

Lessons in anti-semitism. Two Jewish boys stand condemned by the slogan on the blackboard "The Jew is our greatest enemy", 1930s.

bewildered men, their clothes crumpled and their heads shaven, would be taken care of until they could return to their families, often many miles away.

Although only eight years old in 1939, Gerda Solomon clearly recalled her departure. Her father had already spent nine months in the concentration camp at Sachsenhausen. Her education came to a stop when Jewish children in Czechoslovakia were no longer permitted to go to school, and even the Jewish schools were closed. She and her brother were sent, ostensibly as children of the family chauffeur, from their village home to Prague, their parents following. "My father had belonged to the Social Democratic Party and through that we managed to get visas for England; what we could not get was the Gestapo stamp on them. So day after day my father went to one of the Gestapo places, and my mother and I to another, standing for hours in long queues. In any case my brother and I were down on a list to go to England with the Children's Transport. We should have gone earlier but our relations said to my mother, 'If you send the children out, you don't know if you will ever see them again'. So one transport after another went and we weren't put on it. Eventually news came that there was only one more transport leaving Prague and my father put his foot down. 'I don't care what happens', he said, 'the children must get out'. So at twelve o'clock at night—I shall never forget it—we were woken up, taken to the station and put on the train."

Many people recalled the strain of the days preliminary to departure. For Helga Loeb, whose mother was a widow dependent on her pension, there were no wealthy relatives abroad to come to their rescue. "Everybody was busy rushing to the consulates, sewing outfits and selling possessions. What a relief when our permits to join the Children's Transports came through; we too could join in the hectic rush and our mother was free to take up a domestic post that had been offered to her in Liverpool. Although I was only twelve, I travelled right across Vienna alone to fetch our documents. For some reason this was considered safer and I felt immensely proud of my responsibility."

For most children, the first news of their parents' success in getting them a place on the Children's Transport was a letter telling them to be at the local station at a certain date and time. Train loads of children passed through Germany, converging on the Hook of Holland or Hamburg. On the journey they were cared for by members of the Reichsvertretung fur Juden in Germany and the Kulturgemeinde in Vienna[6], who were under oath to return when they had delivered their charges. "These were the unsung heroes of the day" said John Grenville, Professor of Modern History at the University of Birmingham, who himself had come by the Children's Transport. "The Nazis made it clear that if they defaulted, the operation would come to an end." Older children were given the charge of younger children. One girl of fifteen, who had had some brief training in a children's nursery, was told to take care of an infant and make up its feeds. "This at least left me no time for tears, and I couldn't help being cheered when I thought of the suitcase full of lovely new dresses and blouses my mother had made for me. But I still remember her sad face."

In some cases children were strictly segregated by age. "My younger sister and I were separated at the station" recalled Helga Loeb. "I don't remember seeing her again until we were being sorted out for our foster-parents at Norwich. Cruel though this seems in hindsight, we just took such hardships for granted." Among much gratuitous unpleasantness by the Nazis, only one parent was allowed on the platform to say goodbye. "My mother endured the anguish of parting with her three sons alone" recalled Professor Grenville. In the case of Ernst Aris, however, both parents saw the boys off and then drove rapidly to a point where they could wave to them on the train. This was the last glimpse the family was to have of each other. Yet another refugee, then a small child, was moved to tears forty years afterwards as she re-visualised the group of aunts and uncles, cousins and grandparents who came to the 'bus stop, none of whom she was to see again.

The children were allowed to take very little money (twelve marks said one, fifteen shillings said another) and no jewellery. Ernst Aris's brother had a silver watch, but a kindly guard told him to put it out of sight. They were allowed one suitcase each, which was filled with the best clothes their parents could afford, often bought by selling their few remaining possessions. Some boys arrived in the plus fours then fashionable in Germany. They were to look strange, as did their long mackintoshes and large hats, alongside the more casual English wear. Henry Warner, who went to work in the Birmingham jewellery quarter, remembered the amusement of the girls in the workshop at his clothes, and longed for the time when he had earned sufficient money to fade into the anonymity of flannels and pullover. Most of the children seem to have been spared the sadness of their parents, because they did not realise the parting was probably forever, and indeed many of the fathers and mothers pinned their hopes on the ability of their children to find them guarantors or get them out of Germany in some way. In most cases this hope was misplaced. One girl tried to persuade an English relative to take her cousin as a domestic. "How can you expect me to let her come here as a servant" argued the lady. "It would put us on the wrong footing." "You don't seem to know what is happening in Germany" was all she could reply. It was an impossible task for a young girl.

Every refugee interviewed remembers some details of the momentous journey to this country. Lia Lesser from Prague, one of the youngest, recalled the hard wooden seat she occupied for so many hours as she made the long journey across Europe. The older children were conscious of a great feeling of freedom and relief as they crossed the German frontier. Many came via the Hook of Holland and saw the Dutch railway stations crowded with sympathisers, pressing drinks, chocolate and their blessings on the children. "They also brought us postcards to send to our parents" recalled Gerda Solomon. "I still have mine."

The sea journey seems mostly to have been accomplished at night, and many do not remember the boat at all. They were settled eight to a cabin; some were sea-sick on the rough crossing, others slept throughout.

On arrival at Harwich "dog-tags" were placed around their necks and the children, still half asleep, were shepherded into buses for Dovercourt, a near-by seaside holiday camp[7].

Students and voluntary workers from the various refugee committees received the children in a large reception hall and gave them cups of steaming cocoa. Three of the people interviewed remembered vividly their first slice of English white bread and butter. Two found it delicious after their accustomed rye-bread. A third tossed it to the seagulls. Every effort

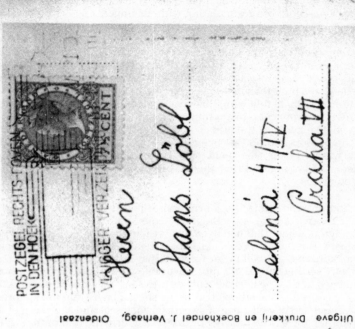

Postcard sent by Fritz Löbl, brother of Gerda Solomon, to his father in Prague announcing their safe arrival in Holland, 1938.

was made to put the children at their ease. "A little man sang *Under the Spreading Chestnut Tree* gesticulating with his fingers on his bald head"; to another group a muscle man showed off his strength. At last the confused and weary travellers were taken to the chalets lining the sea, where they were to sleep. Coming from Central Europe, few had seen the sea before; even Ernst Aris from East Prussia, who had spent holidays on the Baltic coast, was awe-struck at the thundering waves. The wooden chalets had been built for summer visitors. Many of the refugees arrived in the winter of 1938/39 following the Kristallnacht and found them cruelly cold. "We slept in our coats or anything we could lay our hands on" said one child, who, like many of the others, had come from a middle-class home, where the parents had not yet been turned out of their centrally-heated flats. It was often at this point that the euphoria of the adventure dwindled, as they realised that this was no holiday journey. Many were deeply homesick.

Some children who made the journey via Hamburg and Southampton, were able for two days to enjoy the novel experience of luxury aboard the SS Washington, a liner that had been put at their disposal by the American Government. But the sight of a small baby put out in its pram to air on deck, struck a chord one girl will never forget. What of the parents, and of the child itself, setting out alone into an unknown future? Apprehension overwhelmed her, as she became truly aware of her own predicament. But she was reassured as she stepped on to the special boat-train for Victoria. A kindly hand had placed a bag of sweets on each seat and she was met in London by her uncle, who took her by taxi on a whirlwind tour of the sights of London. "He had only been here two days, but he seemed to know everything."

In the last months before the declaration of war, sheer pressure of numbers made it almost impossible to match children to foster-homes. "Our fate seemed to be entirely a matter of chance" said Professor Grenville. "I found myself on the railway station at Harwich, where I was suddenly separated from my two brothers. An elderly gentleman in an elderly car took me to a preparatory school in Essex. I lost touch with my brothers for several weeks, and was homesick, frightened, and completely bewildered." Lucy Benedikt described Saturday and Sunday afternoons at the camp. "People came and looked us over ... 'I want a blue-eyed child ... so big'."

Lia Lesser's future was determined in an even more casual way. Her mother had been in correspondence with an English lady, and she was taken to London to await being claimed. The children were being dealt with in alphabetical order, and a school-teacher from Anglesey found to her dismay she had been allotted a child whose name began with Z. Worried as to how she was to make the long journey back to her home the same day, she asked for a substitute. This was Lia Lesser (Blum as she then was), a fortuitous occurrence for her, as it resulted in an exceptionally happy childhood. She slept throughout the long journey, "but my guardian told me that when we changed at Crewe some sailors carried me to the Holyhead train, and sang to me for the rest of the way. It was bright moonlight when at last we arrived at Bull Bay. 'Mouse' as my guardian was always called, took me by the hand and we walked together up to a white farm and then through three gates that led to her bungalow. A large cat sat comfortably on the table in the lamplight and I knew that my troubles were over."

Lia Lesser in Anglesey, 1939.

Gerda Solomon and her brother were also fortunate. "A Czech gentleman came along and took charge of us. After three months in a Czech hostel in Broadstairs we heard our parents were in England. They were housed in a tiny gypsy caravan in Surrey, where my father did farm work for one pound a week. It was dreadful for them not being able to afford to come and see us. But at last a wealthy couple, who had taken it on themselves to teach the refugees English, gave them tickets to Broadstairs, as a birthday present for my mother. You may imagine the reunion."

In some cases England represented only a staging post, where children might stay until the arrival of visas made it possible for them to proceed to America or elsewhere, where their parents hoped to join them. The most fortunate had relatives or friends in this country, but very often the relatives were refugees themselves, in no position to take on an extra burden. Many were taken in by Jewish families in Britain who undertook to bring them up as their own children, but even for the most warmhearted there were problems.

One kind and sensible lady felt her foster-child would be happier wearing the same uniform as her new school-mates, and dyed her bright jersey dark brown. The child bitterly resented the loss of the rainbow colours her mother had given her. For another ten year-old the shock of separation from home was so great that she would neither speak nor allow anyone to touch her long, thick hair.

"It was the little hurts that were the worst" confessed a refugee who had been ten years old when she arrived. Her scattered family had been brought together one Christmas by a kindly Quaker doctor who employed her widowed mother, formerly a professional person, as his housekeeper. But this reunion was spoilt for her little daughter, who was heartbroken at seeing her mother emptying the family chamber-pots.

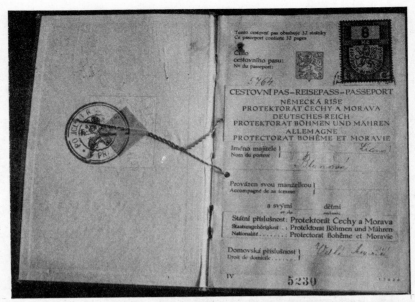

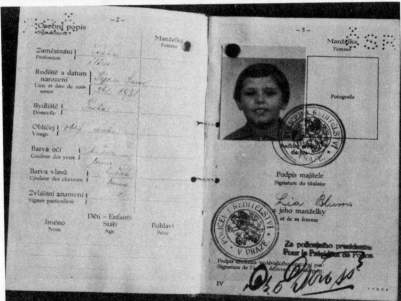

Pages from Lia Blum's passport

The psychological impact on all these children must have been appalling, even for the best-balanced, who determined to learn English and settle into their new background as quickly as possible. The psalms proved an unexpected inspiration to one such child. "I think a Bible must have been left by my bed. I used the psalms deliberately to learn English and as a source of strength. They were my mainstay."

The three Aris brothers with their mother (left) and an aunt, 1935.

Often groups of people, schools or churches collected the money necessary, and one or more of their members undertook to care for a child. In the case of the Aris brothers this was highly successful: "Three families from Long Crendon in Buckinghamshire made themselves responsible for me and my two brothers. We were ten, eleven and nearly fourteen years of age. The father of one of the families was Professor of Classics at Glasgow University; the second a colonel in the Indian Army and the third a bank manager. They were good, loving people, who did their best to make us happy. Their old houses, which I now realise were very beautiful, seemed queer and cold to us, with their quarry tile floors, and the oak beams on which we kept hitting our heads. My eldest brother soon went to work on a farm near Gloucester, belonging to two ladies of the Fry's Chocolate family. My other brother and I joined the Professor's son as boarders at Thame Grammar School." Ernst Aris was quick to notice the difference between German and English schools. "Over there, we had classes of seventy or eighty. A master ruled us with a long stick. Often he had the whole class bending over." At the outbreak of war, he and his brother came in for a certain amount of ragging, "even to being called 'little Nazis', but we gave as good as we got" and soon settled down to make some enduring friendships. Professor Grenville noted how in Germany anyone who was slightly different was picked on and mocked: here he stood out in clothes, language and outlook, but was always treated with the greatest sympathy by boys and masters alike. The Quakers, perhaps by reason of their early persecution, were deeply committed to helping the refugees. It was through Mrs Edith Fox of Woodbrooke Quaker College in Birmingham, that Ruth Price, who had helped so many concentration camp victims, came to be adopted by the congregation of a church in Rubery on the outskirts of Birmingham. It was June 1939 and the need was urgent. At Mrs Fox's request, the Vicar asked for a volunteer to take a fifteen-year old girl: a sixty-year old lady, who ran a small drapery shop, came forward.

The Aris family house in East Prussia.

Mrs Fox had been in touch with Quakers in Holland, and through them with Ruth's family. She had sent the girl a postcard showing a pretty cottage in the country, and Ruth anticipated with pleasure the thought of this as her future home. Moreover several of her friends were already in England. At first she was disappointed with the little store at the end of a drab row of terraced houses, and, knowing nothing of the language, bewildered by the elderly people around her. The only money she had were the twelve marks she had been allowed to bring with her, so that she could not visit her friends, and even the few coppers for the tram-ride to the Foxes at Woodbrooke constituted a problem. She became worried that her education seemed to have been forgotten, nor was she even permitted to work. Eventually a place was offered to her at the Edgbaston Church of England College, and an organisation called the Birmingham Adult School Union collected sixpences from its members for her fares and expenses. "Somebody gave me an old tennis racquet and a second-hand school uniform ... I could have been happy, but war was approaching. My mother unsuccessfully applied for a domestic permit, and my father, who had been an interior architect, attempted to emigrate as a carpenter."

With the outbreak of war the school was commandeered as a Fuel Office. The pupils scattered, Ruth to Edgbaston High School. After four terms

WAR ORGANISATION OF THE BRITISH RED CROSS
AND ORDER OF ST. JOHN

To:
Comité International
R de la Croix Rouge
Genève

074924 · 15 JUL 1941

Prisoners of War, Wounded and Missing Department.

ENQUIRER
Fragesteller

PASSED P.73

Name   *SCHULVATER.*

Christian name   *RUTH.*
Vorname

Address   ....

Relationship of Enquirer to Addressee   *DAUGHTER.*
Wie ist Fragesteller mit Empfänger verwandt?

The Enquirer desires news of the Addressee and asks that the following message should be transmitted to him.
Der Fragesteller verlangt Auskunft über den Empfänger.   Bitte um Weiterbeförderung dieser Meldung.

*LIEBSTE ELTERN. BIN GESUND
UND SEHR GLÜCKLICH ZUHAUS UND
IN SCHULE. OHNE NACHRICHT
VON EUCH UND AMERIKA. GRÜSSE
KÜSSE   Ruth.*

Date   *1·4·41.*

ADDRESSEE
Empfänger

Name   *SCHULVATER.*

Christian name   *E. ISRAEL.*
Vorname

Address   *KUXHAVENERSTR. 6ᴵ*
       BERLIN · N.W. 87.
       GERMANY.   26 MAI 1941

The Addressee's reply to be written overleaf.
Empfänger schreibe Antwort auf Rückseite.

Letter sent through the Red Cross by Ruth Price to her parents, April 1941.

of schooling she obtained her School Certificate, and eventually became a teacher.

For a time she received Red Cross messages from her parents and was able to tell them she had met the young man she was eventually to marry. "They answered, rather to my surprise hoping for an immediate engagement. They must have been very anxious about my future. Later I heard they were deported and perished in Auschwitz. I think they were together. That is my only consolation."

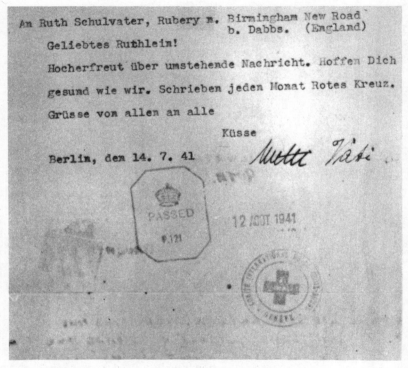

Reply to the letter from Ruth Price, August 1941.

Helga Loeb from Vienna, her sister Iolanthe Fox, and their mother, also received sympathetic help from the Quakers. The mother acted as housekeeper to Lucy and George Cadbury, and her daughters were welcomed with her into the Cadburys' home. "They were so generous, not only with money, but with their time. I was rather a disturbed teenager, not doing very well at school. They taught me not to take the easy way, that duties came first. I now see the three separate strands that brought me through to be a strong personality, my mother's affection, the kindness of the Jewish family that rescued me and the personal care and tolerant understanding of the Quakers."

As well as the Quakers, Christadelphians also felt a special responsibility for Jewish victims of the Nazis, and many opened their homes and institutions to the children. A strange story is told by Ruth Simmons. A lad from a rural district in Poland had been placed with Christadelphians on a primitive dairy farm in Worcestershire. He was looked after by a very elderly lady and her farmer son. As he approached his sixteenth birthday, Bob, as he was now called, was summoned to the Tribunals and Ruth Simmons was sent to reassure him. She arrived at milking-time, the farmer motioned her to a big shed which she entered nervously. Immediately a vast herd of untethered cows surrounded her. Bob meanwhile continued calmly with the milking, whilst his future was discussed. All was well, he was not interned and it was obviously a very suitable placement.

Nearly forty years later, Ruth received a telephone call from America. An uncle of Bob's, who had emigrated to the States, had died and his solicitor wished to get in touch with his nephew. It was a long shot, Ruth had heard nothing of him in the interim, but she decided to see if anyone knew of his whereabouts.

Apart from the motorway roaring above it, the farm seemed almost untouched by the years. It was still as ramshackle, shabby curtains still flapped from the open windows, there was still no electricity. The old lady had departed, but her son, now in late middle-age, sat on the same ancient leather sofa, its springs sagging to the floor. He was in the process of basting a large and succulent rib of beef, throwing the surplus fat on the fire so that it roared up the chimney. "Bob's having a bath" he called out, "like he always does on a Friday before he goes for a binge in town. He won't show himself till he's completely dressed, just like all the Jews." Returning to his cooking, he chuckled ruminatively, "We live well here ... 400 acres and they'll all go to Bob."

Bob eventually came down, squarer and going bald, but otherwise not much changed and was moderately interested in Ruth Simmons' news.

Two fifteen year old girls were never chosen by a family. "We were too old for fostering." Grete was sent to learn mothercraft in Liverpool, where she had to deal with mentally disturbed children as well as normal ones. Anna, who had come from a family of intellectuals, found herself in a small town in the Midlands with a couple who ran a greengrocer's shop. "I went to school but they expected me to do the housework. I was very spoilt at home and never even made my own bed; now I had to make theirs as well. I'm sure they thought I gave myself airs, and I see now they were kind-hearted. But I was very unhappy." It was gradually dawning on both girls that they would never see their parents again and both admitted to having cried nearly the whole time.

It speaks for the resilience of the human spirit that most of the people interviewed have, outwardly at least, achieved successful lives. Yet tragedies were not uncommon. Simon and David, two brothers, whose parents felt at the time they could not leave Germany for business reasons, were given free places at Rugby School. On leaving, Simon was offered a position in a firm which gave him the prospect of studying for a BSc on day-release. His parents meanwhile had emigrated to the United States and wrote that he should join them, leaving his younger brother in England to complete his education. Simon was reluctant to throw up his chances of a good career; moreover, the submarine war in the Atlantic was at its height and he was extremely apprehensive. Ruth Simmons, in her official capacity, pleaded urgently with the parents, but they were adamant.

The ship was torpedoed and Simon was drowned. After that incident, no more young people were sent overseas.

Trude was fostered by a cultured family, who recognised that she was gifted, and determined she should have every educational advantage. She was successful at school and in her later career. But although she was showered with presents, she could apparently sense no loving warmth in the family's attitude and deep down felt she was unwanted. She committed suicide.

John Grenville was another obviously talented child but, in his case, his education was considered only of limited importance. The fees for his Essex preparatory school were paid by an anonymous benefactor who, while expressing interest in his progress, never became personally involved, and the boy was cared for by the Portsmouth Refugee Committee. The Regional Committees varied in outlook, but the general view was that the refugee children should not have advantages over English children who were similarly dependent on public charity. Moreover, it was considered likely to promote anti-semitism if the professional market were suddenly to be flooded by German-Jewish doctors and lawyers.

His preparatory school had given young Grenville an excellent classical education and he was offered a scholarship to a public school. The Portsmouth Committee, however, felt he should become self-supporting as soon as possible and decided that he should leave school and train as a tailor in Leeds.

John Grenville's father had for a time been held in a concentration camp, but, perhaps because he had been a judge in a Court of Appeal, he was given a visa for England and found work in a factory at Croydon. His attempts to bring his wife over on a domestic permit failed. Although John Grenville was now comparatively happy in his school-life, he was able to see his father only about once a year and he was very frightened for his mother's fate. "I even wrote to the King."

The boy's father tried to persuade the Portsmouth Committee to allow his son to take up his scholarship, offering to support him as far as he could. But the Committee threatened to renounce any interest in the boy if its instructions were not carried out. Eventually a compromise was reached. John Grenville was to attend a Technical College in Cambridge, where he would learn the building trade. But the boy had made up his mind to become a scientist and set out to educate himself with a correspondence course paid for by his father. When in his innocence he told the Cambridge Refugee Committee of his efforts, they replied it was against the regulations of the Technical College and warned he might be expelled. On the contrary, however, he was helped by the head-master; he gained his building certificate but went to work as a laboratory assistant.

Unfortunately the fumes of the laboratory affected his health and he now decided to become a historian. He found himself a job as gardener's boy at Peterhouse, Cambridge, where he shocked the College by asking to be allowed to use the library. It took some time to obtain permission and it was only granted on condition that he did not attempt to enter the University of Cambridge as a student!

On the outbreak of war, the London School of Economics was evacuated to Peterhouse and one of the students tutored Grenville for the Inter-Arts Examination. He obtained a place at Birkbeck College and handed in his notice to Peterhouse. They accepted it with regret, noting that they felt he had the makings of a Head Porter!

John Grenville thought that his earlier unhappiness and his struggles had left a permanent scar. "I had to become more English than the English, play cricket, drink in pubs. I always felt I was acting a part."

He went on to a successful academic career, and in 1969 became Professor of Modern History at the University of Birmingham. "But it was only when I gained a Commonwealth fellowship, aimed not so much at academic excellence but to represent English scholarship at its best, that I managed to shed my inferiority complex about being a German refugee."

Another apparently well-adjusted businessman admitted to being beset by the overwhelming necessity of the English 'stiff upper lip'. Such feelings of insecurity were admitted by many of the refugees, and even when they appear to have been overcome, they sometimes return with old age.

"I noticed my greengrocer over-charged me" said one very assimilated lady, "and I was about to go back and tell him so, when I instinctively felt, no, better not make myself conspicuous. 'But for heaven's sake why?' I realised, nevertheless, I couldn't conquer this old fear, welling up from fifty years ago."

Such seems to be a common experience, even among those who came to this country as quite young children.

References and notes

1. Sherman A.J.S. *Island Refuge* (1973) 171. 181-184.
2. Presland J.A. *A Great Adventure* (1944) 3-4
3. Presland J. ibid. 2
4. Presland J. ibid. 9-10
5. Jüdische Gemeinde — Jewish Community Centre
6. Reichsvertretung fur Juden — This was the official organisation in Germany during the Nazi period, which was empowered to deal with Jewish affairs. Emmi Simson worked there and recalled "It was enormous, with departments for education, agriculture, mortgages and banks, among many others, and was the only body of its kind recognised by the Nazis."
   Kulturgemeinde — a similar organisation in Austria.
7. *Manchester Guardian* 3 January 1939. Description of Dovercourt Camp reprinted in *Movement for the Care of Children from Germany Ltd. First Annual Report 1938-1939.*

Oath of Allegiance.

I, *Hilde Eisner*

swear by Almighty God that I will be faithful and bear true allegiance to His Majesty, King George the Sixth, His Heirs and Successors, according to law.

(Signature) *Hilde Eisner*

Sworn and subscribed this *19th* day of *July* 194*7* , before me,

(Signature) *Elias P Hollander*

Justice of the Peace for *The City of Birmingham*

A Commissioner for Oaths.

Name and Address
(in Block Capitals)
{ E. P HOLLANDER
55 PORTLAND ROAD EDGBASTON
Birmingham

Unless otherwise indicated hereon, if the Oath of Allegiance is not taken within one calendar month after the date of this Certificate, the Certificate shall not take effect.

Wt 9186   50 bks/2/47   Wt & Sons Ltd   69o/1712—**24**

Oath of Allegiance sworn by Dr Hilde Eisner (see p. 116)

6

Bunce Court School

Three sisters merit special praise for their dedicated work in the care and education of refugees. They are Anna, Paula and Bertha Essinger, who left Germany in 1933 when it became obvious to them that Nazi Germany was no place to bring up children in honesty and freedom. [1]

Anna Essinger ran a boarding school on progressive and co-educational lines in the best liberal traditions of the Weimar Republic, at Herrlingen in the Swabian Jura district. She was a Jewess who had become a Quaker and as such had contacts with the Rowntrees and Cadburys in Britain [2]. With their help she transferred the school to Bunce Court, Otterden, Kent. There was no objection from the Board of Education, the Ministry of Labour or the Home Office, and the school was able to start on 6 October 1933. It was a large manor house set in 25 acres of beautiful parkland and gardens. In those days no one seemed to understand just why they had come away with the children [3].

By 1935 it had become well-established with an open air theatre. Some children were accepted without payment of fees in the hope that changed circumstances would enable them to pay later. This did not always prove possible. The school attracted some interesting children, mostly from professional backgrounds. There were a number of German teachers with Weimar connections, and even Communists. There was also a nucleus of local teachers [4]. At this point Bertha Kalin joined her sisters at the school as matron, organising the daily running of a boarding school and looking after the very individual needs of pupils and staff. She had left Germany for Grenoble in 1933, but when her husband died in 1935 she came to Bunce Court. It was she who ensured some German-Jewish continuity and understanding for a large number of students [5].

The civilised running of a progressive pupil-orientated school continued until 1938. The "final solution" cast its hideous shadow into every Jewish household. Planning and orderly evacuation became impossible and the sisters at Bunce Court recognised that the prime necessity was to save life. Many children arrived bewildered and frightened in a strange land, without parents, without security and without familiar faces and things. They came through the reception centre of Dovercourt where they presented enormous problems as no one knew the children or their background. At Bunce Court they found a warmth and sympathy which could hardly replace, but certainly substituted for their home ties. There was much public sympathy for these pathetic little brands plucked from the burning, and private gifts enabled the school to build two extra dormitories to take in some of the children. Some were temporarily housed in two annexes, one a former hospital at Faversham, and the other in a charming old farmhouse at Chilham, which for about a year accommodated a junior school for the youngest children. By September 1939 children from the annexes were enabled to return to the main school as further dormitories were built.

In May 1940 all men and boys over 16 years of age were interned and this was followed by the internment of the cook and three 16-year-old girls. Then in June, Kent was declared a defence area and the school was given three days to quit. The notice was extended to a week while the sisters frantically searched for accommodation in a safe and suitable area. Most large houses were already requisitioned but they finally acquired Trench Hall in Wem, Shropshire. It was much smaller than Bunce Court but they managed to accommodate one hundred and twenty-five children. The local people at first looked askance at this sudden invasion of young people from the Continent, and as for the children themselves this was yet another traumatic experience. They had been driven away from Germany and now they were driven away from their beautiful school in Kent. The teachers too had their troubles. Husbands and friends had been interned and some deported to Australia or Canada.

It was the move to Shropshire which brought the school into the care of the Midlands Region of the Refugee Children's Movement. Some of the younger children broke the long journey in Birmingham and were given lunch at the Regional Office. From then on Ruth Simmons kept in regular contact with the school and was enthusiastic about the warmth and general air of happiness. A progressive committee had already been formed in Shrewsbury and they encouraged the school to put on plays and concerts. It was this same committee which organised a memorable recital by Dame Myra Hess, the celebrated pianist, at Shrewsbury School. A leaking roof and an ancient piano failed to deter her, and when a string broke, she humorously apologised and carried on. A large sum of money was raised thereby for the refugee children of Shropshire [6].

Three ex-Bunce Court pupils have given an account of their schooldays there. They are Lily Aron, Joachim Auerbach and Kurt Rose. The atmosphere was spartan. Up at 7.00 a.m., on with your track suit and run. There was gym, boys and girls together, until 7.30. Then 7.45 breakfast, followed by cleaning up bedrooms, toilets and corridors, as there was a very small domestic staff.

Lessons were from 8.45 to 11.00. Children were encouraged to "talk English, talk English!" Modern languages, maths, crafts, workshops, music, repairing clothing were all on the curriculum, but facilities for physics and chemistry were few. Lessons continued after 11.15 to 12.45.

After lunch, from 2.30 to 4.00 it was practical work, gardening, potato peeling and general cleaning. The school grew all its own vegetables supervised by the biology teacher. From 4.00 to 6.00 p.m. it was homework and after that they were allowed to hear the 6 o'clock news on the Headmistress's radio. They did not go out much as they were so isolated, but all agreed it was a happy time. Those who had nowhere to stay during the holidays remained at the school and occupied themselves with games, gardening and reading.

There were no religious services and no observance of Jewish festivals unless they were specifically requested. Joachim Auerbach celebrated his Barmitzvah (Confirmation) there but he did not read his Portion of the Law and this had to be done by the Rabbi. However, before each meal pupils stood behind their chairs and observed a minute's silence for contemplation. Miss Essinger was strict but very much respected. "Tante Anna is coming" would put a stop to unruly behaviour, but she had the children's welfare at heart and was always approachable. She formed the necessary link between the memory of a Germany they had left behind and a new life in an alien land and an unknown language. "Miss Essinger never refused an appeal to care for a disturbed or unhappy child" recalled Ruth Simmons. "It was a challenge to her".

A picnic lunch in the office of the Refugee Children's Movement. The children are on the way back to their school in Kent after the war, 1946.

After they left the school, many of the pupils came to Birmingham, where they were accommodated in the refugee hostels. Ruth Simmons found opportunities for suitable work for them and many went into the Forces.

A considerable number proceeded to university and achieved success in academic life and in industry.

Long after the school closed, Miss Essinger's pupils continued to visit her. It was largely due to her efforts that they were able to become worthy citizens of the country of their adoption. [7]

References

1. Ex inf. Kurt Rose
2. Ex inf. Lily Aron
3. Essinger, A. *Bunce Court School* 1933–1943
4. Ex inf. Lily Aron
5. *AJR News* July 1986
6. Ex inf. Ruth Simmons
7. Ex inf. Joachim Auerbach and Lily Aron

7

The Hostels

A mock radio programme written by the first warden of Elpis Lodge Hostel, Dr Hirsch, for a party to mark its closure in 1948, included the following dramatisation:

"Do you remember the cold winter nights, when you groped your way through the dark, blacked-out Gough Road and at last opened the door and were glad to find warmth and light inside? In spite of all the difficulties, the air-raids, the jobs, the duties, those were happy days, spent in a sheltering home.

"Here we are back in the living-room of Elpis Lodge. It is rather chilly but the old stove does all right. Scheyer has brought in the anthracite and Ungar has swept it clean. Are we all together? Everybody got his slippers on? Anybody late? Oh, yes, Pressburger of course, all breathless." "Sorry I'd promised to get some trousers finished. Are we playing Monopoly tonight? What's on the menu? Plenty of sausages? But it's Friday night and that means fried fish. You could tell that anyhow by the miaows of Blackie and Tiger, faithful mothers of forty-two children.

"Anyway here comes Goeke, fresh from his Friday bath, a long one, a hot one, last time it overflowed. Tykoschinsky is giving forth as usual; 'the world is facing a big famine.' Kupfermann shouts back, but Schneider sits between them, undisturbed, reading his comics.

"There's Schwersenz in the old-timers' corner. He knows all the gadgets of the house, and Hertz, repairman of broken chairs, Rudo and Brodman want to go out tonight. Doors are locked at 10.30 sharp, but don't worry they will find some subterranean way in!

"Here comes Meyerstein with his fiddle and the Loeser brothers, Peanut the writer and Max the painter. Kurt Gingold really knows how to enjoy life, he's crazy about ballet and the theatre, and here's Harry Keller, the mad barber. Ernst Aris's hair has never recovered from that last haircut—he is there too, looking serious. He is thinking about his BSc. When he has got that he will have a car of his own.

"Gutter wants to talk about the latest inventions in the plastics industry, but Harry Goldman is trying to fix up a bit of gambling; Solo, Poker, Newmarket. Here's Harry Ritter the photographer with curly hair. Everyone teases him with the old German saying *Krause Haare, Krauser Sinn*—curly hair, curls in the brain!

"And last of all little Rogo, the youngest of us all. He is going to London soon to learn tailoring.

"How it all rings still in my ears, seven-thirty in the morning. Get up Abusch, get up Rogo, get up Abusch, Rogo, Rogo."

The porch at Elpis Lodge, 1947. Harry Goldman is in the foreground.

Until the outbreak of war, there had been a constant stream of refugees to England and several hundred Germans, Austrians and Czechs were living in Birmingham. These were further augmented during the invasion scare of 1940 by refugees who were precluded from living in coastal areas. Several hostels were established by the refugee organisations and by various individuals to meet the urgent need for accommodation, particularly for young people. Elpis Lodge in Gough Road housed boy trainees in industry, and there was another hostel for boys and girls nearby at 34 Wheeley's Road. There was a hostel for Czechs in Hagley Road. A house was run by the Friends' Committee in Sutton Coldfield and Amelia Mueller opened her home to a group of boys in Handsworth. The Vicarage at St. Mary's Church, Selly Oak, was loaned as a temporary hostel for girls, and after that closed down, Canon Guy Rogers, Rector of Birmingham, and Mrs Rogers gave the Old Rectory in Sir Harry's Road, Edgbaston, to the Refugee Committee. Besides housing many young people, this was the Regional Headquarters of the Refugee Children's Movement, the organisation responsible to the Home Office for bringing ten thousand young people to England, nine hundred of whom were in Birmingham and the Midland counties.

In 1939, the Birmingham and Coventry Christadelphian Ecclesia offered to provide a home for Jewish refugee boys to be run on strictly orthodox lines. This was Elpis Lodge, which was placed under the leadership of Dr and Mrs Albert Hirsch. Dr Hirsch had formerly been headmaster of the well-known "Philanthropie Schule" in Frankfurt and the couple were described in *The Christadelphian* as "people of culture and learning whose hearts will be in their work". They proved warm-hearted and sensible and provided their charges with a real home.

Dr Abraham Cohen dedicated Elpis Lodge at an opening ceremony on 21 April 1940, an appropriate date as he pointed out, because this was the Eve of Passover, the Festival of Freedom. He added "once again the Christadelphians have come to the rescue of the Jewish people".

Elpis Lodge was a substantial Victorian house set among lawns and shaded by an ancient cedar. It had been thoroughly modernised with new bathrooms and kitchen. The rooms were "light and airy" ("freezing in winter" observed an old boy) and comfortably furnished. There was a grand piano, a radio and games for the boys to enjoy.

On 1 May, fifteen boys, aged from fourteen to fifteen and a half years, arrived. By August, there were twenty. Three of them were fresh from internment, but now all were in work of a practical nature to enable them to attain independence as quickly as possible.

Four boys were in the jewellery trade, three in tailoring and the others included a tool-maker, an upholsterer, a garage-hand, an electrician, a woodworker and a baker. One boy, a junior clerk to a firm of accountants, was studying for his matriculation.

Dr Hirsch advised the boys on their careers. He always tried to seek out natural aptitudes, and to take into account family background. Some families had been tailors for generations, and the father of the boy who did woodwork had specialised in turning chessmen. The boy learning upholstery hoped one day to join his brother who followed that trade in Argentina. In 1942, at an exhibition held at Elpis Lodge to show examples of work being done, "two easy chairs were upholstered in a way which showed sound craftsmanship".

Dr Hirsch also cared deeply that those boys who were being trained in practical trades, so that they could support themselves as quickly as possible, should not be entirely deprived of the way of life previously enjoyed by their families. He aimed to raise the level of taste above the standard of the cinema and encouraged the boys to go to concerts at the Town Hall. Musical evenings were held at the hostel and individual talent fostered.

Peter Meyerstein took violin lessons. There were classes in English literature and history under the direction of a qualified teacher. Dr Hirsch himself instructed the boys in Old Testament and Jewish history. The Christadelphians maintained a continuing interest, and one member of the Ecclesia gave lessons in shorthand.

The standard of living at Elpis Lodge was frugal, in any case a commonplace of wartime conditions. The boys made a weekly contribution of half their earnings, and were allowed to keep a quarter for pocket money. The rest was saved for them. In the first six months, the average cost of food and cleaning materials was 10s.11d. (55p) weekly per head. The average weekly total of running the Hostel, including remuneration of wardens, domestic staff, lighting and heating was 29s. (£1.45) per head. This was reduced to 24s.6d. (£1.23) by the boys' contributions. It speaks well for the care exercised by the wardens over an eight year period, that the level of expenditure was maintained at practically the same level despite a rise in the cost of living.

In 1942, only eleven boys were resident at Elpis Lodge. Some had become self-supporting, or had joined parents who had managed to settle in England. Similar trades were being followed, but they now included a laboratory assistant, a plumber's mate and an optician in training. In 1944, a boy who hoped to join a relative sheep farming in Australia got his first experience of animal care at the Botanical Gardens, where he helped to look after a bear, a baboon, several rhesus monkeys and an alligator.

Of all the boys who passed through Elpis Lodge, very few had both parents in England. For the rest, the sole contact was the rare Red Cross message, and many had eventually to come to terms with the sad fact that they would see their families no more.

It was possible to interview only three Elpis Lodge "Old Boys".

Harry Goldman, who was born in Hamburg, came to England with his brother in 1938. He was eight years old when he was brought over by the Refugee Children's Movement, and after being fostered in various homes in London and Birmingham, he arrived at Elpis Lodge at the age of twelve. For a long time he was the youngest boy and he was to look back on his stay in the hostel as perhaps the happiest period of his life.

"I suppose everybody made rather a fuss of me. Dr Hirsch realised my Barmitzvah (Confirmation) was coming up and it was arranged that Revd Wolf Lewi should teach me my Pasha (portion of the Law).

The Refugee Club childrens' party. Elpis Lodge, 1947.

"On the great day, after I'd read my portion, we came back to Elpis Lodge to a wonderful spread. It was an unforgettable party and I don't believe I missed out on anything, except that my parents were absent. But I was luckier than most of the boys—at least I knew they were out of Germany. My father had gone to Shanghai and my mother was in England in a sanatorium. She came later to Elpis Lodge as a cook.

"Under Dr Hirsch, discipline was strict but very fair. We couldn't go out till we'd done our allotted tasks—washing up, polishing, cleaning the windows. But otherwise we were encouraged to develop ourselves. I played fooball and went to the Rink for skating and ice-hockey. Dr Hirsch was a good pianist and helped me to appreciate music. But I must admit playing cards was our favourite recreation. Of course there was plenty of mischief, but nothing more that I remember. Everyone was "Digging for Victory" at the time and Dr Hirsch thought we should try our hand at tomatoes. One morning before they were ripe, I got up early and painted them all red. I got clouted for that.

"I went to the Hebrew School and although some people say it was pretty rough, I enjoyed it there.[1] I was rather in advance of most of the boys and won a scholarship to the Technical School. Afterwards I started on an apprenticeship in engineering and I've stayed in that line ever since. The hostel changed when Dr and Mrs Hirsch left for the United States in 1945 and Dr Martin Deutschkron took Dr Hirsch's place.

He was good fun and we liked him but he hadn't got quite the same touch as Dr Hirsch, who managed to keep order quietly, without apparent effort. We ragged Dr Deutschkron a lot and once gave him a bad fright, surreptitiously letting of fireworks. He took it all in good part, but somehow the atmosphere was different."

Rudi Hart came to England with the Refugee Children's Movement in 1939. At fourteen years old he was one of the first members of the hostel.

"I came directly from a large refugee camp at Clayton near Norwich, which housed between four and five hundred boys in army barracks. The atmosphere at the hostel was a great improvement on the impersonality of the camp. I settled down quite quickly in my new home, and to the happy uneventful life there. There were rules and regulations, but on the whole it was quite easy-going and informal. We boys mixed well, and the same age groups were kept together in the dormitories. Sometimes there were interchanges and visits between the hostels, particularly Wheeley's Road, which was quite near. Whenever there was a special occasion in the Community, we went to the Communal Hall at Singers Hill to join in, but although Dr Cohen solemnly warned us to behave ourselves, as we were now part of the Birmingham Jewish Community, there was not much social contact between the local Jewish population and the refugee boys. As a result I made few friends within the Community. At the age of fourteen we were found work, and as I was interested in furniture making, I served an apprenticeship. Today I am well established in my own business in Birmingham."

At eighteen the time came for Rudi Hart to leave Elpis Lodge. "I regarded England as my home and had mastered the language. It was only when one or two boys came to the hostel from the German concentration camps at the end of the war, that I reverted to speaking German."

Joachim Auerbach, whose parents died tragically at Auschwitz, came to Birmingham when he was sixteen. He had been a pupil at Bunce Court and, in spite of many problems, he was determined to continue his education. He was advised to study commercial subjects, including accountancy at the College of Commerce, and went on to take an external degree in economics at London University.

Martin Deutschkron, Dr Hirsch's successor, was a gifted linguist and had taught German, French and Latin at King Edward's High School for Boys since 1940. He lived to be eighty-eight and never lost his intellectual ability. His energy was phenomenal: a small, impish man, seldom seen without his beret, he had a quirky sense of humour, especially relishing a tale against himself.

"Good God", he ejaculated one day during the war, to the delight of his pupils, whom he was taking to help on the land. "I promised you we were going plumming, but now it seems we're going pea-ing."

In Germany Martin Deutschkron had been an active member of the Social Democratic Party, and as such particularly wanted by the Nazis. He had to go into hiding, taking cover in different houses from night to night until he was able to escape to England. He was forced to leave his wife and daughter behind and they lived underground in Berlin throughout the war.

Thanks to his appointment at Elpis Lodge, Martin Deutschkron was able to offer his family a home. They were suffering seriously from malnutrition on arrival and it took many months for them to recover from their experiences.

By 1948 it was obvious that Elpis Lodge, which had fulfilled such a useful function, was now no longer needed. The objectives of the hostel had been achieved, and it was agreed by the Representative Council of Birmingham Jewry and the Refugee Children's Movement in London that the obligations which the Christadelphian Ecclesia had so generously undertaken could now be terminated.

The Refugee Committee seems generally to have been fortunate in its choice of hostel wardens. "Melly" Mueller of Handsworth had lost her own family in Austria but made a haven for many youngsters whose parents had likewise perished. She was remembered affectionately as "The Missus", until she died in 1986 at the age of ninety.

Mr and Mrs Echt from Danzig were in charge of 34 Wheeley's Road, which housed thirty refugee boys and girls. They had seen an advertisement offering the post to an English-speaking Orthodox couple, and though they possessed neither qualification, they were the right people. As at Elpis Lodge, another rambling Victorian house in Edgbaston became a true Jewish home. Henry Warner recalled the Friday night suppers with *benshing* (grace after meals) and traditional songs. "We didn't feel we were refugees, just young people in a warm and loving home. We made friendships here that have lasted a lifetime; in fact it was here that I met my wife."

Ursula Warner had previously been placed in a family near Wheeley's Road, where she had not been very happy. "When I first went to the hostel, I used to go back there to collect my letters. One day the family was out.

I could see an air-mail letter: I couldn't wait, managed to get a window open and climbed in. Afterwards I couldn't get it to shut. I realised I had done something dreadful and was very frightened. I looked along the road and saw someone I half-recognised as a German refugee, and asked him to help me. This was my future husband.

"None of us at Wheeley's Road had any money, but we were happy", continued Ursula Warner. "I suppose because we didn't know what was happening in Germany. We danced to the gramophone every Saturday night and sometimes on Sundays we'd go to Bewdley or Stratford. But we had to work very hard, and it was our job to keep the place clean. Mrs Echt could be a bit of a dragon. When we'd finished dusting, she'd put on a white glove and run her fingers around the ledges to see they were clean. Like Elpis Lodge, we 'dug for victory' too. We each had our own little patch in the big garden, and we were able to enjoy the vegetables we grew. The canal was at the bottom. Sometimes, in hot weather, we swam in it.

"I had a job with a local hairdresser, but afterwards I went to the jewellery quarter. I loved working with beautiful things." Her future husband also worked in the jewellery quarter as a press-tool maker for a firm which manufactured cigarette cases and powder compacts. They had recently installed some German machines and Henry Warner was able to make himself useful interpreting the instructions.

Ursula Warner's firm went on to war work with the outbreak of hostilities and as an alien she was no longer permitted to work there, so she obtained employment with an electrical wholesaler. With the invasion scare of 1940, Henry Warner was interned and sent to Canada. On his return, the Warners were married.

Wedding of Henry and Ursula Warner, 1941.

"I was only nineteen", recalled Ursula. "As I had no parents, I had to go to the magistrates' court to get permission. We had a wonderful wedding, conducted at Singers Hill with full ceremony by Dr Cohen and the Chazan (Cantor), Revd Lewi. I wore a light grey suit with a hat and veil. My navy blue shoes cost me ten shillings (50p) from Ravel, an outrageous extravagance. Afterwards Mrs Echt put on a splendid reception at Wheeley's Road. We were only sad because our parents weren't there."

Lucy Benedikt was another girl who came to Wheeley's Road after some unsuccessful placements. She had enjoyed an excellent education at the Pestalozzi[2] School in Vienna, and when she arrived in England at the age of fifteen, she longed to continue her studies. But the Refugee Committee were adamant that its charges must stand on their own feet as quickly as possible, and found her a post at an accountants' office in Corporation Street, Birmingham.

"I was a sort of Girl Friday, doing a bit of typing and making the tea, and I badly wanted something a bit more demanding. I was very pleased when my boss introduced me to a lady who ran a comptometer school in the offices on the other side of the landing. She understood exactly how I felt and gave me lessons in comptometer operating completely free of charge, using the then new Sumlock machine. In due course I qualified and got a job with a big firm, Fisher and Ludlow. Later I joined my parents in the United States. They had a hard time at first to make ends meet, but thanks to my friend I was able to fulfil my academic ambitions. I graduated as a social worker from Hudson College, with a fellowship later from Columbia University. All this time I supported myself by earning a good salary as a comptometer operator during vacations."

Lucy Benedikt was transferred from Wheeley's Road to St. Mary's Vicarage, Selly Oak, in 1941. It was an inter-faith hostel for girls only and was run by Quakers. Archer Tongue, now Chairman of a Committee in Lausanne fighting alcohol and drug abuse, was deeply involved.

"We were closely connected with the nearby Quaker College, Woodbrooke. I once saw Pandit Nehru there.[3] It was a very good environment with great emphasis on music, singing and the creative arts.

"It became all the rage at St. Mary's to go vegetarian—we all had to change our ration cards for special ones for extra cheese and nuts. We slept in a large room overlooking the churchyard, where we were still young enough to play 'Ghosts' It was fearfully cold but it was the fashion to think 'fresh air is good for you'—our face-cloths froze overnight on the basins. There were mice too—they scampered across the floor at night, chasing our cotton reels.

"Often in bed we'd have serious discussions. What would we do if the Nazis invaded Britain? Would we be able to disappear into the countryside? What about our accents? Under all the fun and liveliness, we worried about these things. Above all there were the dreadful fears about deportations and other terrifying rumours of what was happening in Germany. My parents managed to get on the last boat to the United States in 1941, but for most of the girls it was silence.

"After eighteen months, St. Mary's Vicarage closed down. We moved to the Old Rectory in Sir Harry's Road, a beautiful Georgian house. I remember the elegant curved staircase. One girl who fancied herself as an actress played Juliet to her boyfriend's Romeo from the landing, or Lady Hamilton from the films, floating downstairs in an imaginary feathered picture hat. Mrs Goldschmidt was Warden here. Her husband was blind, but a good listener and a great favourite with the girls. Here again there was much emphasis on music and I learned to play the recorder.

"But meanwhile my parents were insisting that I should join them in America, and I went in a convoy on a banana boat. We used the North Atlantic route. The weather was atrocious and there were icebergs; the Captain nearly put back. It wasn't until the end of the journey, when we were approaching New York Harbour, that we ran into submarines. We stood by the life-boats with the purser's wife, who acted as a kind of matron to us girls. She carried her canary in its cage, saying, 'Children, if anything happens, we won't have much of a chance'.

"It was frightening, but I enjoyed the journey, if only for the wonderful food. We had an egg every day—and bananas. We hadn't seen them for years."

When peace came in May 1945, the boys and girls who had come to England prior to the war had grown up. At eighteen, when they were well-established in employment, they were helped to find lodgings in the city. Many had volunteered for the Pioneer Corps, from which they were often transferred to other Services. This was an opportunity to escape from dull jobs.

On demobilisation, many opted to continue their education and some proceeded to university. Several gained outstanding success. One boy taught science at Eton, another became a consultant geriatrician, and there were several university professors.

The hopes that the parents of these children had cherished had been brutally destroyed. However, to the lasting credit of the Refugee Committee, and especially Ruth Simmons, the young people who came to the Midlands were encouraged by such means as night-schools and day-release schemes to stretch their potential to the fullest extent, thereby achieving a truly satisfying way of life.

Notes

1. This opinion of the Hebrew School was not unanimous. One girl found the teachers "had no compassion for us and made no allowances that we spoke a different language and came from a different cultural background. Only Benny Winter, his wife and her sister, Rebbitzin Rabbinowitz, showed us sympathy".

2. Pestalozzi, J.H.(1746-1827). A Swiss educational reformer who advocated teaching methods which followed the gradual unfolding of the child's development. His principles have long been absorbed into primary education. (*Encyclopedia Britannica*).

3. Pandit Nehru. (1889-1964). Prime Minister of India from 1947.

8

By Fair Means or Foul

Most of the people interviewed emigrated from Nazi Germany through recognised means, either by guarantees, domestic nursing or trainee permits or such official schemes as the Refugee Children's Movement. There were some, however, who could not fit into these categories, or who were led by chance, quick wits or the courage born of desperation, to take their fate into their own hands.

André Drucker came from a family that had suffered from the chronic depression which had haunted the Austrian economy between the wars. He was put through a technical school in Vienna to learn the textile trade, but afterwards found it very difficult to make a living. A flair for writing poems, plays and short stories helped him and he composed political songs in the satirical style of his better known contemporaries, Brecht and Weill. These he performed in the back rooms of coffee houses and in beer gardens with great success. Such activities were illegal. At the same time he was an active member of the Communist Party and once represented the Austrian Workers' Theatre at a Party Conference in Moscow. He was not surprised when, after the Anschluss, he found his name on a list of subversive persons, and left Vienna for Prague where he had relatives. This sanctuary was brief.

"I was in the Wenzelstrasse in March 1939, when the Germans marched into Prague. A Communist comrade had connections for helping refugees and they led me to the Polish border. We sheltered in a little house from which you could see the German guards patrolling the frontier. They walked towards, and then away from each other the length of a few hundred yards. At a given signal, while they were apart, we ran across. It was frightening. People had been shot there before. We made our way to Kattowitz and stayed there in a mill. Here, in Poland, we felt safe under the influence of Colonel Beck[1]. Unbelievably, I met a cousin selling cinema tickets! She gave me a meal every night and taught me something of Polish gastronomy. She got me on to a train for Gdynia and from there I took ship to London. It was a crazy old hulk that should have been laid up, but it was good enough for us refugees. There were hundreds of Slovak peasants on board with huge bundles, all fleeing from Hitler. We chugged through the Kattegat and the Skagerak, past many German ships. The Polish soldiers on our boat told us that on occasion the Germans had stopped and boarded their ship, and taken people off to prison.

"For five days and nights we sailed through a force nine gale, lying on the deck or propped up against the funnel. At last we passed under Tower Bridge. A Quaker refugee organisation took us over and looked after us. For a few days I walked about London exploring, then I took the train to Birmingham where I had a married sister, thankful to be on the last lap of my journey to freedom."

Chance twice played its part in determining the fate of Werner Abrahams who, like André Drucker, had found very temporary safety in Prague, in his case as a refugee from Germany.

"In 1935 things were becoming very hot in Germany. My father was a founder member of Kaufhof, a group with shops all over Germany. He was coming out of his office one day when some Nazis in uniform stopped him to ask, 'Are there any Jews working in this store?' My father replied, 'Well, there are some down the other end'', and escaped to some relatives in Czechoslovakia.

"All our assets were frozen in Germany. Our relatives in Prague owned a factory making nuts and bolts, but they bought their machines in Germany. They told their suppliers that payment was to be taken from my parents' frozen account and in this way we managed to salvage some funds to set up a textile business in Czechoslovakia.

"This proved very successful. I carried on with the pre-medical training I had started in Germany as I had ambitions to become a doctor. But my parents insisted I should also learn a trade that would be useful in emergencies. I trained as an upholsterer and this became more valuable to me when we had to cut and run again.

"In 1937 my father and I were out walking. A very high-ranking Nazi officer came up to us and asked my father if he had once been his boss in Germany. They recognised each other and he warned my father if he did not leave immediately, he might not live to see the day.

"My father managed to get to England because of a patent he had obtained in some highly technical method of electro-plating plastics. Chance, once again, stepped in. The Home Office forgot to issue a permit for my mother and me. We did eventually manage to get to Italy, but we were marooned for weeks in Milan. When we did at last see the White Cliffs of Dover, it was only six weeks before the outbreak of war."

Despite their experiences, fate, on the whole, seemed to be in favour of the Schotts. Sidney (Siegfried) Schott was manager of a large scrap metal firm in Germany, and, perhaps because of his military record in World War I, he kept his position until the Kristallnacht. This event was particularly ominous for the Jews of Hanover, where they lived, since it was the home town of the unfortunate Grynspan who had set the fearful ball rolling in Paris by shooting the German official, von Rath.

In 1936, while on holiday in Switzerland, the Schotts and their thirteen year old son, Walter, struck up a friendship with two Jewish lads from Birmingham, who were staying at the same hotel. One was Gerald Blumenthal, many years later to become the Treasurer of the Birmingham Hebrew Congregation, the other his friend, Arthur Green. In their extremity after the Kristallnacht, the Schotts begged the boys to see if they could help their son to get to England. The boys, by their own efforts, raised enough money to obtain a permit for Walter and arranged for him to live with a young couple, Ivan and Cora Liebermann.

The parents, meanwhile, were struggling in a vicious circle. They had no passport and could not obtain one without a visa, yet they could not acquire a visa without a passport. In desperation, and in return for a very large sum of money, they bought a visa for Cuba. It was arranged that their son should travel with the Refugee Children's Movement to England.

Else Schott embarking in the SS St. Louis at Hamburg, 1939.

The time drew near for the Schotts to embark, and still Walter was in Germany. They became frantic, particularly as Sidney Schott had been threatened that if he did not pay certain taxes, for which he was patently unable to find the money, his son would not be allowed to leave. They decided to stay, and telephoned Bloomsbury House. But the Refugee Committee insisted they must go. Walter would leave in four days' time with the next Children's Transport.

In May 1939 they left the boy with trusted non-Jewish friends and boarded the luxury liner, St. Louis[2], for Havana, where they had relatives. The ship, captained by a sympathetic German, contained nine hundred and twenty-five refugees. But during the journey the Cuban government changed and the refugees were not permitted to land. For ten days they sweltered in the harbour at Havana. Small boats brought letters to the passengers but there was no news of Walter. "We felt sure he had not been allowed to leave Germany." Else Schott recalled her anguish. "I just wanted to die." This torturing suspense lasted for many days, but at last relief came with a radio-telegram announcing their son's arrival in Birmingham.

All this time the Captain had been trying to help his passengers. He attempted to land them at Miami, but President Roosevelt could not see his way to admit the unfortunates. Finally they were forced to set course back to Europe with gun-boats following them up the English Channel.

Rumour had it that the dreaded camps were being prepared for them in Germany. But at the last moment England, France, Holland and Belgium agreed to divide the majority of the unwanted refugees between them. The American Jewish Joint Distribution Committee in Paris were in charge of the operation; those who were not allocated virtually received a death sentence.

"At Rotterdam we were pushed off into small boats. There was no water, the lavatories were stopped up and we slept in the hold, but after the St. Louis nothing mattered and at least we weren't going back to Germany." Once again, fate was on the Schotts' side. Their son being in England, they were given permits to join him, and for this reason, no doubt, they survived[2].

Walter, meanwhile, was happily installed with the Liebermann family. "They were gentle people. Ivan Liebermann loved playing Chopin on his grand piano. Alas, he was killed in North Africa, when his Air Force station was bombed." But that summer Walter spent getting used to his new life, gardening and going to cricket matches at Edgbaston. He attended Bournville Grammar School. "I had language difficulties, of course. They gave me a copy of Macbeth" But he learnt more from following the fate of the St. Louis in the newspapers and on the radio. The joy of being free was overshadowed by terrible tension until the family were reunited. Once again, the Blumenthals came to their rescue, taking Sidney and Else Schott into their home as a domestic couple.

Revd Shlomo Forscher from Czechoslovakia, who was Cantor at the Singers Hill Synagogue from 1968 to 1969, experienced a very different but almost equally harrowing journey by boat in 1939. "We'd nowhere to go ... except to make our way illegally into Palestine. We came by train from Prague to Vienna. We embarked on a boat down the Danube to the Rumanian port of Sulina. This took three weeks. There we hired a cargo boat. It had to be fitted out for seven hundred people to live and sleep on it. We took food for only twelve days, but our journey lasted one hundred and seventeen days. Water was very scarce; we couldn't wash at all. Health conditions were appalling.

"When we reached Palestine we had to land in darkness, but we were caught by the port police and put into a military camp. From there we were taken to an immigration camp and thence we somehow found our way into a town. We worked hard and lived in very poor conditions ... nine of us in a single room ... we could sleep only in shifts."

But at least they made their way to safety, unlike the passengers on the ill-fated SS Struma which in 1942 on a similar voyage sank in the Black Sea with the loss of seven hundred and ninety-eight lives[3].

Manele Spielman knew the tensions of the hunted man long before being pursued by the Nazis. He was born and spent his boyhood in the small town of Radlow in Poland. Conditions were primitive. It was only when he was evacuated to Graz in Austria during World War I that Manele Spielman saw electric light for the first time. He recreates Radlow vividly in his unpublished memoirs *The Stricken Tree*, his log-house home, his school, skating in winter, the travelling zoo and the travelling cinema. Both parents had to work hard for a living; his mother ran a tiny drapery store, his father made candles for the Catholic churches. Yet, all is suffused with an atmosphere of warmth and affection. The Sabbath and the recurring festivals relieved the everyday struggle; they enjoyed the *borsht* (beetroot soup) and *cholent* (bean stew) and other special foods in celebration. There were books, too, not only in Yiddish, but Polish translations of Tolstoy, Gorky and Dostoevsky.

Radlow was ruined during World War I and at the age of eighteen Manele Spielman moved to Cracow, hoping for employment with an uncle. Jobs were hard to find. He describes himself as a *Luftmensch* (Yiddish — someone without real occupation, who scrapes a living as best he can) doing odd jobs for an art dealer.

In his simplicity and ignorance he was unaware that he should have registered for military service. He was arrested and taken home to join the Polish army. But having observed the way Jews were treated in Cracow, he felt certain he would be beaten up and gave his soldier guards the slip by treating them to an immense meal with plenty to drink. While they were enjoying themselves he disappeared and went into hiding in the synagogue. With the help of a new name and a forged birth certificate he got across the border and went to Berlin.

"Germany had suffered serious inflation, but it did not worry me unduly as I had no money. By 1930 a certain amount of anti-semitism had started, but the streets of Berlin were full of young Jews who had escaped from pogroms in Poland and elsewhere. One of them persuaded me to join him as a door-to-door salesman in men's suitings. I was nearly murdered one night, sleeping rough. But after a time I built up quite a connection and set up a home where I was joined by my sisters. Then, after a lightning courtship, I got married. Refugees were not allowed to marry in Berlin, we had to go over the border. In due course our daughter was born."

By 1938 emigration was his only hope and Manele Spielman took a course of organic chemistry which he felt might stand him in good stead in his efforts to settle in Texas where he had an uncle. But it grew daily more difficult to find a refuge. "Jews for sale" read a sardonic notice at this time.

One day, he was in a car with some friends when the driver was stopped by some SS men. Everybody was asked to produce their papers, and although they were in order, they were all hustled into a police station. Alone in a cell, Manele Spielman heard shots from time to time and thought his end had come. It was not until a fortnight later that he was suddenly released. His wife, meantime, had had no idea where he was. During the Kristallnacht in November 1938 he rescued a *Sefer Torah* (Scroll of Law) from a burning synagogue. This scroll is now in use at the New Synagogue, Park Road, Birmingham.

As he was Polish, the Germans were liable at any moment to ship Manele Spielman across the border to Poland. He went into hiding, until he heard that his uncle in Texas had agreed to sponsor him, and that he could first go to England "in transit". The couple could not bear to part with their daughter so that she could travel with the Refugee Children's Movement; she and her mother had to be left behind to follow.

"The suspense on the train was almost tangible" Manele Spielman remembered, "and so was the outburst of relief as we passed the frontier and the Nazi officials left. I was placed in a transit camp in Richborough,

Kent. It was just like an army camp, surrounded by barbed wire, and we immigrants were not supposed to leave it. But I was frantic about my wife and child and persuaded the camp commandant to let me go to Woburn House in London. Here I met a Jewish baker who took me home for my first meal of English fish and chips.''

His quest was successful. He was rejoined by his family, released from the camp and work was found for him in Birmingham as a garage mechanic.

Now his anxiety rested on his family in Poland and it was not misplaced. It was many months before he heard their fate. When the Germans occupied Radlow, his mother and one of his sisters were driven into the Jewish cemetery with the remainder of the Jewish community. Here they were forced to dig trenches and when they were ready the Germans shot and buried their victims.

Stories of courage in agonising situations are commonplace. Walter Schott's grandparents, well into their sixties, jumped from a first floor window and scaled a high wall when their shop in Krefeld was wrecked on the Kristallnacht by the Nazis. Their efforts were in vain; they perished in Auschwitz.

Charlotte Singer saved the lives of her husband, her three children and herself by her own bravery.

"The year 1939 had already started and we had no hope of emigration. But on 4 January we heard that the Home Office had granted my husband a stay of one year in England for post-graduate medical study. One of the many degradations we had to suffer after the takeover of the Sudetenland by the Nazis was the surrender of our passports, and the British Consul requested my husband's to stamp with a visa. Much to my surprise the police chief handed it over without question, even agreeing to insert the names of our two younger children so that they could travel with their father to safety. I took the passport to Berlin, it was stamped with a visa for England and I returned in triumph.

"But in my absence my husband had been arrested! He returned late that night, but his passport had to be surrendered again on a trumped-up charge of his not having disclosed some fees paid by a Czech patient.''

There followed weeks of cat and mouse games with the passports and visas of both husband and wife, for Charlotte Singer had found a loophole whereby she could reach England either as a domestic or a nurse. At last she could stand the suspense no longer. "I must have been one of the few persons who dared to enter the lion's den, the Gestapo Headquarters, without being summoned.

"I was shown into a room with a huge desk. Stacks of documents were piled upon it. What was uppermost? Strafakten (documents concerning punishment) of Dr Singer. I lifted the cover. There was his passport. I nearly snatched it and ran, but reason prevailed. How quickly they would have found me. Then 'Heil Hitler', an official in full uniform sat down behind the desk and asked me my business.

Robert and Charlotte Singer, 1955.

"There was a long silence while he was shown the files ... He did not say to me as another official spat out a fortnight later, when I was arranging to follow my husband to England, that the Führer had said *Juda verrecke, nicht verreise* (Judah must perish, not Judah must go travelling).

"His hand seized the passport ... I felt faint ... still without a word he threw the passport across the desk. I caught it and ran through the doors into the street ... Five human lives must have been at that moment on a very frail thread.

"I found out later that the Director of the local Treasury had been responsible for our deliverance. He, Herr Wenzel the police chief, and another courageous German who saved my eldest daughter in Berlin, are not forgotten by me, even to the present day, especially in the first week of February."

Walter Stranz, a practising Christian from Berlin, had the misfortune to be non-Aryan according to the Nuremberg Racial Laws. His father Martin had converted from Judaism to Christianity on his marriage to a lady who was herself half-Jewish, so three of his grandparents were Jews.

By the autumn of 1938 Martin Stranz was no longer permitted to follow his profession as a lawyer, and so, with his wife, he visited the United States to examine possible openings. The outlook was bleak. In any case the strict quota system meant a two year delay before emigration. They returned to Berlin a few days before the Kristallnacht. Martin Stranz was thrown into the concentration camp of Sachsenhausen and his two children were excluded from school.

But the family's salvation lay in Martin Stranz's sister, a lady impressive both in physical build and iron determination. She had emigrated to England earlier and now channelled her energies into extricating her brother's family from their plight.

"She had been an active feminist in Berlin" recalled her nephew, "and through that had met the secretary of Sir Stafford Cripps[4]. On that tenuous basis she pressurised the austere Solicitor-General into guaranteeing a colleague, representing her brother as a distinguished and famous jurist like himself. This was a gross exaggeration; he had a very run-of-the-mill practice in a working-class district of Berlin.

"My mother meanwhile had contacted a former client of my father's who ranked high in the Nazi Party. Whether it was through him, or other representations, my father was suddenly released.

"But he refused to leave without his family. My aunt set feverishly to work again and at one of her innumerable refugee meetings spied a lady even larger than herself. She sat next to her and in conversation it transpired that this lady, a Mrs Freeman, was herself half-Jewish. She had vowed to work for children in need of rescue from Germany and had opened a home for Jewish-Christian children in Watford, Hertfordshire, which she called Welcome House.

"'Splendid' said my aunt, 'you must take my niece and nephew'." Mrs Freeman was nonplussed. She had visualised a group of toddlers, not young people of seventeen and fifteen years old. But nobody could resist my aunt's steamroller tactics. She went on to persuade a Quaker organisation to guarantee my mother, and so in April 1939 we all came to England together.''

Kathleen Freeman, 1940.

The Stranz children attended grammar schools in Watford, paid for, Walter Stranz thought, by some committee. Otherwise the remarkable Mrs Freeman shouldered the burden of twelve children by herself. As some left to join their parents, she replaced them with others, an astonishing record of personal sacrifice and devotion.

The only port in the world where no visas were required was Shanghai[5]. The prospect was uninviting. ''The city was nothing but a dark jungle of overcrowded brick boxes ... Rents were astronomical even for the tiniest room carved out of someone's already too small apartment ... the employment situation was impossible ... thousands of refugees already there had exactly the same skills you possessed, whatever they might be, and the Chinese glutted the manual labour market."[6]

The Welcome family, 1940. Walter Stranz is in the back row on the right of his sister (with pigtails).

Herbert Goldman, father of Harry Goldman, born in Hamburg in 1905, was one of the many who in desperation bought a sea-passage for Shanghai. He arrived on 15 May 1939, registered as a tailor (unemployed) and was issued with an identity card bearing his fingerprints.

In May 1940 he volunteered to join the French Foreign legion (Tonkin). With the fall of France in that month, the Japanese military pressure on French Indo-China had increased. Their army was in occupation of the neighbouring parts of south-west China and from there in December 1940 they attacked the frontier town of Langson which lay on the railway to South-West China. Here Herbert Goldman first saw action. The Japanese pressed on from there to Western Thailand to secure the route to Malaya, and in order to buy Thai support, had given them the part of Western Indo-China which was under French sovereignty[7]. This included the town of Mailin where Herbert Goldman was later cited as "having conducted himself well, notably on 12, 27 and 28 January 1941 under bombardment by Siamese planes and under machine-gun fire from Japanese 'planes". He was awarded the French Colonial medal with bar.

By July 1942 he appears to have returned to Shanghai, now under Japanese occupation. The Germans had been agitating for their Japanese allies to act more positively on the Jewish problem and in the same month the Gestapo "Butcher of Warsaw", Colonel Meisinger, arrived in Shanghai with proposals for a pogrom. The Japanese rejected the idea, but set up a ghetto in Shanghai, the first in Asia. Meanwhile Herbert Goldman, in accordance with Chinese and then Japanese custom, was included in a

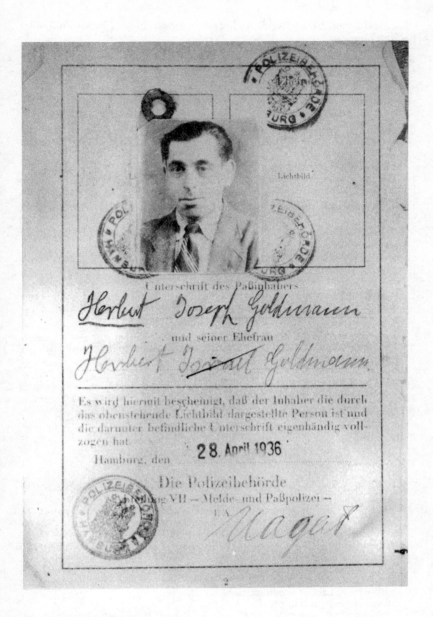

Herbert Goldman's identity card, 1936.

"Mutual Responsibility Bond", being given a guarantee of good conduct by his neighbours.

With a few horrific exceptions there was no torture, nor were there any executions, and the Japanese tried to use their good conduct towards "their Jews" in an attempt to avoid unconditional surrender to the United States. In this they were completely unsuccessful.

Starvation, disease and bombing wiped out many of the inhabitants of the Shanghai ghetto, but Herbert Goldman survived and was included in the census of 1944.

In May 1946 he wrote to Charles Jordan of the American Joint Distribution Committee for the Rescue of German Refugees[8], pleading to be allowed to travel to England. His wife had been in hospital in England for the past twenty-two weeks. "My whole family needs my assistance urgently ... I am very sad about this misfortune."

But he received no satisfaction and in May 1947 asked Mr Jordan for his help again.

"I read in the newspaper that preference is to be granted to those who have a marriage partner and their children in England. Fifty persons left some time ago but I did not count among them."

This time he was more successful. Passports and a visa for six months only were issued, and he departed from Shanghai 12 July 1948.

Herbert Goldman was reunited with his wife, but unfortunately it seemed the events of the intervening years had placed too much strain upon the marriage. After a time they separated.

References and notes

1. Colonel Joseph Beck (1894-1944) was Polish Foreign Minister from 1932-1939. He tried to keep the balance between Poland and Russia. "He did not believe that Nazi Germany constituted a threat to Polish security because of the irreconcilable antagonism between Nazism and Bolshevism". Leslie R.F. *History of Poland since 1863*, Cambridge University Press 1980 p. 203.
2. The story of the SS St Louis is told in *Voyage of the Damned* by Gordon Thomas and Max Morgan-Witte (1974).
3. Wasserstein B. *Britain and the Jews of Europe. 1939-1945.* (1979). pp. 143-157.
4. Sir Stafford Cripps (1889-1952). A member of the war-time Cabinet and the subsequent Labour administration.
5. Wasserstein B. op. cit. 8
6. Tokayer M. and Swartz M. *The Fugu Plan.* (Hamlyn Paperback edition 1981). pp. 191-192, 223, 234-259.
7. Ex inf. E.S. Kirby, Professor Emeritus, The University of Aston in Birmingham, who translated Herbert Goldman's documents from Chinese and Japanese.
8. American Jewish Joint Distribution Committee. Founded in 1914. Several American relief organisations joined to help Jews in need all over the world. Charles Jordan of the American Jewish Joint Distribution Committee disappeared on a rescue mission in Czechoslovakia.

9

The Internment

With the outbreak of war on 3 September 1939, all visas from Great Britain were cancelled. Between 1933 and 1939, about 76,000 people had succeeded in reaching this country.[1] Between 1939 and 1945 few had the good fortune to be added to these numbers.

From the outbreak of war, there was fear of infiltration by enemy agents disguised as refugees; nevertheless, during the period of the so-called "phoney war", large scale internment was delayed. About one hundred Tribunals were set up throughout the country, before which all aliens had to appear. They were divided into three categories: (A) who were to be interned immediately; (B) who were exempt from internment, but subject to certain restrictions; and (C) who were exempt both from internment and restrictions. By January 1940, 186 in Category A had been interned and 8356 in Category B subjected to restrictions.[2]

The Spring of 1940 saw a change of mood. The invasion of Denmark and Norway in April and the Low Countries and France in May, together with apprehensions of a possible invasion of this country, caused alarm. But it was the breathtaking speed with which the Germans overran Holland that produced almost an anti-alien hysteria. The uncanny German success was put down to the activities of a "Fifth Column".[3] Spies, disguised as nuns, domestic servants, schoolchildren and other unlikely people, who to all appearances had been leading blameless lives, were suddenly believed to have been committing sabotage and attacking civilians. Others were thought to have been dropped from the sky by parachute. By 11 May, all adult male refugees residing near the eastern and southern coast of Britain had been interned.

Refugees from Hitler's Germany would seem likely to have been the last people to threaten national security, but in the prevailing atmosphere many authorities were unable to distinguish between Nazi spies and those whom the Nazis had tormented. Even the tribunals had difficulty in sorting out friendly from enemy aliens. Some pointed out that "those people are nationals of an enemy country and however much they dislike the government in power, deep down they must have a love of their native land".[4] Others feared the long arm of the Gestapo. Refugees who had relatives still in Germany might be persuaded into treachery by threatened reprisals.

By mid-May 1940, the whole of Category B men and women were interned and early in June it was decided that almost all men in Category C should be behind barbed wire in hurriedly constructed camps up and down the country. Eight thousand of these internees were shortly shipped overseas to Canada and Australia. [5]

Henry Warner was one of those from Birmingham who found himself unexpectedly sent to Canada. "We were moved from one place to another, ending up in Army tents near Liverpool. From there we were driven to the docks, put on board a large ship and taken below behind barbed wire. We thought we were going to the Isle of Man, but after a bit of zig-zagging about, somebody said, "that's Ireland". We were very cramped in our hammocks. There was a lot of dysentery and long queues for the toilets, but we didn't worry too much. Much worse were a number of Nazi prisoners of war among us in their uniforms. One of the German civilian internees wasn't a Nazi at all; he was the Kaiser's grandson, a splendid man, first rate at swabbing the decks."

By the beginning of July 1940, 30,000 men and some women had been interned. Such was the stringency of the times that few exceptions were made, not even for established people like Emil Rich who had important war contracts. Many young men wanted to volunteer for military service, but were turned down as aliens. "But you accepted a friend of mine", said Kurt Rose from Berlin. "Yes, but he's an Austrian so he's a friendly enemy alien."

Only the irrepressible humorist, Henry Freeland, could have viewed this strange time as a comedy, which he describes in his long and detailed poem *A Song of Internment*. (See Appendix to this chapter.)

The behaviour of the two courteous policemen who roused Henry Freeland at dawn that day early in July 1940 and asked politely if they might examine his home, must have been an extraordinary contrast to the dreaded knocking on the door by the Gestapo. Elsewhere, a young man was advised by a friendly officer not to forget his tennis racquet!

"I'm not ready yet", said Kurt Rose to the policeman sent to fetch him. "All right, I'll be back at eight-thirty", came the obliging rejoinder. He was taken to a police cell, but the door was left open and an appetising lunch was sent in from a nearby restaurant. Heinz Shire, working on a farm as a holiday job in Northern Ireland, was quietly advised to slip back across the border to Dublin in neutral Eire, where he was a medical student.

The internees were warned they would be shot if they tried to escape, but otherwise the most threatening experience was the toilet parade, when they were escorted in parties of twelve by soldiers with fixed bayonets for a three minute session!

Henry Freeland and Frank Linden were taken to a converted holiday camp at Seaton in South Devon. "The sun shone and the sea sparkled, but what good was that to us when Hitler's armies were waiting across the Channel and we knew we would be the first victims of a Nazi invasion." There the internees experienced their first air-raid warnings. "Into the chalets", roared the Sergeant Major, brandishing a pistol. The same Sergeant Major initiated them ferociously into the intricacies of roll-call, which was held twice daily. Otherwise, the internees' time was their own. After a short

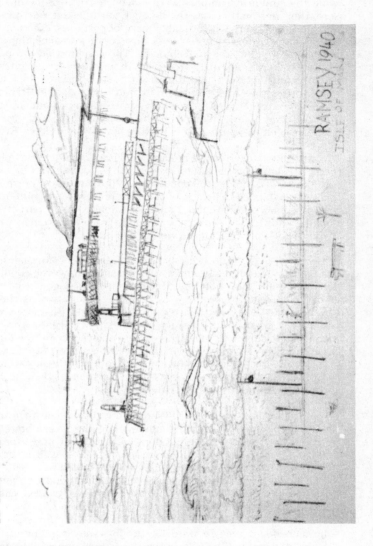

View from the camp at Ramsey, I.o.M, sketched by an internee, 1940.

while the sunburnt campers were moved north to Bury in Lancashire. Here, their destination was the derelict, rat-infested Warth Cotton Mill. Appalled, they were led through a maze of corridors, dominated by huge wheels, hung with slimy green moss. Rusty cranes creaked high above their heads. The weather, too, had changed. The wind rattled through in noisy gusts and rain rumbled on the roof. Two thousand men were interned in the building, four hundred locked in at a time in vast cavernous workshops. "We had twenty-six taps between us. You had to paddle to them to wash and clean your teeth. As for wash-days, we had to boil our shirts in tubs in the yard and hang them on barbed wire to dry. Oh, we Viennese washerwomen were proud of our white linen!" sang Henry Freeland.

Three weeks later, Henry Freeland and Frank Linden parted company. Henry Freeland was sent still further north to Loch Gilpert in Scotland. "It was a luxury train. People kept asking us if we were comfortable." Frank Linden was shipped to the Isle of Man. There were nine camps for men and two for women on the island. Italian internees were for part of the time in Douglas, and Germans in Ramsey and Onchan. The women were in Port St. Mary and Port Erin on the west of the island.

Crossing to the Isle is notoriously rough and many began their internment there with a bout of sea-sickness. Once on shore, however, conditions were not unpleasant. Many hotels had been requisitioned, and inside the barbed wire the internees were free to organise themselves as they wished. Although they were not allowed on the beaches, the camps were all in positions of great natural beauty, overlooking the sea; several internees spent their leisure sketching. The women enjoyed more freedom than the men. They were allowed the run of Port Erin and Port St. Mary, and were permitted to swim from the beaches. Once a month they were taken by coach to meet their husbands in a former ballroom at Douglas. Eventually a camp was set up for married couples.

The orthodox Jews were housed separately, their domestic arrangements supervised by a rabbi, but every one came together to celebrate the Jewish festivals. H.L. retains the programme of a cabaret party for Chanukah 1940, and Passover was celebrated in some style. As well as the obligatory sweet red wine from Palestine, and the hard-boiled eggs with salt water, the Seder meal included chicken soup with traditional matzo balls, roast chicken and *chremslich*, a special Passover delicacy of pancakes stuffed with fruit, nuts and spices.

Volunteers soon came forward for the everyday running of the camps. Some went down to the docks in Douglas to help unload ships which came in every day from the mainland. Others worked in the camp post office, where letters had to be censored, or in the Bank where special camp money was used. Yet others were busy on the camp newspaper. There was an out-pouring of poetry, both lyrical and satirical. Many passed the long days reading. Frank Reinach got through the complete works of Dickens in the eight months of his internment. "I would never have managed Pickwick Papers except for the Island", he admitted. There were interminable schools of poker.

Rations were distributed. Those who fancied themselves as cooks had ample scope. At one camp a chef from the Savoy Hotel was interned, and in that house gourmet cooking was the rule. Another camp boasted a Viennese coffee-house. Generally, these internees, like the islanders,

Celebrating festivals in the Isle of Man, 1940-41. (a) Passover

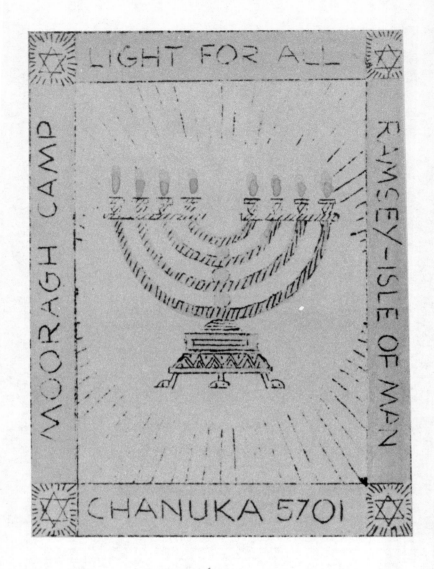

Celebrating festivals in the Isle of Man, 1940-41. (b) *Chanukeh*

fared better than those on the mainland. Just after Victory in Europe in May 1945, an RAMC officer, invalided out of the army, had his convalescence speeded up by the unheard of luxury of egg and chips and to this day he declares the Manx kippers the most succulent he has ever tasted. But the armchairs in his hotel, recently vacated by the last of the women internees, were not comfortable. These ladies had set up a cottage industry, making soft toys and selling them to the local people; the stuffing they had used came from inside the furniture.

The island doctors and dentists soon found themselves overwhelmed. H.L., a qualified dentist, assisted one of the local men, and under the supervision of the inevitable fixed bayonets, escorted patients to X-Ray. Herr Professor G, one of Europe's most distinguished ophthalmologists, carried out eye-tests.

There was indeed an extraordinary profusion of professional talent on the island. The artist, Kurt Schwitters[6], painted portraits of the internees and their guards. Musicians such as Peter Stadlen[7], Paul Hamburger[8] and Peter Gellhorn[9], the composer, Franz Reizenstein[10], and many others were on the Isle of Man at one time or another. The members of the most famous quartet of our time, the Amadeus[11], came together as ''prisoners'', as they liked to say in after years. Light music was provided by the duettists, Rawicz and Landauer[12], well-known on the BBC. For all these people music was of overriding importance and they gave of their talents generously.

No wonder the atmosphere was stimulating. A number of Oxford and Cambridge dons among the internees were specialists in their fields, notably science and social science. They were prepared to lecture and, as several people observed, ''you could go to university''. The most popular speaker, however, was a local clergyman, the Revd John Duffield, who taught English history. He was rebuked by his parishioners for his pains, ''hobnobbing with the enemy''. At the height of the internment, the attitude of the islanders does not seem to have been friendly.

Despite all the diversions offered, each refugee was burdened with his own anxieties. The presence of Nazi prisoners of war made life difficult for some. Frank Reinach lived in a house which accommodated thirty-two internees, four of them Nazis. He was unfortunate enough to have to share a bedroom with one of them. ''He had lived in England all his life, but the last thing he used to say to me at night was, 'of course, you know, Hitler's a very great man, he'll soon be here. You should join the National Socialist Movement, because we will obviously win the war''. Sometimes fighting broke out, but the overriding anxiety for each individual was his own family. A few wives who had not been interned managed to visit their husbands, but the majority in Birmingham were in domestic service and the fares made travelling out of the question.

Less than one month after the hasty internment of Category C men, the tide of public opinion began to turn. On 2 July the Arandora Star, a Blue Star liner filled with German and Italian refugees bound for Canada, was torpedoed by a German submarine off the west coast of Ireland and sank with immense loss of life. Second thoughts brought doubts as to the wisdom of wholesale internment. It was becoming obvious that the procedure was no advertisement for British democracy and that valuable allies were being locked away who were ready to give skilled help in the war effort. By the end of July the Home Office announced that certain categories would be

House - Cleaning

-..... and ~~to~~ think that I have got the Nobelprize '

Distinguished lavatory cleaners on the I.o.M.

considered for release: the old and sick and those with dependants, those on important war-work, scientists, doctors and dentists, and those who were willing to enlist in the newly formed Auxiliary Military Pioneer Corps.

Many wished to volunteer for the Pioneers, which mainly involved digging trenches and latrines, and required a certificate of medical fitness. The Isle of Man had only one medical officer, and release was painfully slow.

The situation was soon to be relieved in a romantic way. An opera singer among the internees had volunteered for duty on the docks at Douglas. His English wife, who was a relative of Winston Churchill, had taken up residence in the town, so that she might see him every day, though they were never able to speak. The opera singer volunteered for the Pioneer Corps and, impatient for his release, his wife reported the medical bottleneck to the Prime Minister. Two more medical officers were shortly despatched and the husband and wife were reunited on the return boat home, "Mona's Isle".

This story was told by Thelma Chadwick, wife of one of the medical officers. She herself was arrested one day on the docks by the Military Police. Her family had befriended several refugees and while on a visit to her husband, it was her habit to await the incoming boat to look for familiar faces. It took her some time to convince the police that she was not an escaping internee, but the wife of an English serving officer.

The panic over the "Fifth Column" died down as soon as the invasion scare receded. In the camps restrictions were relaxed. Internees could now follow the progress of the war on the previously forbidden radio and newspapers and books were no longer censored. Further categories of internees were progressively released. By August 1941, only 1,300 refugees remained interned in Britain; by July 1942, there were between three and four hundred and by April 1944, only twenty-five.

The danger of a Fifth Column among German refugees proved to be almost completely without basis.[13] The refugees who had been sent overseas returned. Henry Warner had spent six months studying for his matriculation in Ontario, and a further two months on an island in Lake Champlain. One day, the Commandant sent for him and told him that he, with forty-nine others, were required in Britain for war-work. He returned after a freezing winter journey via Greenland, in company with a boat-load of homesick Canadian volunteers. On disembarking at Gourock in Scotland, the first thing he set eyes on was a poster, asking "Was your journey really necessary?"

As they returned, the refugees did what, from the beginning they had so earnestly wished to do, namely to play their part in the war effort. By January 1941, 4,610 had been enrolled in the Pioneer Corps and many more were active in the Home Guard, the Auxiliary Fire Service and Air Raid Precautions. Gerhard Salinger, who became an Air Raid Warden, was told he could only go on duty accompanied by an Englishman, but, he asked, if a fire-bomb fell, did he have to wait for an Englishman to put it out? As a result, this regulation was rescinded.

For the majority of refugees who had elected to stay in this country after the war was over, their main consideration was the speediest possible naturalisation.

Appendix

A Song of Internment

It is impossible to do justice in translation to Henry Freeland's long and witty poem. Every verse contains allusions to old German folk-tales, nursery rhymes, proverbs and popular sayings. It is however a valuable source of information about conditions in the internment camps of Great Britain during World War II.

A sample is given below, followed by a very free translation by the late Leonard Corfan. The poem may be read in full in the War Poetry Collection, Language and Literature Department of the Birmingham Central Library.

The police arrive early in the morning to collect the prospective internees and take them to Hope Street Barracks, Birmingham.

1940

Am 4 Juli früh am morgen, man lag im Bette ohne Sorgen
der Vöglein Lieder auf den Bäumen, umgaukeln uns in unseren Träumen
Junggesellen warn allein, Eheleute warn zu zwein
so ist bestimmt in Gottes Rat, dass jeder seine Ruh'statt hat.

Eingehüllt in tiefem Traum, an Störenfriede glaubt man kaum
doch starkes Klopfen an der Tür spricht in keinem Fall dafür
dass man ohne viel' Getue konnt' beenden seine Ruhe
Besagte frühe Morgenstund' hat statt Gold'nen Fluch im Mund

Man blickt durchs Fenster mit Verzagen, wo unten steht ein schöner Wagen
egal ob Chrysler oder Ford, jetzt interessiert uns nur ein Ort
wohin der Kaiser geht zu Fuss, gleich ob er willes oder muss
dieses war ein guter Plan, was Gott tut, das ist wohlgetan.

Zwei Herren schienen sich zu drängen, gleichzeitig durch die Tür zu zwängen
der eine bärtig, der and're kahl, doch beide waren sehr jovial
sagten ohn'jegliches genieren, sie kämen her zum internieren
das wirkte, wie ein Blitz, so grell, und sieh, das Unheil schreitet schnell.

Die Herren schienen interessiert an allem was im Haus passiert
und von unten bis nach oben wurden Fächer aufgeschoben
und in grösster Windeseile, sie lasen jedes Briefes Zeile
selbst einen alten Liebesbrief las der tüch't'ge Detektiv.

Noch 'ne Umarmung und ein Kuss, die Trennung schnell erfolgen muss.
dann sass ich schon im Wagen drin, der weichgeferdert fahrt dahin
zu 'ner Militarkäserne, Hope Street, in nicht weiter Ferne
in's erste Stockwerk tat man sperren, circa 150 Herren

...

mit aufgeplanztem Bajonett führte man uns zum Klosett
dieses war ein guter Streich doch ein bess'rer folgt sogleich.

Im Klosett musst' man sich sputen, erlaubt war'n netto drei Minuten
nicht alleine or zu zwein,stets ging man zu zehnt' hinein.
hervorragend organisiert wurde man spaziern geführt
man wollte uns damit beweisen, wem Gott will rechte Gunst erweisen.

After many adventures and a spell in a sea-side holiday camp in Devon,
they are brought North and incarcerated in the ruined Warth Cotton Mill in
Lancashire. Here they exist for a time, under appalling conditions,
hilariously described.

Das nun folgende Kapitel, hat WARTH MILL als seinen Titel
Manchester-Bury heisst der Ort, noch seh' ich ihn in einemfort
in meinen Träumen um mich schwirren wo man wurde fast zum Irren.
einstweilen sass man noch im Zug, vom fahren hatten wir genug.

...

Manchester. Man führt uns durch viele Strassen, noch war der Eindruck
ein'germassen
nach langer Zeit fällt unser Blick auf eine drahtumzäunt Fabrik
ein jeder starrte schreckensvoll,der Anblick war ja einfach toll,
doch fürchterlich war's erst von innen, dem Schicksal keiner konnt
entrinnen.

die Spucke allen weg tat bleiben, der Zustand war nicht zu beschreiben.
wie man dort herein uns führte, durch dunkle Gange,
schmutzbeschmierte,
eine verfallene Fabrik, reserviert für uns zum Unglück.
vor Hunger uns're Mägen toben, und das Wasser kam von oben.

Zum dichten sträubt sich meiner Feder, grünbemooste Riesenrader.
an der Decke Transmissionen über unsern Köpfen tronen.
der Kaffee schmeckte ja ganz gut, doch zum lachen war uns nicht zumut
seid mir gegrüsst, ihr teuren Hallen, zur Kontrolle musst'man auch noch
wallen.

...

Zum waschen und zum putzen Zähne, gabs sechs und zwanzig
Wasserhähne
um die sich schlugen welche Freude, allmorgentlich 2000 Leute
um diese Chance zu benützen, stand man in tiefen Wasserpfützen
was klappert die Mühle am rauschenden Bach, dabei gab es immer
tucht'gen Krach.

Dort gab es viele alte Leute, die auch gehalten war'n als Beute
ich z.B. einen weiss, mit weissem Bart, ein Mummelgreis
öfters sah ich ihn zu zwei'n mit einem Herrn, der nur ein Bein
doch auch diese war'n zur Stell, wenn man anstand zum Appell.

Wenn man wollte Wäsche waschen, musste man 'nen Trog erhaschen
man kochte sie auf offenem Feuer auf dem Hof, vor dem Gemäuer
man hängt alsdann den ganzen Hauf, am Stacheldraht zum trock'nen
auf.
stolz war man auf das weisse Linnen
wir lust'gen Wiener Wäscherinnen.

Their final destination is Loch Gilpert in Scotland, where they pass the remainder of their internment, by comparison in luxury.

Translation.

Early in the morning on the fourth of July (1940) we were asleep without a care. The birds were singing in the trees, fluttering around us in our dreams. Young people lay alone, married ones in pairs, as God has willed it, everyone has his resting place.

Wrapped in deep dreams, we scarcely thought our peace would be disturbed. A loud knock come on the door. It was obvious there would be no more rest. The early bird catches the worm.

We looked through the window with sinking heart. Down below stands a fine car, a Chrysler or a Ford, what does it matter? What is God's plan is a good plan.

Two gentlemen squeeze through the doorway together — one bearded, the other clean-shaven. They were very jovial and showed no trace of embarrassment. They said they had come to intern us. You could have struck us down with a feather.

The gentlemen seemed interested in everything in the house, drawers and cupboards were opened upstairs and downstairs, they read every letter, even our love letters.

One more kiss and embrace and we must part. Then into the car which took us to the barracks in Hope Street. There were about one hundred and fifty men on the first floor.

...

They took us to the lavatories, guarded by fixed bayonets. That was a good joke, but there was better to follow.

We had to hurry in the lavatories. We were allowed just three minutes, not alone or in couples, but in companies of ten. These excursions were excellently organised and showed us who was truly favoured by God.

Warth Mill was our destination, Manchester-Bury was the name of the place. I can still see it in my dreams, and even that is enough to drive me mad. But for the time being we were still in the train, we were fed up with travelling.

...

Manchester. They took us through many streets. It didn't look too bad. Then we noticed a factory surrounded by barbed wire. Everybody started up with horrible foreboding.

I was flabbergasted, the conditions were indescribable. It was really horrible inside. We went through dark corridors covered with dirt, a derelict factory, unhappily reserved for us.

Out stomachs rumbled with hunger and water fell from the leaking roof above.

My pen can hardly describe the huge wheels covered with green moss. On the roof cranes tower above our heads. The coffee tasted all right, but we weren't in the mood for laughing. Believe it or not, we then had to go for inspection.

There were twenty-six taps for washing and cleaning one's teeth. Every morning — what fun — two thousand people were milling around them. To get a chance of using them you had to stand deep in puddles of water. Just like the mill at the babbling brook, there was always a lot of noise.

There were plenty of old people, one I knew had a white beard, a real old dodderer. I used to see him with a man who had only one leg. Yet they were always there to answer roll-call.

When you wanted to do some washing you had to get hold of a tub, it had to be boiled on the open fire in the yard in front of the wall. Then we would hang the whole lot on the barbed wire to dry. We jolly Viennese washerwomen were proud of our white linen!

References and notes

1. These figures are given by the refugee organisations; however, some may have emigrated.
2. Wasserstein, B. *Britain and the Jews of Europe* (1979), 84-86.
3. ibid. 90
4. ibid. 94
5. ibid. 96-99
6. Kurt Schwitters (1887-1948) Avant-garde artist and writer.
7. Peter Stadlen (1910-) English pianist and writer on music of Austrian birth.
8. Paul Hamburger (1920-) Mainly an accompanist, also taught music and translated.
9. Peter Gellhorn (1912-) Conductor, pianist, composer.
10. Franz Reizenstein (1911-1968) English composer of German birth, also pianist and chamber musician.
11. Amadeus Quartet, String quartet founded in London 1947, disbanded 1987 on death of one of its members.
12. Maryan Rawicz (1898-1970), born in Poland.; Walter Landauer (1909-1983), born in Vienna. Piano duettists, famous for their performance of light music.
13. Wasserstein, B. op. cit. 91

Worcester Home Guard, 1940s. Emil Rich is fourth from the left in the back row.

10

The Alien Pioneers

In the autumn of 1940, when the cities of England were bracing themselves for the oncoming Blitz, lovers of the arts in North Devon were to be offered an unlooked-for treat. The War Office had lighted on the little seaside town of Ilfracombe as training ground for the Alien Companies of Pioneers, and some very unusual Pioneers were on their way.

Two or three months after the Isle of Man had been turned into an internment camp, a recruiting officer appeared with an invitation to those eligible to take the King's Shilling. Many young men accepted the offer with alacrity, among them Kurt Rose and Werner Abrahams, both from Birmingham. They found themselves shortly in Ilfracombe, "proud of our uniforms and ready to salute anyone else in uniform, be he postman or fireman". The hotels were taken over as billets and musical talent was soon found in abundance. A symphony and a chamber orchestra were formed and concerts became a feature of that war-time winter. The Alien Pioneers also included professional actors and a dramatic company put on plays, variety and a Christmas pantomime.

Kurt Rose and Werner Abrahams were transferred to Catterick in North Yorkshire where a quarter of a million soldiers made it the largest training camp in the country. Many of the native Pioneers were scarcely able to sign their names, and had to be given the simplest tasks. The Alien Pioneers, however, retained their smart appearance and discipline, carrying out with enthusiasm their often drudging work, and off duty winning table tennis and chess championships. "Don't pull my leg, soldier" expostulated a Commanding Officer on being told of the exploits of these unlikely newcomers.

"There was no war in Catterick" said Kurt Rose, "we had to come on leave to Birmingham for that." But he soon began to earn a distinction of his own, organising dances which revolutionised the social life of the camp. The once reluctant ATS girls (only six to two hundred and fifty men) were now tempted to such entertainments as *A Night in Paris*, with a splendid buffet prepared by an Austrian chef, and two bands for non-stop dancing.

"The Austrian influence was everywhere. We swapped our tea ration for coffee, and for a time came down to the delicious smell of coffee and hot rolls. Reading our newspapers, it almost seemed like a Viennese coffee house! But this pleasant state of affairs didn't last long. By mid-winter we were under canvas on the Yorkshire moors, thankful for a cup of tea made by boiling snow, and using the water to shave afterwards.''

Kurt Rose in uniform.

Werner Abrahams, meanwhile, had marked his arrival at Catterick with a BBC interview for the Six O'Clock Post-Script on the radio. ''I pointed out that while I was in British Army uniform, my father was still detained on the Isle of Man. Whether by coincidence or not, he was released in forty-eight hours.''

By spring 1941, the Alien Pioneers were posted to South Wales where, at first somewhat inefficiently, they tackled stone-breaking. ''We used sledge-hammers, the stones kept jumping to one side and wouldn't break, but eventually we got up to our quota.'' They were cheered by the hospitality of the Welsh farmers and at Passover they were entertained for *Seder* by the little Jewish community of Merthyr Tydfil. ''We managed to get a lift by cement lorry and appeared, apparently covered with flour, for the Festival of Unleavened Bread!''

It was during this posting that Kurt Rose was honoured in embarrassing circumstances. One afternoon he and a friend took French leave to go swimming in Langland Bay, near Swansea. "The water was ice-cold and we noticed a boy far out in difficulties. We dragged him in half-drowned but, as we had no passes, got dressed and made off pretty smartly. But the Press got hold of the story and a fortnight later we were summoned back to Swansea by the police. "Have you got a girl in trouble?" fumed the Commanding Officer. But the Chief Constable only wanted to compliment us, and my friend and I were awarded testimonials for gallantry by the Royal Humane Society."

After 1943, it became possible for aliens to be enlisted in the combatant forces. Werner Abrahams rose steadily from the ranks and by D-Day was one of the few officers in the British Army with a German passport. A motor-cycle accident prevented his landing on the Normandy beaches. But Kurt Rose was more successful and was stationed at Caen. Here, after the bombardment, a young Jewish couple with a baby staggered from the ruins. "Everybody rushed to give all they had to this first Jewish family to be found on the Continent. We had the job of clearing out barges. One of them contained chocolate, and as we marched through the town we handed it out to the children."

Towards the end of the war, Kurt Rose was posted to an interpreter's course in Brussels. "There were still a few Jewish families here, who had spent the war in hiding. Passover 1945 was the first time this remnant of a community could be together, to take part in affairs, and to know the Germans were really defeated. The Jews of Brussels were joined by thousands of troops for a *Seder* in the great department store of the Galeries Anspach. The restaurants ran all around the galleries and they were packed ... ATS girls, Americans, Free French, every uniform you could think of."

Kurt Rose had by now left the Pioneers for the Intelligence Section of the General Services Corps, where he was attached to a "T (Target) Force". The targets in this instance were distillation plants cunningly concealed, often in disused quarries on the Dutch-German frontier. "Britain was badly in need of oil at this time. A major, seconded from Shell, was in command of the unit, and we became very successful in locating these plants."

It was in a small town on the border that Kurt Rose came across a Jewish family who had hidden underground throughout the war. "They had had a small haberdasher's shop, but little remained of it. As luck would have it, we ran across some Canadian troops who were about to seal a warehouse full of blankets, curtain materials and towels. 'We could set this couple up', I pointed out to my Shell major. The following Friday night they asked us to supper and gave us each a pair of leather gloves, the last bit of stock they had left. I still treasure mine."

Nearly a quarter of a century later, Kurt Rose, now director of the internationally known fashion enterprise "The House of Lerose", was setting up a new factory in Holland. The haberdasher's son telephoned, asking to meet him. His parents had died, but he had not forgotten the corporal in the British Army who had managed to re-start the life not only of his own family, but of five other families beside.

From the Dutch border Kurt Rose was sent to Wilhelmshaven. "The streets were black with German Marines, marching eight abreast, ready to give themselves up. I could see the shadow of the SS insignia on the uniform of one colonel we arrested, although he had ripped off all his decorations. His hand shot up to his breast pocket to take a poison capsule, but the guard pounced"

At this point, Kurt Rose's military progress was halted by a serious car accident and he was invalided home for a year. "I was posted then to a Regimental Holding Unit at Bielefeld, but nobody knew what to do with me! So, I got myself somehow to Berlin, where I made myself so useful as a translator in court cases that I was given an official posting. Six months later I was demobbed."

Werner Abrahams recovered from his motor-cycle accident and was sent to India. "I was posted to an Indian Holding Unit, in charge of loading ships for Burma. They were very large ships and it was very hot. I had to supervise a labour battalion. As soon as I went to the bow of the ship, the Indians went to sleep in the stern, and when I went to the stern, they were asleep in the bow!"

He moved on to Burma, and one day, whilst under canvas in the jungle, he received a telegram from New Delhi ordering him to report to a special unit of the WEC (Wireless Experimental Centre). "I thought this stood for Western European Campaign and hoped it meant going back home. On arrival, a Colonel Blimp-like figure interviewed me. He took me first for a wireless expert, then as a Japanese-speaking linguist, and as I was neither of these I was nearly sent back to my unit. 'This mistake has cost me my promotion', I cried, and the Colonel took pity on me. Twenty-four hours later I was a Staff Captain

"For the rest of the war I travelled the length and breadth of India. The Indian and British governments had agreed to share the expenses of the campaign 50-50. It was my task to contact local commands and take back the counter-proposals. I was just a carrier-pigeon with a brief-case that had G.R. (Georgius Rex) stamped on it."

Walter Schott was never in the Pioneers. He was sixteen years old when war broke out, and went straight to the Recruiting Office. "Come back when you're grown up" advised the recruiting officer. He reappeared the following year and was told to wait for his eighteenth birthday. By this time it was possible for aliens to join the RAF.

Walter Schott had spent the intervening years working on the land. "I was pretty tough. When I was on the threshing machines, I had to carry two hundredweight of wheat on my back, and get it up to the lofts. The initial training at RAF Cosford didn't worry me, but unfortunately I caught pneumonia. This made me two months late for the flying school and so I never got into a bombing unit. But I flew small 'planes and reconnaissance 'planes." Before long he was ordered into the RAF Intelligence because he spoke German.

With the liberation of Belgium, Walter Schott was moved to Ghent, seconded to the Air Disarmament Wing. "Every airfield captured had to be stripped of technical material which was shipped back to England. The secret documents had to be read and translated for the Air Ministry in London. I had to learn thousands of new words; although it was German it was almost a new language. During the Ardennes offensive in the winter of 1944 I was moving about in forward positions the whole time. Every airfield in Belgium, Holland and Northern France was bombed, and with the flying bombs there were enormous casualties. But the job did have its compensations. The team lived on a comfortable train with an excellent cook to look after us. Once, when we were in the French sector, we invited the local station master to a meal and he arranged for us to be hooked on to a leave train for five days in Paris!

"Germany seemed to be totally destroyed. We weren't allowed to fraternise with the local population, and having no contact with individuals we became hardened. But we did try to do something for the children. I got quite friendly with the nuns of a convent nearby, who lent us a Father Christmas outfit which we needed for a children's party. And all the time we were coming across Jews who had been in hiding all through the war.

"Towards the end of my service, I was stationed at Hanover, near Belsen, and I contacted several friends who were survivors, in fact I attended the first wedding in Belsen. I spent a great deal of my time trying to trace the fate of my grandfather who was in Theresienstadt before he perished at Auschwitz. We set up a sort of postal service for survivors; at that time there was no post out of Germany. We arranged for their letters to go to England, and from there they were forwarded to America and Palestine.

"I shall never forget Germany at this time. Tens of thousands of people on the move from east to west. Every little village was crowded with refugees ... people just milling around ... it was chaos.

"Of course, many forms of aid were being offered, medical treatment, food and money, but there seemed no permanent solution. Attempts were being made to help displaced persons into channels of self-rehabilitation. But they didn't seem to be wanted anywhere. Gradually, movement started into France, the Balkans, over the Alps to Italy and thence into overcrowded and unseaworthy boats in the hope of illegal entry into Palestine.

"About this time I became involved with the Jewish Brigade which was working with the refugees in the German cities. Papers were being passed around for volunteers. I applied for the Palestine Police but heard no more of it.

"In 1947 I was demobbed and returned to Birmingham to build up a home. It was not very long before the establishment of the State of Israel ... I still regret that perhaps I missed a chance ... "

Walter Schott succeeded in building up an electrical business and married an Israeli girl. They have three daughters, all of whom have left Birmingham to live in Israel.

Home Office No. E. 5051

Certificate No. **AZ 28355**

BRITISH NATIONALITY AND STATUS OF ALIENS ACT, 1914

CERTIFICATE OF NATURALIZATION

Whereas   Hildegard Eisner known as Hilde Eisner

has applied to one of His Majesty's Principal Secretaries of State for a Certificate of Naturalization, alleging with respect to   herself the particulars set out below, and has satisfied him that the conditions laid down in the above-mentioned Act for the grant of a Certificate of Naturalization are fulfilled in   her   case :

Now, therefore, in pursuance of the powers conferred on him by the said Act, the Secretary of State grants to the said

Hildegard Eisner known as Hilde Eisner

this Certificate of Naturalization, and declares that upon taking the Oath of Allegiance within the time and in the manner required by the regulations made in that behalf she shall, subject to the provisions of the said Act, be entitled to all political and other rights, powers and privileges, and be subject to all obligations, duties and liabilities, to which a natural-born British subject is entitled or subject, and have to all intents and purposes the status of a natural-born British subject.

In witness whereof I have hereto subscribed my name this   day of

July 1947.

A. Maxwell.

HOME OFFICE,   *Under Secretary of State.*
LONDON.

PARTICULARS RELATING TO APPLICANT

Full Name	Hildegard EISNER known as Hilde EISNER.
Address	Flat 1, 933, Bristol Road, Selly Oak, Birmingham, 29.
Trade or Occupation	Doctor of Medicine.
Place and date of birth	Ratibor, Upper Silesia, Poland. 24th June, 1899.
Nationality	German.
Single, Married, etc.	Single.
Name of wife or husband	- - -
Names and nationality of parents	Isidor and Frida EISNER. (German).

(For Oath
see overleaf)

Certificate of Naturalization issued to Hilde Eisner

116

11

The Professions

It has been said many times that the expulsion of the Jewish professional men and women from Germany was a significant factor in its defeat in World War II. The outstanding example in Birmingham of the truth of this statement is Sir Rudolf Peierls who worked on the Atomic Energy Project at the University of Birmingham from 1937 to 1963. He tells his story in his autobiography, *Bird of Passage* (1985)[1]. Robert Frisch, his assistant, performed the "first experiment to show up the fragments into which the uranium had split, and proposed the name fission for the new phenomenon".

Sigbert Prawer, now Taylor Professor of German Language and Literature at Oxford University, was lecturer at the University of Birmingham from 1958-1963; Leslie Brent, Professor of Immunology at Queen Mary's Hospital Medical School, was a medical student at Birmingham University and Vice-Chancellor's Prize Winner in 1968. John Grenville has been Professor of Modern History at the University of Birmingham since 1969. Sir Nicholas Pevsner, art historian and editor of the Penguin *Buildings of England* series in forty-six volumes, was research assistant at the University of Birmingham 1933-34.[2]

Robert Schneider came to England in 1933 and became Consultant Physician and Reader in the Department of Clinical Pharmacology at the University of Birmingham. He researched into fat metabolism and intestinal absorption.

Scholars like Herman Kober were helped by the Society for the Protection of Science and Learning. It was fortunate for him that he had been in the habit of spending two months each year in Cambridge on research in mathematics. Through this he obtained a research grant at the University of Birmingham. Thus his wife, also a mathematician, and his family were able to reach England in the summer before the outbreak of war.

Herman Kober was awarded the degree of MSc by the University of Birmingham, followed by the DSc in 1943. During the Second World War he produced a *Dictionary of Conformal Mappings* for the Admiralty, which remained a standard work for a long time. He taught mathematics at King Edward's School, Camp Hill, from 1943 to his retirement in 1962.

The lawyers who got away could not, generally speaking, hope to practise in this country. They had to find alternative ways of earning a living, like Walter Seelig, who retrained as a chiropodist. Ernest Shire, formerly a barrister in Breslau, turned to teaching German language and literature at Trinity College Dublin, where ironically he organised the celebrations for the birth of Goethe in 1949.

Hermann Kober, 1970.

Some of the doctors were able to find work in their own profession, but only after obtaining a British qualification. Many went to Edinburgh or Dublin where the examinations were said to be easier. An English medical student remembered receiving valuable coaching from a well-known German pathologist, a specialist in cancer, in return for helping him with English medical terminology.

In 1934 there was an outcry, led by the Daily Express, that foreign doctors would swamp the native practitioners, and Lord Dawson of Penn, the King's physician, considered that "The foreign doctors who could usefully be absorbed or teach us anything could be counted on the fingers of one hand"[3].

As late as 1938, a resolution to stop foreign doctors practising in England was debated at the British Medical Association's Annual Conference in Plymouth. Birmingham's Dr Solly Wand vigorously reminded the members of events in Germany, "which you don't know, or don't want to know", and the motion was unanimously rejected. The doctors' turn was to come when the war began to draft medical men into the Forces and refugee doctors were able to replace them at home.

It was possible to interview only very few doctors in Birmingham. Some still felt bitter at the chilly reception they had at first received from their colleagues. The widows of two doctors affirmed that although their husbands had emigrated in middle life, with a solid reputation behind them, they never attained the status they had enjoyed in Germany before the advent of Hitler.

Robert Singer had served with the Austrian Army in World War I. He was taken prisoner in Russia and spent five years as doctor in a camp, working with the Swedish Red Cross. He had practised for many years as Ear, Nose and Throat Specialist in the little Silesian town of Neisse near the Czech border. Until 1 October 1938, when all Jewish doctors were forbidden to practise, his surgeries remained crowded, and his patients included a number of high-ranking Nazi officials, who came to consult him under cover of darkness. So his apprehensions were lulled and he did not seek to escape until almost the last moment.

In November, after the Kristallnacht, he was rounded up with other Jewish men of the town and taken to Buchenwald. Here he was forced to stand for sixteen hours at a stretch, an experience from which he never fully recovered.

After unimaginable hardships, he and his family managed to escape separately, and were reunited in London shortly before the outbreak of war. Had he come earlier, he might have taken a British qualification, but he had left it too late and had no money. His guarantor, a cousin and a refugee himself, was in serious financial difficulties and could not help. Robert Singer, with no work permit, spent his days trying to find an opportunity to practise his profession all over the world: in India, in Afghanistan and in China. Meanwhile they were dependent on his wife's scanty earnings. Her work permit was only for a "domestic, living-in", but as she said, "Hadn't I promised God that if ever Robert came back from Buchenwald I would never leave him". So she worked, unofficially, as governess, dressmaker and charwoman, always in dread of investigation by the police. It was while cleaning a doctor's flat that she found some copies of the *British Medical Journal* in his waste-paper basket and took them home for her husband. An advertisement offered the post of Honorary Ear, Nose and Throat Surgeon at Golden Square Hospital in London. Robert Singer applied successfully. "It was unpaid work, but three times a week he was happy in his own profession, wearing a white coat ... he already looked quite different." This post saved him from internment.

Meanwhile their two younger children were being fostered by Christadelphians in Birmingham, where they were being educated. By autumn of 1940 the air-raids were becoming serious and Charlotte Singer felt she must be with her children. Robert Singer was reluctant to leave Golden Square and in Birmingham could get no work except gardening for which he was unfit. Now the family experienced real hardship, moving their lodgings from pillar to post. At last they found sanctuary with a tailor who, with his family, slept in an air-raid shelter, leaving the bedroom free. One day the tailor went to Dudley Road Hospital to apply for the job of porter. He persuaded Robert Singer to go with him and as a result, two months later, he was offered the post of Junior Medical Officer at the Geriatric Hospital, the Western Road Infirmary. Although now over fifty years old he remained for seven years, always being promised promotion which never materialised. "It was not what we had hoped for, his skill was wasted ... but he earned double my wages in half the time" recalled Charlotte Singer. "He had a single flat for night duty ... it was a treat to visit him, have a hot bath and a good, cheap meal in the canteen." Towards the end of the war he was back at his own work as Ear, Nose and Throat Surgeon at All Saint's Mental Hospital, temporarily replacing a consultant who had been called up. In 1956, aged sixty-five years, he became Ear, Nose and Throat Consultant at the Outpatient Department of Dudley Road Hospital. This was the happiest part of his career in Birmingham and he remained there for six years, working in the last months from his wheel-chair.

Louis Lindenstein, 1947.

After serving in the First World War, Louis Lindenstein worked for many years in Nuremberg as an orthopaedic surgeon. But in contrast to Robert Singer, his career was rudely interrupted by the Nazis as early as 1933. Very few Jews were allowed to remain in practice in the town and Louis Lindenstein's part-time Government work came to an abrupt end. He was no longer allowed in the town clinics and his beds were limited to the Jewish Hospital in nearby Fürth. His son was sent to school in Switzerland and later to England. He decided to join his brother who had already emigrated to America, but with the strict quota[4] imposed by the United States, it was obvious that his turn would not come for a very long time. So he and his wife decided to go temporarily to England. Their old friend Hanna Simmons managed to get them a guarantee and they arrived in Birmingham a few weeks before the outbreak of war.

The family were for a time in very straitened circumstances, having to accept help from the American brother. However, they managed to rent a small house in Poplar Avenue, Edgbaston, where, one after another, relatives and friends came to join them. Irma Lindenstein called it "the house with elastic walls".

Both Louis Lindenstein and his son were interned but the father was released on medical grounds. As the war progressed he was put on the Temporary Doctors' Register. Soon he became Casualty Officer at the General Hospital, Birmingham, mostly treating victims of the air-raids. "He worked every day from 9 a.m. to 3 p.m. with student assistants and was paid £5 weekly. With that and the occasional locum we could write to America and tell my brother-in-law we were at last independent." Irma Lindenstein, now over ninety years old, recalled their first holiday in England with child-like pleasure. "We only went as far as Clent for a few days, and the landlady looked rather oddly at the foreign names on our identity cards but it was a wonderful triumph."

Later Louis Lindenstein went to the Accident Hospital and the Western Road Infirmary where he performed small operations, removing glass, treating burns and cuts. It was a far cry from his position in Nuremberg, but he and his family were now happily settled in Birmingham, and when their number came up on the American quota, they no longer wished to go. Unhappily Louis Lindenstein's health was already deteriorating and he died in 1950.

Joe Hirtenstein sat for his final examination in medicine on the day the Nazis marched into Prague, 15 March 1939. His brother Arno, also a doctor, was arrested next day as a Communist. When he was released, six weeks later, the brothers decided they must leave the country.

After abortive attempts to escape to England, and then Palestine, they bought visas for Shanghai, to be reached by boat from Genoa. But once they had arrived in Italy they made their way into France where they were promptly arrested by French police. They returned to Italy, then back to Nice, where they went into hiding. Arno managed to get a permit for England but Joe eventually joined the Czech army in exile. On the collapse of France, he was shipped to Liverpool, where to his surprise he was greeted as a hero.

This Czech army consisted mainly of middle-aged intellectuals and was over-weighted with doctors. Joe Hirtenstein was released and sent during the blitz to a hospital in Barnsley, Yorkshire. Here he learnt a great deal of traumatic surgery. Later he moved to hospitals in Manchester and Northampton.

In 1945 he volunteered to return home to help liberated Czechoslovakia. He found his parents had perished in the Holocaust and his eldest brother had been shot trying to get across the frontier into Hungary. His youngest brother had joined the partisans, but had been fatally wounded the day before the arrival of the Red Army.

Joe Hirtenstein went to work in the Theresienstadt concentration camp, a searing experience. He next joined a surgical team at a large hospital in Prague and here he admitted a patient whom he recognised as his uncle. He had been in Dachau and later died.

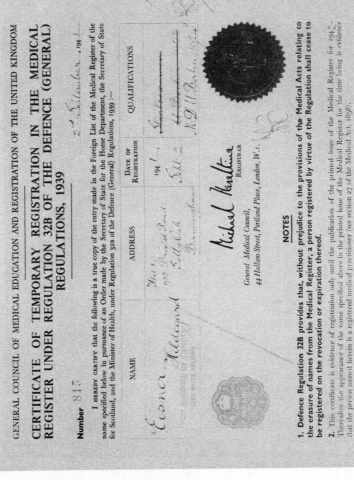

Temporary medical registration of Hilde Eisner, 1941.

122

Joe Hirtenstein realised that to further his career in Czechoslovakia he would have to join the Communist Party. Generally the British Government did not favour the return of refugees to England but in this case the application was granted.

In 1946 he took the post of Resident Surgical Officer at Walsall General Hospital and was gradually upgraded to Consultant Orthopaedic Surgeon. In 1950 Arno established an Eye Department at Selly Oak Hospital. He later transferred to Wolverhampton and at the same time worked, like his brother, at Walsall General Hospital.

Joe Hirtenstein retired from hospital practice in 1980 and took up the hobby of bee-keeping. Arno died in 1985.

The shattering experience of finding her own surgery sealed against her by the Nazis had a lasting effect on Dr Hilde Eisner, shadowing the remainder of her life. She came to England on a domestic permit, but eventually returned to medicine as an anaesthetist at Walsall General Hospital. But she remained a solitary person, devoting almost her entire earnings to the cause of Israel. She planted eighteen thousand trees there in her mother's name, and generously endowed scholarships for medical studies, especially in Ashkelon. After her death her only treasures were discovered in her handbag—a bundle of crumpled letters from her student beneficiaries.

Hilde Eisner plants trees in Israel in 1970 in memory of her mother who died in the Holocaust.

Among other members of the medical profession and its ancillaries, whom we were unable to interview, were an ear, nose and throat surgeon, a psychiatrist, a psychoanalyst and two radiographers. There was also a pharmacist.

Sophie Levy studied speech therapy in Germany at the pioneering Ewing School for the Teaching of the Deaf. She was one of the earliest practitioners of her profession in this country and taught for many years at the Royal School for the Deaf in Birmingham. She was particularly skilled in dealing with problems of hearing and speech impairment among refugee children.

Dentists were in a somewhat better position than doctors because their qualifications were recognised in this country. Bernard Borkon in Breslau and H.L. in Berlin heard that German dentists with as good qualifications as their British counterparts (or preferably better) might be put on the Foreign Register of Great Britain. Bernard Borkon came to England in November 1935 and because Woburn House thought his chances were good, they allowed him £1 weekly to stay for two months. He was successful and obtained a work permit from the Home Office, although it was indicated to him that he might consider India. If he stayed in this country, however, he must work outside London, starting a practice of his own from scratch. On no account must he be accused of taking possible work from a British dentist. Bernard Borkon came to Birmingham, managed to rent a flat and sent to Germany for his dental equipment. "When it arrived, the Simmons family became my interior decorators. It is wonderful what you can do with the wooden cases in which the contents are packed. It took quite a while to make a living, but once established the patients proved loyal. One recommendation led to another. We formed a Society of Continental Dental Surgeons, and met twice a year to discuss our problems and methods."

Bernard Borkon supplied a set of figures based on the Dentists' Register of 1951, enumerating foreign dentists who were registered in the years 1933-1939.

1933	2	1937	19
1934	5	1938	3
1935	47	1939	1
1936	48		

All these dentists were still practising in 1951.

Bernard Borkon always believed that there were one hundred and twenty applications in 1935, the year he applied, of whom sixty were accepted. The list, however, shows only forty-seven. Possibly the remaining thirteen had gone overseas.

H.L. was less fortunate. Despite two visits to England in 1937 and 1938, and eventual success in registering, he was unable to get a work permit. Had it not been for the war, he would have gone to Afghanistan. As it was he was able to work only short spells as a locum tenens before he was interned. On his release from the Isle of Man, he took a post with a Dental Association, with which he remained until it closed down in 1972.

Nursing was the only alternative to domestic service for the young women refugees.

Herta Linden had tried without success to obtain a domestic permit when she heard there were opportunities for Jewish girls to train as nurses in England. "I wrote straight to Woburn House and within a week I had been accepted. We had to have the equivalent of the School Certificate, luckily they accepted my qualifications—I would never have managed the examination in England. I went to stay with relatives and very shortly was notified of an opening in Grantham, Lincolnshire.

Herta Linden at the "Woodlands" Royal Orthopaedic Hospital, Northfield, Birmingham, 1947.

"At the hospital I was made to feel very welcome, but rather as an exotic bird. Few of the Grantham girls had come across a foreigner before—I was taken home to be shown off to parents. But in 1940, as an alien, I had to leave the hospital and went to stay on a farm as a mother's help. The farmer's wife had formerly taught in a very high class boarding school in Ascot—I learnt a lot from her about the do's and don'ts of English life." She returned to the hospital six months later. "You're more like us now" remarked her friends, perhaps a trifle disappointedly.

Herta Linden came to Birmingham to complete her training and here she met and married a fellow refugee—Frank Linden.

The most agonising experience for Robert and Charlotte Singer concerned their daughter Eva, whom they had had to leave behind in Germany. At seventeen she was too old to travel on her parents' passport and too young for a domestic or nurse's permit.

The best hope lay with the Children's Refugee Movement provided she came before her eighteenth birthday. Time and again her parents were assured she would be on the next transport, only to be disappointed. Finally it was arranged that she should leave four days before her birthday. Even as her parents traced the course of her journey from Hamburg to Southampton on the map, the telephone rang. It was Eva, sobbing bitterly that she had been left behind again, and the next transport would be too late.

And then a miracle happened. The Singers' guarantor asked them to come immediately. They found with him a Berlin friend, "a big shot in the Hilfsverein (German Committee for Jewish Relief), one of the few Jewish people allowed to travel backwards and forwards between Berlin and London. He promised he himself would take Eva to Tempelhof Airport with the necessary papers, and she arrived two days before her eighteenth birthday." With gratuitous beastliness, the Nazis assured her that, flying without being in an official group, she would never be admitted to England and would be back in Tempelhof by evening.[5]

Eva had determined to take up nursing. She went to Birmingham at the invitation of the same Christadelphians who were caring for her brother. She started as a probationer at the Women's Hospital, Sparkhill, but was interned for many months on the Isle of Man. On their release the Matron refused to re-admit the refugee probationers. "They have a bad reputation." None of the other girls had parents to speak for them, but Robert Singer wrote a "careful letter" to the Matron. He did not receive a reply.

Eva was the only one of these probationers who continued nursing and she was forced to start again at a hospital in London.

Ilse Lewen, deputy matron at Highcroft Hospital, Birmingham, 1955

Ilse Lewen from Wuppertal came to Birmingham on a domestic permit but was a self-confessed failure as a cook. Nursing however was another matter and she quickly rose to the top of the tree in Birmingham hospitals. Once the invasion scare was over alien girls were allowed to train in TB, fever and mental hospitals. Ilse Lewen opted for the All Saints' Mental Hospital. She was made much of by the staff, but eyed with suspicion by the patients. "I never said I was a German, just a Jewish refugee. I can't repeat the patients' language when they heard this."

Ilse Lewen qualified as a Registered Mental Nurse, and after general training progressed to become Deputy Matron of Highcroft Hospital in 1955. In 1960 she was appointed Matron at Rubery Hill Psychiatric Hospital.

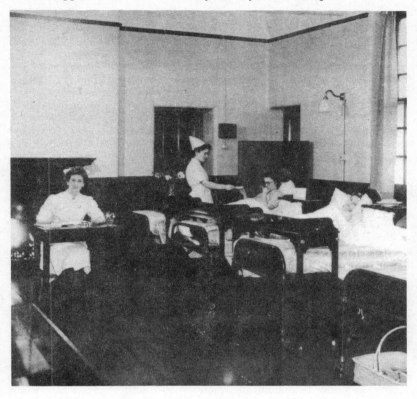

Nelly Hewspear persuading an anorexic patient to eat at the Maudsley Hospital, London, 1945.

Nelly Hewspear took up TB nursing at a Surrey sanatorium. With the fall of France in May 1940, the Matron turned this young girl out, without the slightest concern for her welfare. Despite her desperate attempts to help her family — her parents were still in Austria (to perish later in Auschwitz) and her brother somewhere in Belgium on the run from the Nazis—her efforts were unsuccessful although she was rewarded only by the arrival of her sister two days before the outbreak of war. Nelly Hewspear managed to get a post in a private nursing home, "just a domestic, running up and down three flights of stairs with trays". Later in the year refugee nurses were allowed to return to the hospitals, but, like Eva Singer, Nelly Hewspear had to start again at the sanatorium from scratch. Nevertheless she qualified in 1942 and transferred to a hospital in Kingston-on-Thames, where quite by chance she met her sister, also training as a nurse. It was the time of the "doodle-bugs".[6] A company of Welsh Guardsmen were parading in Richmond Park and received a direct hit. "There were few survivors. We had beds in corridors, everywhere."

Nelly Hewspear volunteered for fire-watching but was refused, as was her application for nursing service with the army ... "I was well treated and had made many friends, yet I still cried at night in bed. My sister had qualified as a psychiatric nurse and for a time we both worked at the Maudsley Hospital in London. We had some notable patients, including the author, Arthur Koestler."

In 1946 she married a pathologist, David Hewspear. They lived for a time in Gloucester where she became a district nurse. "An elderly lady employed two nurses paying us 2s.6d. (13p) an hour each out of a tin box. We had to cycle everywhere, in winter across snowy fields, often to administer morphine."

Nelly Hewspear had ambitions to become a doctor and started to study, but her education had been too much interrupted for her to be able to cope with the pre-medical examinations.

At the impressionable age of sixteen, Ruth Shire suddenly found herself transported from the small, old-fashioned Jewish community of Siegburg, near Bonn, into a progressive family with roots in the Oxfordshire countryside. Mr and Mrs Wood, her hosts, were committed Christians, but broad-minded and very liberal in attitude.

Ruth Shire's education had not been much interrupted in her German backwater. Until she left for England in 1937 she was able to continue at the same school; indeed until 1935 Hebrew had been taught to the Jewish pupils as part of the curriculum.

She remembered the Wood family as remarkable people. "They were anxious above all that I should maintain my Jewish background and took me to a synagogue in Oxford as often as possible. Mr Wood was a retired civil servant from the Ministry of Health; now he was occupied in helping to run the Wingfield Hospital, where he had introduced a Spanish surgeon with completely new ideas about the treatment of fractures as practised in the Spanish Civil War. Mrs Wood became a billeting officer, finding homes for children to be evacuated from London. This was where I had my first insight into social work."

Ruth thrived in this stimulating atmosphere, quickly adapting to a life where horses and dogs were of great importance, and yet where plans for an enlightened new world were daily subjects of conversation.

Mr and Mrs Wood worked tirelessly for the refugees, mostly for the "non-Aryans" with only tenuous Jewish connections. They arranged for Ruth's parents to come to Oxford and when her father was interned in 1940 she went to live with her mother. Here she worked for the Co-operative Society for a time, delivering milk, and learnt to know the villages and smallholdings around Oxford.

In 1941 she applied to train as a nurse and once again found herself among forward-looking professionals, this time in an Emergency Medical Hospital in Middlesex. The premises were simple hutments, but there was little of the traditional hospital discipline; the nurses were young and the matron was a woman of new ideas who liked the refugees. The doctors were mostly in the Socialist Medical Service and enthusiastically lectured the nurses on the coming of the National Health Service.

"It was at about this time" recalled Ruth Shire, "that I had a strange experience. It was my half-day and some friends had driven me to Virginia Water. Looking at this peaceful scene in the sunset, I suddenly felt I had reached a watershed, that I was stepping out of one part of my life and entering another. I felt I was no longer a refugee, a second class citizen, but an ordinary young woman and that here I belonged."

Ruth Shire completed her training and then characteristically embarked on a completely new field in Occupational Health Nursing. At that time this could only be studied in Birmingham where the city was doing exploratory work in preventive medicine.

Here she met her future husband, Dr Heinz Shire. She returned to Occupational Health Nursing after bringing up their family and remained for eighteen years until her retirement.

Lia Lesser trained at the Queen Elizabeth Hospital in Birmingham and rose to be theatre sister at the Birmingham General Hospital. Brought up by understanding Christians in remote Anglesey, she always knew she was Jewish. "There were Hebrew books in my luggage, and a pendant showing Moses receiving the Law on Mount Sinai. I felt rather lost on coming to Birmingham, so I looked up Singers Hill Synagogue in the telephone directory. They welcomed my return after all these years, taught me about Judaism and gave me a pair of Friday night candlesticks which I use to this day." Lia Lesser eventually married into an old-established Birmingham Jewish family.

Hetty Leyton started to train as a laboratory assistant a few months before leaving her native Vienna in 1939. It was 1941 before she was able to continue, and then only because of her fierce determination against overwhelming odds. In 1970 she was at last able to realise her early academic ambitions when she gained an honours degree in psychology and sociology at the University of Birmingham. She became a psychiatric social worker and now specialises in the new field of incest survival.

"Goethe's Faust was a strong influence in my life" she claimed. "My father's enthusiasm for German literature resulted in my knowing parts of the play before I could read or write."

Gifted with intellectual curiosity she did well at school, but her favourite subject was drawing, and she started to study fashion design in her spare time. "But as I grew older I was drawn to medicine, I think partly because of the message of Faust which teaches that only by helping others can one achieve happiness." But the Anschluss of 1938 intervened and she was forced to leave school without matriculation.

"My father had a friend who was a Reader in Pathology at the University of Vienna, and he introduced me to laboratory technique. From there I went to the Jewish Hospital where I was promoted to Senior Technician. Meanwhile things went from bad to worse in Vienna. I was never actually molested myself but I saw Jews being ill-treated and the police turning their backs. At the hospital we kept a ward cleared for street incidents. Once, when I had to ring up the blood transfusion centre, a voice replied: "Aryan blood for a Jewish swine? Let him croak." From then on, the staff at the hospital supplied their own blood.

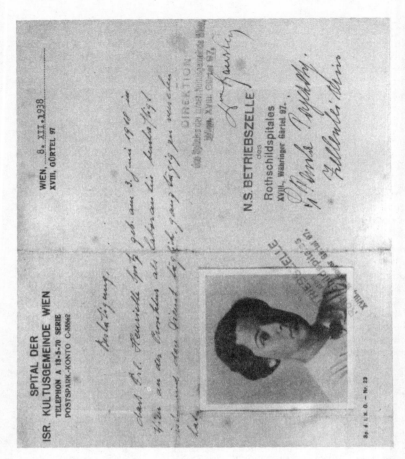

Hetty Layton's pass, allowing Jewish medical personnel to go out after curfew, Vienna, 1938.

Hetty Leyton's father was so shocked by the entry of German troops into Vienna and the subsequent murder of one of his friends in the street that he suggested the whole family should gas themselves. He was given an opportunity to escape, but could not envisage life elsewhere than in his beloved city, so he and his devoted wife made the fatal decision to stay. Their daughter-in-law was already in London on a domestic permit, endeavouring to arrange a visa for her husband who was occupied winding up his business to hand it over to the Nazis. Hetty herself obtained a nursing permit and left for England in March 1939.

She was sent to a hospital in Leytonstone. After three months' trial she resigned.

"It was nothing from morning to night but bedpans and bedmaking. I felt buried alive. I longed above all to use my mind but I was learning nothing. On a salary of thirty-three shillings (£1.65) a month, I couldn't even save anything to visit the few people I knew.

"The only alternative to nursing was domestic work. I was introduced to an elderly lady as a sort of lady's-maid-companion." This lady was about to leave for Scotland to spend the summer at her daughter's home near Birnham Wood and Dunsinane. "It was Macbeth come alive for me! I was thrilled and even happier when her son-in-law gave me the run of his library. I had known nothing of the long Scottish summer evenings, and once I had put my lady's clothes out for dinner, I was free to take my book into the woods and sit reading until it was dark, looking out over the River Tay."

When the outbreak of war was announced, Hetty Leyton was begged to stay, where she could have a "safe war". The house was to be turned into a convalescent home, and she could have done very useful work.

But she returned to London, determined to take an active part in a war she felt to be hers. Besides, she wanted to resume her laboratory work. This the Home Office would not permit, but she was sent as nurse to a First Aid Post in London's Dockland. She was paid two pounds weekly, out of which she had to set aside fifteen shillings (75p) for the rent of a room she had managed to find in Kensington and five shillings (25p) for her fares to work.

During the early months of the war there was little to do at the First Aid Post and she voluntarily worked in the laboratory of a local hospital. But in August 1940 she was suddenly dismissed. Dockland had become a restricted area.

The Blitz had now started and everyone who could manage to do so left London. This included Hetty Leyton's landlady. Now she was not only unemployed, but she had nowhere to lay her head. "Moreover I was extremely worried about my parents. I had heard nothing from them since the outbreak of war and I was frightened to send them Red Cross letters in case a connection with England might draw on them more suffering at the hands of the Nazis." She was never to see them again.

"After immense difficulties I found a room in what I afterwards discovered to be a red light district. Once the girls realised I was not in competition with them they were friendly enough, and I was grateful for this, as most of my acquaintances had fled the bombing. It was a very lonely time for me, and also a time of near starvation, as I had no work-permit. My unemployment benefit was one pound weekly and that meant five shillings (25p) to live on. I suppose I could have gone into one of the refugee hostels, but I couldn't bear the prospect of sharing a room and I felt I might not be free to pursue my interests.

"Even at the First Aid Post I'd managed to take a course in English literature. I couldn't go to the Refugee Club, because I hadn't the few pence for a cup of tea. Once, on a day of icy rain, I found the Labour Exchange closed for lunch and I took shelter in a nearby Woolworths. There was a most fantastic smell of freshly baked buns. I knew if I bought one I'd have no money for the 'bus home, and I couldn't afford to wear out my shoes. So I went out into the rain again.

"There were plenty of jobs to be had in the little garment factories off Oxford Street, because so many girls had gone into munitions, or were sewing uniforms. Having no work-permit I was not permitted to take such employment, but I found a good friend at the Labour Exchange. Even now I can't speak of her without being moved — she was so sympathetic. She would send me to a workshop where I would earn money on piece-work for a few days until the Home Office caught up with me. Then she'd send me to another one where the same thing would happen again. But I'd never realised about the Christmas shut-down and this proved the hungriest time of all. I spent most of the day in bed.

"All these months the Blitz had been in full swing. I used to watch the fires over London from my room. The First Aid Post was bombed and all my friends there were killed. But the shortage of labour had made work permits easier to obtain and when the Labour Exchange reopened after the holiday I was offered the job of book-keeper in a small gown factory. I learnt the rudiments of book-keeping in one night, although later on I did take a Pitman's course!

"But I still longed to get back to laboratory work, and when I heard the Home Office would grant permits for this, I applied to every hospital whose address I could find. Eventually I was called for an interview to a Psychiatric Hospital in Hampshire, which had partially been taken over by the Navy. It was the night after the most terrible blitz on London. I managed somehow to get down to Hampshire by the afternoon and found a different world — full of sunshine and spring flowers.

"On my return to London I telephoned my sister-in-law. There was no reply. I made my way to Swiss Cottage where she worked as a housekeeper. A direct hit by a land-mine had bombed the house into the ground. Only the telephone fixed to a back wall remained and it was still ringing out. My brother, who had reached England only a few days before the war, had by now been interned in Canada. It took three days before his wife could be identified and I had to break the news to him.

"I enjoyed the work in the Hampshire hospital, but it was not far from Portsmouth and as an alien I had to move again when the Second Front was opened up. Haematology had become of absorbing interest to me and I applied for a post in blood-testing at the Public Laboratories in Birmingham. It was here I met my husband and finally settled."

The outlook for undergraduates in Germany after 1933 was even more bleak than for those who had qualified. Few were able to resume their projected careers, even when they had escaped to other countries, and most of those who remained perished in the camps.

After 1933, the *Numerus Clausus*, which had been rescinded during the Weimar Republic, was re-imposed on Jews at German universities. The fate of the students, as so often in the story of the refugees, depended very largely on chance, in the case of the students where they happened to live or study. Ernest Wolf, a second year medical student in Frankfurt, was dismissed from the university as a Jew and a Socialist and was forced to leave the country in April 1933. His brother Rudi had just qualified as a lawyer but could find no work. He enrolled in a Bauschule (School of Civil Engineering) and as there were no other Jewish students was allowed to continue his studies. When, in 1937, he came to emigrate to the United States he was able to go as a qualified architect.

Gerhardt Kornhauser of Berlin was in his third year as a medical student. He was allowed to continue to the end of the semester in June 1932, but was awarded no certificate. At this time, Leo Baeck[7], the courageous Berlin Reform Rabbi, who later chose to remain with his own people in

Theresienstadt concentration camp when he could have escaped, was organising Hachsharah[8] courses for young people.

These taught practical subjects such as agriculture and building for those intending to join the Kibbutz Movement in Palestine. Gerhardt Kornhauser took a course in signwriting and commercial art, but did not possess the hundred pounds guarantee required by the British Mandate to enter Palestine. He managed to eke out a living, signwriting and designing posters for the dwindling Berlin Jewish Community, but was arrested as a Pole immediately after the Kristallnacht and put on a cattle train for Poland. "After four days and nights we were due to go through the Polish Corridor to East Prussia. At a very small Polish station, the Polish Refugee Committee, who had somehow heard of the train, persuaded the authorities to let us go, if we did not return to Germany." Gerhardt Kornhauser had relations in Cracow and an uncle guaranteed him and other members of the family who were on the train.

Within a week he determined to return to Berlin where another uncle, a friend of the British Consul, had arranged a visitor's visa to England for him and his brother, so that they could visit Australia House and perhaps obtain a passage. He dared not return home; his mother met him at the station with his passport, the visa and a few clothes and he went straight to Harwich, but an English Customs Official noted that, although his visa was good for fourteen days, his passport was only valid for nine. He was returned to Holland under suspicion of being a spy. It took a spell of solitary confinement and a stay of four-and-a-half months in Flushing before his passport was renewed. Even then, he was detained on board another night and his belt, tie and shoelaces taken from him in case he attempted suicide. But at last his credentials were established and he was allowed to join his brother in London.

Frank Reinach was born of Liberal Jewish parents in Kassel. His father owned one of the four private banks in the town, all of which belonged to Jews. "There was little anti-semitism before Hitler and we fitted in well with the general community." In 1932 he enrolled as a law student at the University of Berlin. Here he clearly recalled the burning of the Reichstag on 27 February 1933. "We all knew it was the Nazis who did it, though they blamed the Communists." A chance derogatory remark about the "Fascist post office" was overheard by a Nazi student, who threatened to call in the Storm Troopers and have him arrested straight away. Frank Reinach left Berlin immediately and went underground, staying with various friends. He spent all his time learning English and made good use of the anonymity of the swimming baths. "I was indoors as little as possible. I didn't want to be caught in anyone's home if anything happened." Before long, he recovered his book of entrance as a student to the university, in which it said he had been expelled for Socialist activities. This was partly true as he had been a member of the Socialist Students' Association, so he made up his mind to go abroad. He applied for a passport which, to his surprise, was granted without comment, and left for Switzerland, ostensibly on a winter sports holiday. He made his way thence to England where he was one of a minority of refugee students to be able to continue his studies. With the help of a scholarship from the International Student Service he obtained a degree in modern languages at Birkbeck College.

Several refugees who came to Birmingham as young people went on to teach at schools and universities, but Martin Deutschkron appears to have been the only one who followed the profession in Germany and continued in this city. From the account of his time as warden of Elpis Lodge Hostel he appears to have been a highly individual character.

Walter Stranz, a much younger colleague at Redditch County High School, where Martin Deutschkron taught for some years, remarked "I'm not surprised he didn't keep very good order at the Elpis Lodge Hostel. When the boys ragged and teased him so, we often wondered why he was so keen on teaching. But he had enormous confidence, and when he was teaching, that moment was the most important thing to him. He came to teach French, but he bullied the Head into starting a small German class and he taught Spanish to the Sixth Form and some Russian. He went on well after retirement and even the education authorities were uncertain of his age. He was equally keen on sport, and coached tennis well into his eighties."

The mother of one of his less academically gifted pupils added: "My son went to his flat for lessons. Over 'Kaffee and Kuchen', the atmosphere was so friendly that speaking German became a game, and he passed his examinations quite well."

Dr Deutschkron died in 1982 and with his passing disappeared one of those teachers who has little place in the modern world of education, endearing alike in his eccentricities and enthusiasms.

Dr Deutschkron's daughter Inge emigrated to Israel, where she became German correspondent for the newspaper *Maariv*. She describes her wartime experiences in *Ich Trug den Gelben Stern (I Wore the Yellow Star)*, published in Cologne, West Germany, 1979.

In Germany, from 1933 onwards, the Jewish teachers and their pupils found the schools sooner or later closed against them. Some children spoke of the tears their non-Jewish teachers shed on saying farewell, others were glad to be rid of the taunts they had endured. Most of the pupils entered Jewish schools where they were available, and the Jewish teachers rose to the challenge. Indeed, for a short time there was a cultural renaissance among the Jews of Germany. Jewish artists, actors and musicians, deprived of a wider audience, gave of their best to their own community. A Jewish League of Culture was formed which contained half the members of the Berlin Philharmonic Orchestra. The artistic and musical life of this country benefited enormously from the refugees. As may be imagined most of the people so gifted gravitated to London.

Delia Ruhm, a professional flautist, came to England in 1939 and later settled in Birmingham. She has played with many orchestras in Scotland and England, including the Orchestra da Camera. Among the amateurs Robert and Charlotte Singer organised a string quartet, and there were many enthusiasts who supported the musical life of the city.

References and notes

1. Peierls R. *Bird of Passage*. (Princeton University, USA 1985).
2. Archive of the Society for the Protection of Science and Learning at the Bodleian Library, Oxford.
3. Sherman A.J. *Island Refuge*. (1973) 48.

4. The U.S. quota system is based on a person's place of birth, so German Jews were part of the German quota allowed into the country each year.
5. Gilbert M. *The Holocaust.* (1986) 79
6. Doodlebug or V.1; a robot bomb invented in World War II by the Germans, mainly used to bombard London.
7. Leo Baeck (1873-1956). After the war went to USA as Professor of Theology at the Hebrew Union College, Cincinnati. In London he helped to found the Leo Baeck Institute for the Study of Central European Jewry. Author of *Essence of Judaism* (1961) and *This People Israel* (1965).
8. *Hachsharah.* Hebrew, to train or prepare, specifically for work on the land.

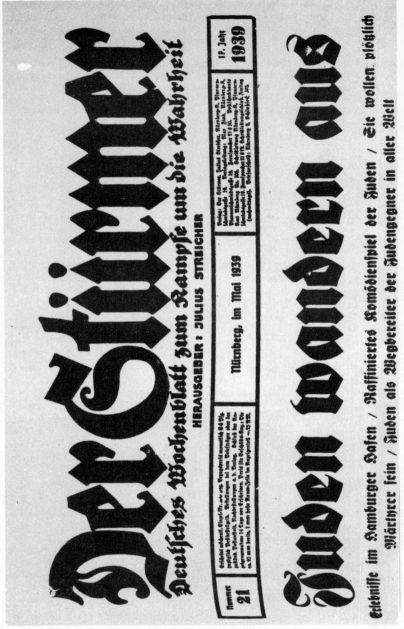

Front page of *Der Stürmer (The Stormer)*, May 1939.

"German weekly in the struggle for truth.
Jews emigrate.
Events in the harbour at Hamburg / Cunning comedy played by the Jews / They suddenly want to become sailors / Jews pave the way for Jew-haters all over the world."

12

The Domestics

Before the Second World War, the "servant question" was featured in *Punch* as one of its regular jokes. Certainly, it was the subject most frequently discussed by middle-class housewives, these "treasures" being perennially in short supply. Places for domestic servants in England were widely advertised in the British press and the Continental Jewish press. From 1933 onwards, apart from nursing, it was virtually the only opening for women refugees, and thousands used this escape route. On arrival they did not always give satisfaction. Some mistresses were sympathetic, understanding the painful situation of these strangers, and in many cases treated them as daughters. But others expected excessive value for the rather poor wages offered. Many forgot, or did not fully appreciate, that the applicants came mostly from professional or middle-class homes, where they may even have been waited on themselves. Unless they had already been driven out by the Nazis, they had lived in the typically comfortable apartments of the German middle classes with parquet floors, double windows against the fierce Continental winter, and central heating. They spoke in horror of the stone floors or tiles which had to be scrubbed, the open fires which scattered ash everywhere and required constant attention, and the draught from doors and windows which the English considered "healthy".

Helen Freeland was one of the more fortunate girls who found a kindly mistress, a voluntary social worker whose self-imposed task it was to rescue unaccompanied young women arriving from the Continent at Victoria Station from "White Slave Traffic". "Many times I had to give up my bed to one of these girls", Helen recalled. "Although it was only 1932, many parents, anxious to leave Russia and Poland, innocently sent their daughters to London, supposedly to be maids in Jewish households. From this base they hoped their girls might be able to arrange for their emigration. But there was a great risk of their being intercepted by unscrupulous agents, and ending up as prostitutes in South America.

"I came to England at the age of eighteen on a student's permit, but I found I was expected to work as a maid. It was very hard work cooking and cleaning, all day alone in the big old house in a London suburb", Helen Freeland continued. "Then each evening I would have to travel to Piccadilly for my English lessons in night school. Another pupil there persuaded me I was being exploited and I left to take a job with a lady

Refugee Advertisements

GOOD Cook, confectioner as well, experienced in all household duties, needlewoman, well mannered, Seeks Post: able to act as housekeeper: best references. Hochstim, Vienna 1, Wipplingerstrasse, 14/14.

MARRIED Couple, Non-Aryan, at present Vienna, urgently seek Employment: experienced gardening and housework: must leave. Address E 39, " M/c Guardian " 2.

MARRIED Couple look for Position, wife excellent cook and all domestic work, man very handy, able to drive car: refugees from Vienna: as housekeepers, caretakers, &c. Write to Goldmann, 6, Eton Avenue, London, N.W. 3.

MIDDLE-AGED Viennese Couple, good cook and chauffeur, butler: go anywhere: moderate salary. Address F 97, " M/c Guardian " 2.

POST for Married Couple Wanted, wife in England, husband still in Prague: excellent general cook, chauffeur-secretary: all domestic work. Box A 458. " Manchester Guardian," 43, Fleet St., London, E.C. 4.

REFINED Viennese Jewess, 43, former head clerk, wholesale textile shop, extremely domesticated, cook general, perf. confectioner, versatile handicrafts, able to teach, requires Position. E 8, " M/c Guardian " 2.

TWO Young Czecho-Slovakians, one general electrician graduate of high technical college, the other radio engineer, desire Trainee Posts. Address Box C 11, Frost-Smith Advertising, 64, Finsbury Pavement, London, E.C. 2.

VALET, Chauffeur, also perfect in cooking, housework, and gardening, excellent testimonials, pleasing appearance, seeks Employment urgently. Kirstein, Berlin W. 50, Nurnbergerstr, 16.

VIENNESE Married Couple, middle-aged, trustworthy, healthy, woman excellent cook, experienced in household, man handyman, mechanic, Seek Post: first-class English refs. Kohl, Vienna IX, Prechtigasse 1.

(a)

Refugee Advertisements

AUSTRIAN Refugee, already in England, 31 years, strong & healthy, wants Farming Trainee Job. Box A 525, " M/c Guardian," 40, Fleet St., London.

AUSTRIAN married couple, Jewish, wife 25, all household duties, good cook, husband, 29, qualified manservant or butler, seek Situations, together or separately. Popick, Wolfsaugasse 19/25, Wien 20.

CZECHOSLOVAKIAN, 31 years, trained Children's Governess, seeks English Post. J 81, "M/c Guard."

GERMAN Lady Teacher, non-Aryan, in secondary schools, Latin, German, French, English, Spanish, also experienced children's governess, seeks position: excellent references. K 18, " M/c Guardian " 2.

GUARANTEE and Hospitality in Good Family sought for pretty, well-educated, healthy 8-year-old Girl, daughter of Czech engineer. Address L 24, " M/c Guardian " 2.

GUARANTOR asked for my Mother, aged 67, still in Vienna: speaks also English and French: able to household: contribute for maintenance already provided. Address J 268. " M/c Guardian " 2.

HUNGARIAN Solicitor's Daughter (29), cultured, trained musician, fluent French and German, desires Hospitality au pair, Manchester district, June to August: sympathetic with old people, experienced with children: English refs. K 64, " M/c Guard."

IN Great Despair.—Married Couple, with girl (11) and with affidavit to U.S.A., implore benevolent persons to help by guarantee until visas will be given in October: woman (31), origin Catholic, very good in all housework, good dressmaker, man (40), Jew, clever, accept any kind of work: both adaptable, laborious. Replies to Karp, Vienna XX, Hannovergasse 11/7.

MARRIED Couple, still in Vienna, speak exc. English, Want Pos'n: wife perfect cook: husband butler, driver, expd. handycraftsman. Write to Mr. Hans Köhler, Vienna VI, Mollardgasse 70. Ref. in England, Marianne Porges, 15, Sandy Lane, Stretford, nr. M/c.

RELIABLE Married Couple, childless, 43, ask kind-hearted people for Post: wife excellent cook, husband chauffeur, gardener: capable: perfect English: English ref. Louis Lackenbacher, Vienna 1, Wiesingerstr. 1/20.

TRAGIC Couple in Prague, must leave, urgently desire Posts: husband chauffeur, gardener, handy man, wife as good cook and all household duties. Freund, 14, Rowan Walk, Hampstead Garden Suburb, London, W. 2.

TWO Smart Viennese Boys, 21, 19, Skilled Welder, Confectioner respectively, threatened by imminent expulsion, seek Trainee Posts: English fluent: English refs. Write J.D., 86, Newman-street, London, W. 1.

TWO Sisters and Fiancée in Germany require Posts, together or separately: all household duties, dressmaking, and millinery: man chauffeur and all outside work. Brits, The Little House, Buxton.

TWO Jewesses, must leave Prague, Beg for Domestic Posts. Cook (32), Dressmaker-Maid (27): sound recommendations: both speak Czech, German, English. Write L. Hodbod, 47, Springside Road, Bury, Lancashire.

UNHAPPY Parents beg kind-hearted People to take care of their Children (boy 12, girl 14) or one of them until parents are able to take them again. Please reply to Klinger, Vienna XX, Reinselmann-gasse, 15/16.

VIENNESE, good appearance, cultured, highest English references, begs to be Received, preferably in motherless Household: experience with children, fluent English, French: certif. Else Braunstein, Vienna III, Weissgerberlände 38.

WHO will take care of German Jewish Girl, 15 years, of good family, until parents emigrate ? Address K 89, " M/c Guardian " 2.

WANTED, Position for my Sister, still in Vienna: perfect in house and needlework. Write to Grunwald, 68, Heywood Street, Cheetham.

WANTED urgently, Guarantor for German Jewish Couple seeking refuge here pending negotiation Australian permit. Nelson, Berlin-Schmargendorf, Ruhlaerstr. 14; or Matheson, 45, Whitehall Road, Aberdeen.

WIDOW, in Vienna, desperate, needs post Housekeeper. Apply Society of Friends, Mount Street.

WINDOW Dresser, 44, prominent expert in textile, cloth, silk, 30 years' experience with large firm, Vienna, export connections, best testimonials, seeks Position. Grief, Vienna 1, Renngasse 13.

YOUNG Jewish Married Couple with affidavits for U.S.A. (wife experienced cook and dressmaker, husband tradesman of repute) appeal to charitable persons for guest-permits for one year: guarantee necessary £200. Kind replies to Artur Zuckermann, Vienna II, Lichtenauergasse 7/18.

(b)

"Refugee advertisements" in the *Manchester Guardian*.
(a) 4 April 1939   (b) 22 April 1939

having a baby. But it was out of the frying pan into the fire. Whenever I came home from an afternoon out, I found the sink piled high with nappies.

"After a time I went to a family leaving London for Leeds, and it was there that I met my husband."

The Quakers, always friends of the refugees, enabled Marya Kleiner to be reunited, after many months of separation, with her daughters, Helga and Iolanthe. Marya Kleiner went as housekeeper to George and Lucy Cadbury, who invited the two girls to join their mother. Helga Kleiner was married from the Cadbury house, and both she and her sister spoke of the influence the Quaker philosophy had had on their lives. Helga felt it had been a great support to her in her career as teacher and child psychologist, while Iolanthe recalled their generosity, "not only with money, but with time. I was a very disturbed teenager, but it was the personal understanding of the Cadburys which brought me through this difficult period.

"My mother had been one of the first women law students in Vienna and it hurt me to see her performing menial tasks for others. I felt, too, that people despised her for being a servant. But now I am able to distinguish the three strands that made survivors of us — my mother's self-sacrifice, the example of the good Jewish people who first took me into their home, and the personal care and tolerant understanding of the Quakers."

Many young people were exploited, however, and one story concerning a ten-year old child might well have come from the pages of Charles Dickens. The little daughter of a family newly arrived from Czechoslovakia was placed in a children's home on the South Coast. Her parents received unhappy letters and when they could save up the fare, her father went to see her. He found her with red and swollen hands. She—the youngest in the home—was kept in the kitchen to do the never-ending washing up.

On the other hand, it is difficult at times not to feel a sneaking sympathy with the employers. Ilse Lewen from Wuppertal arrived on a domestic permit. She had started to train as a dress designer, when her married sister, who was already living in Birmingham, found her a post as a cook. "I hadn't been with my employers long when the lady of the house said to me 'Ilse, I want you to tell me the truth. You have never been a cook in your life, have you?'. On the first day I was there she asked me to make toast. I looked for the electric toaster, but she gave me a fork and the bread fell into the fire. Another day, I burned the potatoes. I also had to light the kitchen range, and once in desperation threw petrol on it, not a lot, but it was a wonder I didn't blow the house up. The children laughed at me because I'd never heard of a banana split. I had to wait on them, too, and sometimes my brother was with them. They ate in the dining room, while I had my meals in the kitchen. My brother was regarded as my superior because he was a trainee, while I was only a domestic."

Nelly Hewspear's brother had a friend who had emigrated to England some years previously. She had only recently left school, and was happy when he sent her a domestic permit as she hoped thereby to find some means of rescuing her family.

"I couldn't speak a word of English, but I managed somehow to find my way to Ealing, where I was to be employed in a boarding house. The people there had little understanding of my position, for I had to share a room off the kitchen with an Austrian Catholic girl. Both my wages and my food were meagre—for dinner it was sometimes a bit of pressed beef and a lettuce leaf out of a cardboard box! I had to work very hard as a chambermaid and once I was told off for reading a copy of Rilke's poems that I had found while cleaning up after a German lodger.[1]

"When the scare against the aliens came with the fall of France in 1940, the landlady felt she couldn't trust me any more. I had met an Austrian political refugee, a scientist, and with his help I found a job with a lady, also a scientist, who was expecting a baby."

Again it was a long day. She rose at 6 a.m. to start polishing the vast parquet floors of the large house, to look after the scientist's four-year old son and even to help with the gardening and decorating. And all this for fifteen shillings (75p) weekly. With the arrival of the baby, things got worse. "The nurse looked after the mother and baby, but everything else was left to me." Like Helen Freeland, she would return from a weekly afternoon off to find all the nappies and dirty dishes waiting.

Ilse Lewen and Nelly Hewspear, both thoroughly disenchanted with domestic service, turned to nursing as an alternative.

Sidney and Else Schott came to domestic service fresh from their horrific voyage on the SS St. Louis. For a few days they stayed with the Blumenthal family who had given shelter to their son, Walter. All the passengers from the St. Louis who had disembarked in England had been guaranteed by Otto Schiff, the banker, founder of the Jewish Refugee Committee. Ironically, it was this generous gesture that became the source of their difficulties. The guarantees were meant to ensure that the refugees did not become a charge on public funds, but it also precluded them from obtaining work permits. The Schotts had little to live on and posed a difficult problem to the local Refugee Committee. They were told that no more money could be found for them, yet one lady member went so far as to warn them, "if you are caught receiving wages, I will have to go to prison for you". In the event, it was Else Schott who went to prison.

A sort of compromise was reached whereby Sidney and Else Schott went to work as a domestic couple in a large household, officially receiving only their keep and pocket money.

"We hadn't been there long when the entire staff, including the nursemaid, left", recalled Else Schott. "My husband and I had to do everything." Despite this domestic crisis, the family went ahead with plans for a large Christmas party. Sidney Schott had to wait at table and for the occasion put on the white jacket he had bought for the ill-omened trip to Havana. "Where did you learn to be a waiter?" he was asked. "At the good hotels where we used to stay", came the reply.

"It was at this party that an immense Rolls Royce drew up and an equally imposing chauffeur knocked at the door. He returned to the car, and helped out a tiny, little man. It was the comedian, Wee Georgie Wood[2]! He wanted to read my palm, but I had no wish to look in to the dark future."

Their employers had scant sympathy for the Schotts' plight. In the exceptionally hard first winter of the war, their quarters were in the attic. "Our sponges froze in the wash basins. My husband found an old electric fire. He mended it and, with the permission of the mistress, we were able to keep the temperature just above freezing. But when her husband discovered what we'd been doing, he became very angry. 'You are stealing my electricity', he accused us.

"After a time we heard of a surgeon's family who needed a domestic couple. 'Don't call me Madam, just do the cooking', requested the lady of the house. But our previous employer was furious when he heard we'd gone, and denounced us to the police for working without a permit. It was the spring of 1940, the beginning of the anti-alien panic. My husband was immediately interned and I was summoned with the surgeon's wife to appear before the Tribunal. 'Did you receive pocket money? Did you receive wages?' I was browbeaten with such questions a hundred times. I still couldn't speak English very well, and somebody from the Refugee Committee should have been there to help me. I did catch a glimpse of the lady who was alarmed that she might be sent to prison, but she rapidly disappeared."

As a result of these appalling circumstances, Else Schott was locked up in Winson Green Prison, mainly perhaps because at this time there was no other place where women refugees could be held in security. "For a time I was kept in solitary confinement and was exercised with a murderess. 'Doesn't she look sad?', I heard a wardress remark.

"Five days later, they put me in a van and drove me to Holloway Prison in London. Here, once again, I was locked in a single cell with a mattress on the floor. But after threatening a hunger strike, I was allowed to mix with some other refugees and given mail-bags to sew.

"After three weeks we were taken to Liverpool. We stayed overnight in a sailors' home, filthy and overrun with rats. But the worst of our trials were now over. Next day we sailed for the Isle of Man, and the women's internment camp at Port St. Mary was like a holiday. I was astonished by the comfortable beds and white bread to eat.

"After a time I joined my husband in a camp for married refugees in Douglas. On our release, we had one more taste of domestic work on a farm in Staffordshire, where Sidney, who had suffered a heart attack on the Isle of Man, was expected to dig graves for dead calves"

They returned eventually to Birmingham, where Sidney Schott found work as a salesman, and Else Schott obtained a post with the Ideal Benefit Insurance Company, where she remained for twenty years.

Like the Schotts, Charlotte and Robert Singer were dogged with problems arising from guarantees. After Robert Singer had endured a spell in Buchenwald, the couple were frantic to get away and implored help from a cousin in London who had been a correspondent for German trade journals. But the restrictions forced on the newspapers by the Nazi Government had swept away his income and there was no question of his being able to provide further financial aid. With no working permit Robert Singer was unable to follow his profession as a doctor and his wife's attempts to support them both were hedged around with difficulties.

Charlotte Singer's solution to the problem was to remain very quiet. "On Sundays I would walk over to Hampstead and study the small advertisements in the newsagents' windows. A needlewoman wanted ... someone to make children's dresses ... to iron ... to repair gentlemen's shirts ... a charlady. If all this work would be permitted to us foreigners, if only I could do it openly."

The family, except for her elder daughter, were re-united in England in May 1939. By June, despite the hazards, Charlotte Singer writes:

"I have become governess to a sweet little person of nine. Her name is Irène, Irina or Irene, according to which language is spoken. She lives in Paris, with her Russian mother (divorced) and now they are guests of her rich aunt with a wonderful apartment overlooking Regent's Park. In the morning lots of sweets and fruit are wrapped up and put in the doll's pram and we walk in the Park ..."

Later "Irina has moved to Switzerland with her doll's pram. I washed and ironed all her and her mother's things as well as the doll's dresses. But Madame, her aunt, still had lots of sewing for me. When I was a governess I had lunch with them in the dining room, but now, being only a seamstress, I have been sent to the kitchen to eat with old Nastya, the Russian cook. I don't mind, because this way I can take some of the good things home to Robert. Once, Madame and old Nastya had a quarrel, quite awful. Nastya came down afterwards crying and I cried too. For the first time I could not be sure that our plight was only temporary, as I had tried to convince Robert and myself. Maybe, when I am sixty-five like Nastya, I shall still be sitting in a maid's room listening to rough words from an employer, God knows where and in what language."

Charlotte Singer had indeed to endure many more months of anxiety and privation before the whole family came together, and Robert Singer was able to take up a hospital appointment in Birmingham. She continued to take any work that offered "but I am mainly a charwoman", she wrote in her diary, "looking after bachelor flats. In one of them a Continental conductor spends his days on the couch. While polishing the floor around him, I try to lecture him. Hope, courage and confidence are instilled by me, all thrown in for one shilling (5p) an hour. The moths are already in his beautiful evening wear. How I wish for him he could wear his tails again, conducting at the Albert Hall. He will not, as Robert will never be able to have his surgery in Harley Street. If only we had all gone earlier"

There were occasional scares. "Once, returning from work, there were two plain clothes policemen waiting in my room. They had only come to investigate a passport mislaid at Bloomsbury House, but the wall near the sewing machine was adorned with dresses in the making and patterns all over the place. I was rather shaky when they left, but they hadn't asked any questions about my working permit.

"The thing which most helped us to forget our sorrow was our music. We joined an orchestra of fellow refugees. I would rather have gone without my lunch to have the 'bus fare for this. Once I returned with my violin—really it was Robert's, mine had been trampled on by the Nazis—and picked up a discarded newspaper on the 'bus with a competition in it. 'Has your life a theme song?' As we had just played Beethoven's Opus 18 No. 4,

I wrote them a postcard about this quartet. A cheque for second prize arrived, a real godsend. Our shoes could now be soled and heeled."

The courage Charlotte Singer had shown in confronting the Nazis in Czechoslovakia sustained her through her long ordeal, and when "by a special miracle the dreadful load was lifted" with the escape of her daughter, her spirits took wing. "Life is really wonderful. I like London with all my jobs ... sitting on the top of the 'bus in the early morning, seeing the sights while on my way to work. I could sing at the top of my voice."

As hostilities progressed, the demand for workers brought a relaxation of the work permits. The refugees, like the entire adult population of Great Britain, were directed to essential occupations. It was partly this that led to the disappearance of the old order of mistresses and maids, a way of life that had so perplexed the Continental girls.

Notes

1. Rilke Rainer Maria (1875-1926). Austrian poet.
2. Wee Georgie Wood, born 1895. Well known for many years in pantomime and variety.

Gültig bis zum ~~31. Oktober~~ 19 36

Arbeitskarte*) Nr. III A 3064/ 05272

für den ausländischen Angestellten

Vor- und Zuname: **Bertold K o r n h ä u s e r**
(bei Frauen auch Geburtsname)

Geburtstag: **19. 2. 15** männl. ~~weibl.~~

Geburtsort: **Berlin**

Kreis: **Gr. Berlin** Staat: **Dt. Reich**

Staatsangehörigkeit: **polnisch**

Beruf: **kaufm. Angestellter**

Unternehmer: **Anton Keller & Co**
(Arbeitgeber, Firma)

Arbeitsstelle: **Berlin C. 2**

Ort (Straße), Kreis **Rosenstr. 16**
(Provinz, Land)

Berlin, den **10.10.** 19 **36**

Der Präsident
des Landesarbeitsamtes Brandenburg
Im Auftrage:

*) Ausgestellt auf Grund der Verordnung über ausländische Arbeiter und Angestellte
vom 23. 1. 33 — Reichsgesetzblatt I S. 26 —.

Einstellung und Arbeitsausübung ohne gültige Arbeitskarte können mit Geldstrafe
oder mit Gefängnis bis zu 6 Monaten bestraft werden.

Vordr. Ausl. Nr. 4

Foreigners' work permit. Berthold Kornhauser was of Polish nationality.

13

The Industrialists

"An open-door policy would have grave effects on unemployment, housing and social policy." So replied Sir Samuel Hoare, British Home Secretary to Colonel Josiah Wedgwood in the House of Commons in March 1938. Pleading for the victims of Hitler's annexation of Austria, Wedgwood had reminded his hearers that "these people were suffering beyond human conception, their money will be taken from them, it is almost impossible for them to escape." Ninety-four people had committed suicide in nine days. His Austrian Refugees' Immigration and Naturalisation Bill proposed that Austrian refugees should be allowed to enter this country freely and become British citizens in much less than the statutory five years. Leave to introduce the Bill was refused by 210 votes to 142.

The *Birmingham Post* speaking for the "ordinary Englishman", considered the Bill "sentimental, hasty and ill-considered". While at pains not to appear unsympathetic and recalling Britain's traditional role in giving asylum to the persecuted, it asked "How many refugees can this country take? Privileges granted to Austrians today, might have to be extended tomorrow to other victims of a Nazi ideology ... Poles, Czechoslovaks, Rumanians and Hungarians ... history is not a safe guide. It was before the days of economic nationalism that foreign refugees, the Dutch, the Huguenots, even the Italians, built up so many of England's valuable industries. Today's foreign refugees come into England as competitors in trades and professions ... we would be overwhelmed."[1]

This opinion was widely held. As late as 1985, a lady recalling the hardship of the nineteen-thirties, the economic depression, the unemployment, so like today's, added: "But in those days the refugees came and took all the jobs." This was clearly far from the truth, with the stringent application of Home Office regulations on work permits. The booklet issued to all refugees on arrival warns: "It must not be said that refugees are taking away work from British workers." They might not even volunteer for any task without permission, "since you may be taking away the possibility of paid work from a British clerk, mechanic or paid servant[2]." Yet the same issue of the *Birmingham Post* of 23 March 1938 which has been quoted above carried the headlines: "Industry on a war footing. Workers urgently needed for essential tasks."

But contrary to the opinion of the editor of the *Birmingham Post*, history was in fact, poised to repeat itself. From 1935 the government had favoured bringing in refugees who had something to offer, be it in art, medicine or industry. It was stipulated that the interests of Britain must come first. If Jews were to be saved it must be to the advantage of this country, not just a simple matter of saving lives[3]. In particular the government was anxious to encourage development in the so-called Special (really depressed) Areas of the North-East and South Wales.

Herbert Loebl in his thesis on the government-financed factories of this period has described the trading estates of the North-East of England set up to attract new industries[4]. They were a godsend to refugee industrialists, who had expertise, but owing to Hitler's crippling grasp on their savings, had been unable to bring any capital with them.

As late as 1974 there were still forty firms in the North-East in existence which had been started by refugees. Completely new industries requiring new skills had been brought to this starving area, ranging from clothing, leather goods and toys and plastics, scientific instruments, building components and mechanical devices. In Lancashire "the chimneys of derelict cotton mills were smoking again, this time for the manufacture of chemicals formerly imported from Germany." New and secret methods of making collapsible metal tubes were introduced, as were tanneries for the manufacture of fine shoe leather[5].

At the Treforest Trading Estate near Pontypridd in South Wales, according to contemporary evidence, at least half the businesses were run by refugees, including Aero Zipp Ltd. In 1938 this must have been one of the first firms to manufacture zip fasteners in this country[6]. In the East Midlands Mac Goldsmith of Leicester established Metalastik, which produced components using a new process for bonding rubber to metal.

Birmingham and the West Midlands were comparatively prosperous during the immediate pre-war period. A number of refugee industrialists were attracted to the district and some were outstandingly successful in introducing new methods and ideas.

Sir Eric Weiss and Dr Kossi Strauss, partners in the international foundry firm of Foseco were attracted to Birmingham as the centre of the foundry industry. "There were four hundred foundries producing brass and bronze, and forty brass and copper mills[7]." Before the electrification of the industry the view after dark from the heights of Kinver Edge or Sedgely Beacon was awe-inspiring, with great tongues of flame from hundreds of furnaces lighting up the night sky.

The foundry industry had changed little since the end of the sixteenth century, when blast furnaces were introduced into the Midlands for smelting iron. Casting was very much a haphazard affair and often contained defects such as pinholes, slag inclusions and poor surface finish. The main consideration was that the casting should be strong enough for the purpose for which it was intended. But in the nineteen-twenties new alloys were being produced which needed lighter castings to tackle heavier loads and stand up to greater speeds. In 1924 Eric Weiss's uncle, Dr Ludwig Weiss, founded a new company in Halle, in Central Germany, which introduced a chemical compound in powder form. When used as a flux this improved the smelting of non-ferrous metals[8].

Dr Kossi Strauss, 1984.

The first Foseco factory, 1933.

The Foseco factory, 1987.

Ludwig Weiss died in 1929. At the funeral Eric Weiss and Kossi Strauss determined to go into partnership in Birmingham where Eric Weiss was working at the time for one of his uncle's agents. Immediately on his return to England he advertised for a backer for his new venture. An elderly man, Frederick Hadley, offered £250, and within a week Foundry Services Limited had been registered as a limited company.

Kossi Strauss continued at the University of Karlsruhe working intensively on new products for the firm. From the start the partners determined that their business should live up to its name. Everything they sold must be scientifically sound and reliable, with a back-up service to instruct those foundrymen who were enterprising enough to avail themselves of the new methods.

Eric Weiss rented two rooms on the second floor of an old building in Spiceal Street, near the Bull Ring, and bought a weighing machine, a sieve and two or three spades and shovels. An assistant was employed part-time to operate a rope-lift which hoisted the sacks of chemicals to the second floor. The products were mixed on the floor and everyone was satisfied, except a tailor on the first floor who complained of powder drifting through the old floorboards on to his suits.

This state of affairs continued until early in 1933 when the tailor must have been gratified to learn that the firm had rented larger premises in Nechells. A month later Kossi Strauss came to England. "You're a fool" said his professor, "Hitler's only after the Eastern Jews." But Kossi Strauss knew better. He brought with him from Germany an analytical balance and a few Bunsen burners and set up a small laboratory in Nechells. Further staff were engaged, mechanisation introduced, debts were paid off and the firm began to show a small profit.

Eric Weiss realised the potential of a product which would exclude undesirable gases from aluminium and in 1933 the firm introduced the very successful aluminium degasser. Kossi Strauss was experimenting in a whole new range of products. He found the primitive conditions challenging, and enjoyed the personal contact he built up with the foundrymen. In return they allowed him to try out his new products on their premises. This was not without its hazards. An explosion once sent a blob of molten aluminium through the roof, descending on his shoulders and scorching his back.

With war approaching, Foundry Services Ltd. attracted many customers in the rearmament industry. Rolls Royce of Derby and High Duty Alloys of Slough, which had set up a large branch factory in Redditch, were among the first to use their aluminium castings. Confidential work was undertaken on the new jet engines and Halifax bombers were also treated with the products of the firm. Hexachlorothene was a vital product for this war work and an essential component; anhydrous magnesium chloride was in short supply. The Ministry of Aircraft Production asked Foundry Services to make it, and in 1940 built and financed a factory for the purpose at Drayton Manor Park near Tamworth. "For the rest of the war, we produced two tons a day, sufficient to supply all the magnesium foundries in the country."

Despite their German accents, neither Kossi Strauss nor Eric Weiss encountered any prejudice. Much of their work was highly secret. "We were even called into Chatham Naval Yard, where technicians were experiencing difficulties in making their big aluminium pistons for submarines. We watched one of these being cast, and were able to use our degasser to eliminate porosities."

After the war magnesium chloride was no longer needed, but Foundry Services Ltd., later Foseco, bought the factory at Drayton Manor Park, leaving Nechells purely for research laboratories and administration. A strong export trade was set up. Many countries had import restriction so the firm started to manufacture abroad, in America, where an agency had been set up as early as 1934, France, Holland, Belgium, Switzerland and elsewhere. The partners travelled incessantly.

The firm continues to flourish. "Today we must employ 5,000 people all around the world" said Kossi Strauss, not long before his death in 1984. "Here in Birmingham alone we have 1,000 people on our books." Foseco gives the lie to the old accusation that refugees cause unemployment.

Building had always been Herman Kay's passion. "I enjoy solving problems. I feel like a musician conducting an orchestra, deeply happy. Sometimes I get so excited, I'm like a *shikar* (Yiddish: drunk)."

He was born in Poland in the early years of the century, but fled to Vienna during World War I to escape the advancing Russian Army. Here he made a name for himself refurbishing old property until he was forced to move on to England as a result of the Anschluss. He spent many years in various branches of the building trade, but was never responsible for a complete house until 1959, when he took part in property development in Birmingham and London. But his real fulfilment was delayed until 1972 when a scheme was put forward to modernise the Birmingham jewellery quarter. Long before the war, it had run down into a very dilapidated condition. The former private houses, some two hundred years old, were unhealthy and their connecting wooden staircases made them a fire hazard. The rooms were divided and sub-divided into the little workshops making petty thieving of gold and precious stones all too easy. The Birmingham Corporation had bought and demolished eight houses in Dartmouth Street and had built a flatted factory. Now they wanted another. Herman Kay obtained the contract; he visualised and brought into being modern airy workshops, all on one floor, easily supervised. The venture was financed by the Norwich Union who lent £600,000. Not only jewellers, but all the related trades were housed in the same buildings, toolmakers, printers and packers, besides a post office and a police station.

The jewellers themselves seemed to have viewed the new scheme in rather a different light. They were comfortable in their dingy premises and unenthusiastic about the greatly increased rentals. It was two years before "Kay's Folly", as it came to be called, was filled, and that only after Herman Kay had personally pointed out its advantages to each prospective tenant.

The jewellers must have realised also that the atmosphere of their ancient workplace would change irrevocably. The old jewellery quarter is now largely a conservation area, replete with restaurants and glittering retail shops. It is rapidly becoming a tourist attraction.

Herman Kay, meanwhile, has retired to Israel, where his two married sons had previously settled.

Emil Rich, although over eighty years old, told his story in a lively and humorous interview. He sat surrounded by a large collection of photographs taken by himself, and many trophies of a successful business career.

"I gained two degrees in engineering at the University of Vienna and I knew all about textile machinery, but like many young Austrian Jews in the nineteen-twenties, I couldn't get a job. Eventually, I was offered the opportunity of modernising a glove factory in Chemnitz in Germany. I hadn't a clue about gloves, but nothing was going to get the better of me. By 1933, when Hitler came, I had built up the firm and we had customers in Finland, Sweden, Norway and England. I liked England best because the people seemed so tolerant.

"I'd married by this time and I could see it was no use staying in Germany. We came to England in 1934. My wife had learnt the technique of glove making, so when we found a little place in the City of London she was able to train two or three workers. We brought the machinery from Germany in boxes and once we'd got it set up I went out selling five days a week. The sixth day I spent in the factory and on the seventh day I rested!

"The Home Office wouldn't give me permission to make leather gloves, only silk ones. 'But what happens if they aren't a success?' I asked. 'Never mind, once you have a permit you'll be much more free', so I took the permit and very soon I was making gloves of leather and fabric.

Emil Rich (left), 1953.

When war came we moved to Worcester. It was a very old glove-making centre and we weren't very popular. But very soon a lot of important people were wearing my Miloré (as we called the firm) gloves. The most important were the airmen. The Air Ministry asked me to produce pure silk gloves. It's the warmest fibre and they were heated with electric elements for flying at high altitudes. At last I was really doing what I'd been given permission for. But I didn't care for the Air Ministry pattern. I made them to my own specification and they accepted it!

"I've supplied gloves to Princess Margaret and Princess Anne. I made the Queen's gloves for the Coronation — the cuffs and gauntlets were embroidered by the Royal School of Needlework. And I've made white gloves for the Assize Judges. It's an old custom to present them when they have no criminal cases to try."

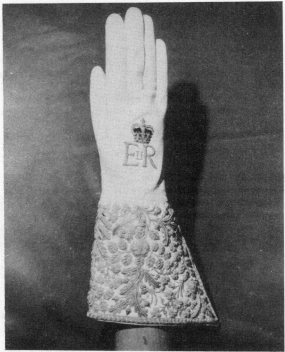

The Coronation Glove, 1953.

Emil Rich was interned in 1940 for a few weeks, but not before he had insisted on making provision for the smooth running of his factory and the welfare of his employees in his absence. On his release he joined the Home Guard. Thanks to his knowledge of languages, he was asked to be the head of the Intelligence Unit. "We haven't got such a unit as yet", said the Commander, "but you can be the only one, and the head of it"!

Even before he was naturalised Emil Rich was badgering the local Member of Parliament in 1948 to help the newly formed State of Israel to defend itself. "If other people won't do it, I'll do it myself", was his reaction on hearing that no one else locally was willing to get involved politically. Later he started the West Midlands B'nai Brith Lodge[9] to gather together the sprinkling of Jewish families in Herefordshire and Worcestershire.

In 1961 he was invited to become a member of the Worshipful Company of Glovers in London, and was given the Freedom of the City of London. He was twice President of the National Association of Glovemakers. During his term of office he established the Glove Guild of Great Britain which started the Glove Fairs of England. This gave a new outlet to the industry.

He retired reluctantly in 1975. "By this time we had three factories, employing three or four hundred people. In my opinion, Miloré gloves were the best of gloves, not only in England, but in the whole world."

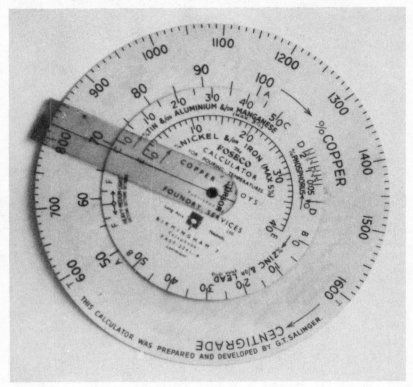

Calculator invented by Gerhard Salinger for Foseco, 1941.

Gerhard Salinger knew Birmingham as an important engineering centre. He was glad to take a post as an order clerk in a factory similar to the one he had directed in Berlin, which manufactured technical instruments, watercocks and sanitary equipment. After the war, he opened a firm of his own making oil-cans and other small items of ironmongery. "There was such a shortage you could have sold anything." Later he specialised in indoor and outdoor thermometers, as well as those for refrigerators and cars.

Heinz Eisner continued in his plastics factory making holloware for industry. A great deal of war-work came his way, for which he had a work permit. Unfortunately, his wife, who had helped him in Germany, had no such permit, so that when he was interned in 1940 there was no one to run this business. However, he was released after three months, and even opened a shadow factory where the demand for his plastics was met by a day and night shift. A few years later the firm built its own factory at Bordesley Green. This continued until the retirement of Heinz Eisner in 1970 and the takeover of the firm by a London group.

Berthold Kornhauser making raincoats in Germany, 1936-38.

The Kornhauser brothers used the expertise they had acquired in Germany and both built up substantial businesses giving employment to many people.

Berthold Kornhauser's retirement, 21 February 1983. (By kind permission of the *Birmingham Post*)

On the strength of his experience in the mackintosh trade, Berthold Kornhauser was sent by Woburn House to Aquascutum. A few months later, at the beginning of the war, he became cutter to Swallow Raincoats in Manchester, making inflatable suits to be worn by airmen who might be shot down at sea. Being of Polish origin he was classed as a friendly alien and so avoided internment. His wife Stella, whom he married in 1940, proved invaluable. "Get a trade" her mother had advised while she was still in Vienna, so she learnt sewing and was able to help with the hand stitching.

"In 1946 we bought a factory of our own in Birmingham with the help of a kind Lancashire man, a property developer who was Mayor of Rochdale. He had made up his mind 'to put the lad right'. We called it 'School Wear' and the backbone of the firm was the gaberdine mackintosh, a sturdy garment worn at that time by every grammar school child. From there we branched out into blouses, sportswear, blazers and every kind of uniform. But with the disappearance of the grammar schools in the nineteen-seventies fashions changed. Uniforms became sketchy, summer dresses were no longer worn. Cloakrooms were hardly used in the new comprehensive schools; children carried their possessions from class to class. The gaberdine was heavy and expensive besides. It was discarded in favour of the anorak, brightly coloured and light in weight. The old strict uniform, once considered so important for discipline and a sense of belonging, is becoming a thing of the past."

Coal scuttles and candelabra are among the items which are being sold to markets all over the world through an unusual exporting organisation operated from Birmingham. This, the British Artmetals Manufacturers' Export Group, was evolved by Berthold Kornhauser's brother Gerhardt. He had used his training in commercial art provided by Hachsharah in Berlin after the ruin of his hoped-for medical career, to enter one of the traditional Birmingham trades, ornamental metal-ware. When in 1964 he sold "Artis", his flourishing firm, he had decided to retire, but remained to run the export group. After a slow start the group ventured into exhibiting at the Cologne Hardware Fair, and orders started to pour in. "We were on the map and followed with fairs at Paris, Lyons, New York and Vienna. Export sales shot up. We are the only industry in this country operating such a group."

Kurt Rose will be remembered as one of those manufacturers who in the post-war years aroused women of moderate income to a sharper awareness of elegance. Of all the refugees who settled in Birmingham, his is one of most spectacular success stories, due perhaps to a combination of luck and the intelligence to take maximum advantage of good fortune when it came.

After leaving Bunce Court School in 1936 he lived as the guest of the family of Joseph Cohen, for many years Chairman of the Council of the Birmingham Hebrew Congregation. Joseph Cohen proved a good friend to the Rosenberg family enabling them, by a bizarre plan, to retrieve some of their treasures from Germany. He arranged a marriage of convenience between the widowed Emmi Rosenberg, mother of Kurt Rose, with an inmate of the Home for Aged Jews, so that she was able to return to Berlin as a British citizen. "Is this English Jewess to take all her silver?" an incredulous Gestapo officer telephoned his headquarters. To their chagrin there was nothing they could do to prevent her.

For a time Kurt Rose worked as a window dresser to a fashion firm with branches all over the Midlands. It was not long before he showed the acute perceptiveness and presence of mind that was later to characterise him in the army and in business. While in Nottingham just before the outbreak of war he decided to attend a meeting of Sir Oswald Mosley's Fascist Blackshirts. Many of Sir Oswald's followers were beginning to get disenchanted with Hitler and the speaker began by disassociating himself from the Nazis. "This is a purely British Movement", he thundered. Kurt Rose had been examining the leaflets which had been handed around, and turning to the back page called out "Then why was this printed in Kassel? Surely, that's in Germany?" The meeting broke up in disorder and when the Blackshirt stood on his soap box in the town square the following week, nobody took the slightest notice of him.

On demobilisation from the Intelligence Corps, Kurt Rose determined to set up in business for himself. Joseph Cohen must have been well aware of the young man's potential, for he lent him sufficient capital to start a small fashion firm with a friend he had met in the army.

"Neither of us knew much about the trade" recalled Kurt Rose, "and anyway it was a difficult time to plunge in. Clothes were strictly rationed, and anything the least bit out of the ordinary was considered unnecessary by the Board of Trade. That meant it didn't come into the 'utility' category and was consequently very expensive. By pleading a war injury, I was able to get a float of one thousand coupons and we started to manufacture, although we hardly knew what to make. [10]

"Then came two strokes of luck. I saw a pinafore dress, uncommon at this time, and realised it had possibilities. In London I managed to get hold of three dress lengths, red, black and green, and had them made up. I took the pinafore dresses around to my customers. They were an immediate success and I received three hundred orders. Soon the manufacturer of the original pinafore dress was making them for me! In pure wool suiting they retailed at 29s.11d. (£1.50).

"Then came the second piece of good fortune. My partner went to a fabric fair, where jersey cloth was exhibited. It struck me that this material, which had never been used for fashion goods, could, if properly treated, be upgraded into something quite desirable. Moreover, it was ideally suited to the changeable British climate. We managed to get some supplies from a firm in Leicester, and although they were rejects, the made-up garments sold well. About this time we heard of a firm in Redditch, run by a Mrs Canning and her daughter, who were producing jersey cloth on circular knitting machines. 'But it's in very short supply', we were told. Then, to my surprise, Mrs Canning asked if I were Jewish. 'It was the Jews who helped me out when my business nearly failed in Manchester. Now I shall help you'.

"Mrs Canning's jersey cloth proved to be the foundation of the House of Lerose, as we now called our business. We had to buy it in ecru and grey and dye and finish it ourselves. Through some loophole in the Board of Trade regulations, no coupons were required for these neutral shades. Soon, we were swimming in coupons! However, clothing soon came off the ration and production soared.

"Meanwhile, on account of the bombing, it had been very difficult to find premises in Birmingham. One day I noticed that the windows on the top floor of a building in Constitution Hill looked as though they hadn't been cleaned for years. The rest of the building was occupied by Midland Typesetters. "You can't have the top floor", said the manager, "that's where the lads play football in the lunch hour." But I persuaded the landlord and we moved in. Eventually, we took over the whole building.

"The next break-through was the introduction of double knitting in 1950. We found a company in Leicester with the first double-knitting machines in the country. About the same time we met a dyer for the double-knitting yarn; the three of us joined up and became a public company.

"We had grown from twelve employees to over one hundred; we built a factory in Henrietta Street, Birmingham, another in Coalville, Leicestershire, and a third in East Kilbride, Scotland, a development area. 'You'll have trouble on the Red Clyde', we were warned, but we've never had a real strike yet. I've always strongly believed in a good friendly relationship with our workers; we had a pension scheme before they became general, subsidised canteens where management and staff eat and chat together, accident and health insurances. Everybody gets a turkey for Christmas and our seventy old-age pensioners each receive a hamper at Christmas delivered personally by one of the directors.

"In 1968 it was decided that we could achieve greater growth on the Continent, and we acquired a factory in Holland, similar to our own, which supplied the Dutch, Belgian and German markets. The director had a fine record of helping Jews in the Dutch underground and proved an excellent colleague.

"On our return to England, after signing the take-over contract, the customs' officer asked 'Have you anything to declare?' 'Yes', I said to myself, 'a whole Dutch factory'."

Not all were so successful. Some had to face disappointment like the engineer who owned a factory and foundry in Germany which manufactured parts for central heating. A British Home Office official came out to inspect it, and when he arrived in this country he obtained the post of managing director of a similar company. In May 1940, when he was working on an important government contract, he was interned. A letter from the Chairman of his Board, a brigadier, vouching for his integrity, was of no avail. He was never afterwards able to obtain a position of comparable status, and his knowledge of central heating, shortly to become commonplace in British homes, was wasted.

Two men, both gifted with creative imagination, who found shelter in the Midlands during these dark days, gave in return something of the sparkle which in happier times had so enchanted British visitors to the Continent.

Manele Spielman had been born in Poland, but had lived for some time in Berlin. Here he was forced to go into hiding but eventually made his escape to England. At first he worked as a garage mechanic, but later set up a small toy factory in Dudley. After the war his business was swamped by the larger companies then developing. "He had the opportunity of acquiring a small shop for ladies' wear", his daughter recounted. "It had been kept by an old lady, and could only have been called dowdy, even by Dudley standards.

Manele Spielman brings fashion to Dudley, 1972.

The windows were crammed with dreary garments displayed on hangers and lit by a single electric bulb. My father developed a passion for window display. He loved the unusual and bought for visual effect, with no thought for whether the item would sell or not. He draped them on modern stylised lay figures which would show them to dramatic advantage. I remember a blouse — almost see-through — with huge polka dots. Dudley people had never seen anything like it. They came in waves, crowding at the windows, pointing."

Manele Spielman's daring paid off. Even if they did not buy the clothes he displayed in the window, they came to the shop, and the business did well.

André Drucker was just such another innovator. After his flight from Vienna in 1938, not only as a Jew but as an active Communist, he found himself in Birmingham where he had a married sister. "It seemed an ocean of houses" he thought as he approached the city by train. He was lucky in finding work overnight as a commercial artist to the Jacey Cinemas, whose director was Joseph Cohen, who had also befriended Kurt Rose. But the urge to continue as a writer, which had already gripped him before his escape, remained uppermost. He wrote poems and short stories, plays for the BBC and features—mostly seeing England with foreigners' eyes—for the *Birmingham Mail*. He was badly paid however and began to feel he was being used by people for his literary talent.

Towards the end of the 1950s, the Espresso Coffee Bar was the rage. The bubbling, steaming machines with their shiny chrome plating were fascinating, though the coffee was often poor. The coffee bars were noisy too, with juke boxes. "It struck me that there must be people in Birmingham who would appreciate the Viennese cafés where you could sit down, read the newspapers and talk over a really good coffee or *schlagobers* (coffee with whipped cream) and eat something small but delicious.

"We opened La Bohème in Aston Street, next to a second-hand bookshop. The café must have satisfied a need for it went like a bomb. I used to go to London each week to collect cakes from a Greek baker. People thought they were Viennese and certainly they were different from anything produced in Birmingham.

"We started a small bakery of our own in Moseley, and then a patisserie in town. This didn't take on at all — I could write there by the hour undisturbed by customers. Then, in the sixties, the tourist trade exploded. Everyone was going abroad on package holidays. People would look in the window and say 'that's just the same as we had in Austria and only one shilling and sixpence (8p)! This completely changed the public attitude. We advertised and found a wonderful German patissier who taught us how to make his exquisite confections. Now we have a dozen cafés, all very profitable."

Poldi Kew and his wife also introduced Birmingham to continental cooking shortly after the war when the maximum price permissible for a meal in a restaurant was five shillings (25p). They produced gastronomic miracles in their small café in Warley. Later they achieved a place in the *Good Food Guide* at their prestigious Deer Park Hotel in Honiton, Devon. In February 1939, Poldi Kew had been foreman of a group of one hundred refugee craftsmen brought from Germany to repair and re-equip the derelict army camp at Richborough, Kent. He "possessed a gift of leadership". The task was completed in a few weeks and the camp became a temporary refuge for five thousand men. Poldi Kew joined the British Army and rose to the rank of Captain. He took part in the liberation of the Belsen Concentration Camp and rescued many people, including his own father. [11]

After a hard struggle Henry Kronheim has built up a successful electrical engineering firm in Wolverhampton. He was born in Güben in 1920, a small industrial town on the border between East Germany and Poland. Güben had always been a strong trade union town, where Hitler had had some difficulty in getting his ideas accepted. Henry Kronheim's father managed to keep his furrier and cap-making business going, but when his son left school, finding work was a problem. They had seen books being burnt in the town square, but the reality of the situation did not touch the boy until he found himself obliged to leave Güben and look for an apprenticeship. This was eventually found in Dresden, where he started to train as an electrical maintenance engineer. At the same time he started a course at the Technical High School, but before long he was thrown out as a Jew and he moved to Berlin.

With the Kristallnacht his father was sent to the concentration camp of Sachsenhausen with the rest of the adult male Jewish population of the town. Henry Kronheim recalled his mother's ordeal. "My father had a large collection of guns. He belonged to the local hunt and used the skins in his work. My mother had to take them to the police station — of course Jews weren't allowed to possess fire-arms. Father was released after a while, but he had a rough time. Being deaf, he couldn't hear the Nazi commands. He had his head bashed in.''

With the help of a loyal maid, his sister and her baby escaped, eventually reaching Brazil. Henry Kronheim managed to obtain a guarantee of one hundred pounds to get to England through a Quaker organisation. His parents saw him off from the Schlesischer Bahnhof in Berlin. ''They knew they would never see me again, indeed they both perished in the Warsaw ghetto. My father, always a practical man, put twelve overalls in my case. 'You need these for earning a living', he said. 'They'll be more useful than best suits'.''

Although war was looming and electrical engineers were shortly to be at a premium, Henry Kronheim had to survive for many weeks in London on a tiny allowance. One day he saw an advertisement in the library for electrical engineers at Harlands in Alloa in Scotland.

''It was hard finding the fare, but the Scottish people went out of their way to be hospitable and I was happy.'' When fully qualified he moved to Wolverhampton where he repaired underwater electrical pumps for the flooded Maginot Line. His work was now so highly specialised that he was unable to join the Pioneers as he wished. ''You're more useful on electrical repair work here than digging trenches in France.'' But he joined the Home Guard. ''As a refugee I had to be in by 10.00 p.m., but when I was on duty I had to walk the streets at all hours with my gun!''

Henry Kronheim was always active in trade union affairs, and in 1943 he became a shop steward. He moved shortly to Goodyear Tyres where he held a highly responsible and potentially dangerous post as high tension electrician, in charge of the whole factory during his shifts.

In 1946 he decided to set up in business in partnership with a fellow charge-hand at Goodyears, specialising in heavy machines and industrial maintenance. As the business prospered he was able to devote more time to his interest in trade unionism and the relationship between management and men. ''First my partner and I were elected to the Electrical Contracting Association, a very exclusive club which looks after the legal position of main contractors and sub-contractors. I was then asked to join the Labour Relations Committee, which deals with relations between employers and employees and furthers relations between trade unions and the Employers' Federation. I was a founder member of the Joint Industry Board for the electrical contracting industry, representing the employers, with Frank Chapple [12] representing the trade unions. This organisation really works. It's not political, simply does its best for employers and employees in the electrical industry. We are the only industry in the United Kingdom to hold its own Industrial Relations Tribunal for unfair dismissal and we've had no strikes.''

Of late years, Henry Kronheim has become increasingly involved in the Educational Training Committee of Electrical Trades. ''It's far ahead in outlook, compared with schemes in other industries, and looks after the lads all the way through to qualification. It comes under the Youth Training Scheme and gets the government grant but there are jobs for these people, despite the recession. They can hold their own against any young electrical engineers from Germany, Holland or Japan."

Henry Kronheim (left), June Kronheim and the Mayor and Mayoress of Walsall, 1964. Henry Kronheim was Regional Chairman of the Electrical Contractor's Association.

"Making handbags has always been a Jewish occupation" said Samuel Prais, who originally came from Kielce in Poland, but lived in Germany for many years. The parents and grandparents of his wife, Berta, had also emigrated from Poland and settled in Offenbach near Frankfurt-on-Main about 1905. The family had been leather workers in Warsaw and in Offenbach they started to manufacture handbags. About this time the tight "hobble" skirt was fashionable making bulging pockets unsightly, so the cloth or leather handbag was much in demand.

Samuel Prais was a wholesaler and traveller, who counted his customers among his friends. When, on Hitler's accession in 1933, they warned him not to come any more, but to leave Germany as soon as he could, he took their advice. "We're not Nazis", they explained. "It's our children. They are in the Hitler Jugend and they will smash up your car. The Nazis are out to kill all the Jews."

Samuel Prais's brother-in-law had settled in London, where he had married and was working in the family business. Samuel Prais joined him. "I sold my business and my property for next to nothing, and anyway I couldn't take any cash out of Germany. So I bought all the metal frames I could lay my hands on, and sold them for export in London. I made several trips back to Germany, buying frames. In 1935 I was given a permit to set up a factory in Birmingham, the centre of the metal and engineering trades. This was a completely new venture as handbag frames had never before been made in England.

"I rented a workshop in Warstone Lane in the jewellery quarter, bought some machinery and started with about twenty hands. We worked long hours and expanded steadily. I was lucky in having a really good man as my landlord. He knew my story and encouraged me to go ahead and buy the factory and more machinery. 'You can pay me later on', he said.

"During the war we made aeroplane parts for the Air Ministry. In 1952 we built a large new factory in Warstock, on the outskirts of Birmingham in what were then green fields. Before automation we employed about five hundred people and even now we have four hundred."

The Prais family firm continues to make handbag frames, but has now diversified into other lines, including clocks, mirrors and photograph frames.

Henry Aron was born in 1921 in Poland and was therefore not classed as an enemy alien, so escaping internment. He had come to England in 1936 as a schoolboy. He left school in 1939, hoping to join the Forces. Having been warned against joining the Polish Army in England on account of anti-semitism he tried without success to enter the Intelligence Service of the Royal Air Force. Without specific training he started in a chemical engineering firm and after the war was sent by the directors to gather information about the state of the trade in Germany. By 1948-9 Germany was beginning to get on its feet again and here Henry Aron discovered a completely new industry. A shortage of nickel meant that a replacement for stainless steel had to be found and the Germans had started making chemical plant with plastic material.

"My company wasn't particularly interested but I realised this new potential, and with a colleague who was a chemist we started on our own. I sold my car and raised £700 capital, and my partner's father, a coach-builder, who had recently retired, allowed us to use his premises. We started supplying the electro-plating industry and gradually expanded, opening factories in London and the North. At one time we had a factory in Israel. Haifa Chemicals had developed a process of making fertiliser which demanded plant made from non-metallic materials. They realised the advantages of plastic, and after asking several people to come out and build such a plant, approached us to start this completely new venture. At one point we were employing eighty people, but galloping inflation in Israel made too many problems for us and we were bought out by our Israeli partners."

Ironically, Henry Aron admits the success of this flourishing business is largely due to his continental connections and his ability to speak English and German with equal fluency. "I have a direct line to Germany, and speak German on the telephone perhaps eight or nine times a day."

Ernst Litthauer was born in Berlin in 1916 into a large, old-established and assimilated family. "They felt so secure and settled, that they could not believe that the Nazi regime would not soon be toppled and democracy returned." Hjalmar Schacht, president of the German Central Bank, who had engineered the economic recovery in Germany after the inflation of 1922/3, let it be known in Berlin in the early days of Hitler, that the established older Jews should stay and the children and young people be sent abroad. No doubt he wanted to avoid the damaging effect of emigration and withdrawal of funds by too many Jewish industrialists and businessmen.

After leaving school in 1934 and a spell in Cambridge to learn English, Ernst Litthauer returned to Berlin and was apprenticed to a family firm. With their help he obtained in 1937 a trainee post with a London firm of tube stockists and engineers. "These were perhaps the happiest days of my life. I had very little money, but enjoyed my work, life and freedom in England, and the friendly social life of the family guest house where I stayed.

"My widowed mother insisted on staying in Berlin as long as possible. She wanted the little money we had in England for her children to study. My sister was then at Cambridge; she is now professor of Social Psychology at the London School of Economics. Early in 1939 we succeeded in persuading my mother and her sister, a painter, to come to England." At the outbreak of war they were invited by their cousin, Kurt Hahn, to stay near the school in Gordonstoun, which he had founded after being forced to leave his German school in Salem. The future Duke of Edinburgh was one of the pupils who came with him from Salem.

Ernst Litthauer was interned in 1940. On his release he found employment in a London firm, making marine Diesel engines. He was accepted for the Home Guard and continued his engineering studies at night. "To my great embarrassment a fire bomb destroyed the newly acquired uniform, before I had worn it even once." His Home Guard duties were in a motor repair shop, but "as I had no practical experience and was useless for any but the simplest tasks, I was made assistant to the quartermaster! As the only 'enemy alien' in the unit I met nothing but friendliness; the sergeant took me to football matches"!

After the end of the war Ernst Litthauer qualified for the Institute of Mechanical Engineers and acquired some accountancy qualifications.

Before the war Rudolf Hahn, the brother of Kurt Hahn, had taken over a small factory in Kings Norton, BKL Alloys Ltd. It made secondary aluminium by smelting and blending aluminium scrap by a process not previously known in England. He built the company up successfully so that at his death it employed over a thousand people.

In 1946 Ernst Litthauer was offered a job by Rudolf Hahn and moved to Birmingham. The manufacture of steel pipe fittings had now been started. These were used in the oil industry and, not being made in the UK had been imported from the USA. The authorities encouraged their manufacture in England to save dollars.

After a difficult start the venture began to succeed. Rudolf Hahn's son, Oscar, a qualified engineer, took over the technical side. The commercial side was entrusted to Ernst Litthauer. Demand in the UK was limited, and he began to build up an export business, travelling widely in Europe and North Africa. As it was thought that his experience could be of use to others, he was made chairman of the North American Executive of the Birmingham Chamber of Commerce and Industry. He was awarded the OBE for services to export.

Oscar Hahn had been elected President of the Birmingham Chamber of Commerce and Industry, the first Jewish president and the first not British born. He also served for several years as chairman of the Midland Race Relations Board, and on the boards of the Birmingham Repertory Theatre

Oscar Hahn (in wheelchair) opening a new factory for BKL Fittings, Redditch, 1967.

The tap manufactured by Gerhard Salinger.

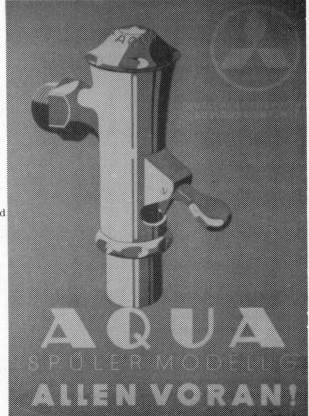

and the Shakespeare Memorial Theatre. He was awarded the CBE. On his father's death he sold the business to Guest, Keen and Nettlefolds and eventually became a main board director of GKN. Ernst Litthauer was made deputy chairman of the BKL Group and managing director of BKL Fittings Ltd., the name given to the Pipe Fittings Division. This continued to prosper after moving to a purpose-built factory in Redditch to the extent that at the time of his retirement in 1979, after 33 years with the company, it gave employment to over six hundred people. While working in Redditch, he was chairman of the Redditch and District Manufacturers Association.

"Fate has dealt kindly with me", he reflected in conclusion, "I would never have developed as I have, had conditions allowed me to remain in Germany. I might have realised an early ambition to become an architect, but I would have remained in the sheltered circle of the family. As it was, I created a new life by my own efforts, and I am grateful to this country for the opportunities it has given me, and the recognition I received."

Frank Gerson was another who developed a new business in England from old family foundations on the Continent. The sale of seed-corn had been an almost entirely Jewish trade in Germany, but Frank Gerson found little opening for it in this country, especially after the entry of Britain into the Common Market. He switched successfully to grass-seed, and now supplies councils and local authorities throughout Britain.

The story of the refugee industrialists in Birmingham bears out Herbert Loebl's thesis that, far from causing unemployment, the newcomers often created work. He estimated that as the war neared its close, 80,000 to 90,000 refugees had been admitted to Great Britain. This is rather higher than the official estimate. By 1947, over one thousand firms had been set up by refugees and these had created work for 25,000 employees[13]. In this the people who settled in Birmingham played their full part.

References and notes

1. *Birmingham Daily Post.* 23 March 1938.
2. *When you are in England.* Issued by the German Jewish Aid Committee. (undated) 18-22.
3. Sherman A.J. *Island Refuge.* (1973) 33.
4. Loebl. H. *Government Financial Factories and the Establishment of Industries by Refugees in Special Areas of North-East England.* 1937-1961. Thesis for MPhil, University of Durham (1978 unpublished) 7-9.
5. *Manchester Evening Chronicle.* 16 May 1939.
6. Ex inf. Tony Glaser, Cardiff.
7. *Fifty Years of Development in Materials Technology.* (pub. Foseco Minsep plc. 1982).
8. ibid.
9. B'nai Brith (Sons of the Covenant) a society founded in New York in 1843 to unite Jews all over the world, through mutual aid, social service and charitable work.
10. Coupons were used in rationing in World War II.
11. Bentwich. *They Found Refuge.* (1956). 103,104.
12. Frank J. Chapple. b.1921. General Secretary of the Electrical, Electronic, Telecommunication and Plumbing Union 1966-1983.
13. Loebl H. op. cit. 9.

(G)

DUPLICATE DECLARATION

BRITISH NATIONALITY AND STATUS OF ALIENS ACT, 1914

Declaration of Acquisition of British Nationality

(1) Name in full.

(2) Address in full.

I,[1] *IRMA LINDENSTEIN*

of[2] *130 POPLAR AVENUE EDGBASTON BIRMINGHAM 17*

being the wife of[1] *LOUIS LINDENSTEIN*

to whom a certificate of naturalization (No. *AZ 30953*)

was granted on or about *22ⁿᵈ AUGUST 1947*, hereby declare

that I desire to acquire British nationality.

(*Signature*)................*Irma Lindenstein*................

Made and subscribed this *8ᵗʰ* day of *September* 1947,

before me,

(*Signature*)................*Jackson*................

~~Justice of the Peace for~~ *A Commissioner for Oaths*

(or other official title)

A Commissioner for Oaths.

Address { *57 Colmore Row Birmingham*

HOME OFFICE
26 SEP 1947
REGISTERED

Declaration of British Nationality issued to Irma Lindenstein

166

14

Through the Distorting Mirror

"I was wearing my ocelot coat", remarked an Austrian lady in a casual tone that was in itself almost a gesture of defiance. The ordinary English person might well have been disconcerted and unable to understand the needs of these apparently affluent foreigners. He would not have known how she was to continue. "I was looking for somewhere to buy two ounces of coffee. We Viennese love good coffee. A well-dressed friend of ours", she added, "a former business associate, was sitting on a park bench in London. He had nowhere to go and nothing to do. A tramp came up and begged a cigarette. 'Sorry', said my friend in his halting English, 'I haven't got one, and believe me I've probably less money in my pocket than you have'. 'Never mind, pal', said the tramp, 'have one of mine'. My friend accepted gratefully. He hadn't had a smoke for days."

Their good clothes were often the only remaining possessions of the refugees who managed to escape in the last headlong rush before the declaration of war. Any infringement of the Nazi currency regulations, or attempts to bring out valuables, carried the death penalty. Real deprivation was commonplace, until wartime necessity relaxed the granting of work permits, and the refugees were able to become self-supporting.

A lack of understanding was shown all too often in official and in private circles. Cruel campaigns of hate were whipped up by the newspapers, particularly during the threat of invasion in 1940. Yet time after time, the people interviewed recalled and wished to put on record the kindness and compassion they had received from English people. When Irma and Louis Lindenstein were at last able to move into a modest house, their neighbours took a lively interest. "They gave us tea as we cleaned up, asked us in for Christmas, and explained English customs to us; when to eat, what to eat and how to eat: they were a great support to us."

Lotte Munz was also put right by neighbours. She awoke one morning to a strange grinding noise which greatly puzzled her. They explained it was a lawn mower, and that it was essential to cut the grass at least once a week, to get the carpet-like effect, so desirable in the English garden.

Hilde Salinger was one of the earlier arrivals in Birmingham, and her husband, an engineer, was able to find work in Aston. "I hated the mean streets, and couldn't help comparing them silently with the spacious avenue where we had lived in Berlin. The local people seemed friendly but distant, and they didn't want to know about my troubles. I thought perhaps they were pro-Nazi, maybe for reasons of trade. But all that changed with the Kristallnacht. The neighbours came up and embraced me. They couldn't understand how a House of God could be attacked. A miner's wife from Hamstead Colliery sometimes came in to help me in the house. She could neither read nor write, but that morning she burst into the house, muttering, 'That Hitler and his gang! Shoot them! Shoot them!''

However, under the stress of war many people seemed to find it difficult to distinguish between Nazis and those whose lives the Nazis had thrown into chaos. "Good God, man, didn't they know you were a German?" expostulated a Commanding Officer, on being handed secret documents by a refugee NCO with many months' service in the Forces. Even in the 1970s, at the end of his teaching career, Frank Reinach would be asked by colleagues on the staff of his technical college, "Are you really English, or are you German? Are you going home to Germany for Christmas?"

Misinterpretations sometimes produced bizarre situations. Frank Linden arrived in England on Cup Final Day. "I thought I'd come into a mad-house … everybody wearing comic hats and swinging rattles." Heinz Shire, as a student in Dublin in 1941, was aroused on Easter Day by soldiers marching to a German military band. "I thought it was the invasion. But it was only the celebration of the Easter Rising of 1916 and the procession was marching along to German military music."

Irma Lindenstein thought it was the polite thing to visit her guarantor one Sunday morning and take him some flowers. He was rather taken aback and seemed to think he was going to be 'touched' for something. On the other hand, the hosts themselves were sometimes bemused by foreign customs. Even Hanna Simmons found the Viennese custom of hand-kissing disconcerting. "They always seem to come when I'm peeling onions or frying fish."

What was the attitude of the refugees of the 1930s to the land of their birth, half a century after arriving in Birmingham? This varied widely. Many people wished to have nothing to do with the country or the people, refusing to speak the language or accept financial restitution.

"I could have spat in their faces", was the reaction of one lady who had been offered a free holiday in Germany by the Bonn Government, as a gesture of goodwill. But others accepted the invitation at its face value, some to visit spas for health reasons, or to see once more the haunts of their childhood. Others wished once again to stand beside the graves of their parents, and yet others to see, and perhaps attempt to reward, the 'Righteous Gentiles' who, at such risk to themselves, had helped them in their hour of need.

Emmy Golding (née Kaufmann) arranged through the good offices of a non-Jewish school-teacher for a memorial to be erected in her tiny native village of Kommern in the Eiffel. It read, 'In memory of the Jewish inhabitants of this village who were murdered by the Nazis'. She returned to see it, accompanied by her daughter who wrote, "We walked down the street and knocked on the door of an old neighbour. After a second of surprise came recognition and the neighbour fell on my mother's neck crying 'Kaufmann's Emmy'! She rushed up and down the street knocking on doors, and there emerged a crowd of people, all exclaiming and talking at once … These neighbours and friends had tried desperately to help the Jews, until they themselves were threatened with deportation if they persisted."

Many businessmen have had close relations with Germany, especially since Britain's entry into the Common Market. Frank Reinach lectured regularly at German universities until his death in 1985. "A new generation has grown up and one cannot really accuse them of what their grandfathers did." Although he considered himself irrational, he, like the businessmen who so frequently visited Germany, still felt he could not take his holidays there.

Heinz Shire was one of many who found difficulty in talking to his German contemporaries, unable to help wondering what they had been doing during those terrible times. But he felt differently about the younger people. "We must get together — the world is too small. In the 1920s, Germans and Jews lived in symbiosis and were a good influence on each other. The proportion of German-Jewish Nobel prizewinners is staggering. They cross-fertilised each other in medicine, the arts and business."

Most unexpected was Louise Bergman's reluctant confession. "I happened to be in Sutton Park at the time of an International Scout Jamboree and I heard the German lads singing all the songs of my youth. I felt ashamed, and yet I couldn't help being moved."

Some of the older refugees are still pulled by cultural ties. Irma Lindenstein, in very old age, still repeats German poetry with pleasure, while music is another strong link. Kossi Strauss' great love was Wagner. "His anti-semitism has nothing to do with his music." But he never found courage to go back to Bayreuth.

Circular to Refugees from Germany and Austria.

In view of the present emergency you should :—

(1) Conform to arrangements made for corresponding British population :—

(2) Obey honourably all directions of the Police.

(3) Be willing to undertake any form of work or service that may be open to you or that you are asked to undertake by responsible authorities.

(4) **AVOID TALKING GERMAN IN PUBLIC.**

(5) Not on any account attempt to go to Bloomsbury House or Woburn House for any purpose. If a maintenance allowance is due to you it will be sent to you at your last known address.

(6) If you are in a private house or lodgings, remain where you are, unless forced to move by the authorities. If you are required to leave your lodgings or the home in which you reside, try to make other arrangements for yourself : failing that go to the local Refugee Committee, if there is one. In any emergency if there is nothing else that you can do, go to the local police and ask them to advise you.

(7) Notify by post card at once to the German Jewish Aid Committee at Broadwood House, Lady Margaret Road, Sunningdale, Berks., any change of address, stating :

> Registration Number(s).
> Name(s) and Ages.
> Former trade or occupation.
> New address.
> Whether maintained :
>> (i) By a friend or relative.
>> (ii) By maintenance allowance.
>> (iii) In a Hostel.

(8) If you are living in a Hostel, the Warden, or person in charge will make all arrangements for you and will, if necessary, seek advice from the local police or from the Committee at Broadwood House Lady Margaret Road, Sunningdale, Berks. **You should, in any case, obey his orders implicitly.**

(9) Arrange, if possible, to listen for radio announcements affecting refugees.

(10) As many refugees are moving and may not receive their copy of this circular, will you please tell your friends of the foregoing instructions and also ask them to send us a post card giving their registration number(s) and latest address.

BY ORDER,

OTTO M. SCHIFF.

Address in the event of emergency :

BROADWOOD HOUSE,

LADY MARGARET ROAD,

SUNNINGDALE, BERKS.

Circular issued by the Board of Deputies of British Jews

15

The Refugees and
the Birmingham Jewish Community

(I) Extracts from Minutes (1933-1945) of Singers Hill Synagogue

The minutes of the council meetings of the Birmingham Hebrew Congregation provide invaluable source material for the history of Birmingham Jewry. They reflect the events and the reactions to them of the leaders of the Birmingham Community. Concern was shown about the plight of the Jews in Germany in 1933. On 26 March 1933, Mr E.P. Hollander (Past President) referred to the matter and said the Congregation would act in accordance with directions received from the Board of Deputies[1].

A month later, it was announced that the Lord Mayor would convene a mass meeting at the Town Hall to protest about the persecution, and that the Rector of Birmingham, the Revd Canon T. Guy Rogers, had expressed profound sympathy with the Jewish people and would render every assistance. There followed a long resolution moved by Mr O. Deutsch (President 1932-41) which was carried unanimously. It stated that the Birmingham Hebrew Congregation expressed profound sympathy with its fellow Jews in Germany ... and protested at their ill-treatment and their position as second-class citizens, their removal from the professions ... In the name of humanity and righteousness it called upon the German government to cease all discrimination against its Jewish subjects and to restore to them the full exercise of the rights enjoyed by them hitherto.[2]

The protest meeting was held at the City Council Chamber and elicited much Christian support[3]. Mr O. Deutsch then raised the question of how German refugees coming to Birmingham should be dealt with. It was resolved to form a Committee consisting of E.P. Hollander, O. Deutsch, L. Salberg, J. Albury, Dr A. Cohen and the executive of the Benevolent Board.[4] The writer was not able to find out when this Committee met and what activities it carried out.

When Commander Locker Lampson MP introduced a Bill into Parliament protesting against the injustices perpetrated on the Jews in Germany and proposing the grant of British nationality to the refugees, a letter was framed by Mr O. Deutsch expressing the Community's thanks. A letter was also to be sent to the Board of Deputies urging similar action by all Anglo-Jewish communities.[5]

Between 31 July and 4 August 1933, the Revd S.I. Solomons, Second Minister, conducted a correspondence with Commander Locker Lampson and Neville Laski, President of the Board of Deputies, on this topic. And there the matter rested. Only one mention of the refugee problem was made in the Council Minutes between July 1933 and October 1938. In April 1936, the Central British Fund for German Jewry made a special appeal for £1,000,000. The Birmingham branch was expected to collect £20,000, to be raised by the four synagogues.[6]

The review of the Council's work at the Annual General Meetings reported by the President of the Birmingham Hebrew Congregation for the years 1936, 1937 and 1938 contain no reference to the refugee question. After Munich, when the dreadful happenings in Germany gathered momentum, Dr A. Cohen, the Chief Minister, preached a sermon on *Kol Nidre* night (the eve of the Day of Atonement) appealing for funds for the relief of Jewish victims of persecution. The sum of £598.16.3d. was raised.[7]

However, at the AGM held on 30 April 1939, Mr Oscar Deutsch reported "an unprecedented strain and stress in world affairs and the considerable suffering of Jews in many countries". An intercession service was proposed for the 17 July, organised by Canon Guy Rogers. It would be a joint service, and tribute was to be paid to the many citizens of Birmingham for the large-hearted manner in which they had come forward to succour Jewish refugees. At the same AGM, Mr B. Silverstone, Foundation Manager of the Hebrew School, stated that a number of refugee children were attending the school and he found them very happy there. He also drew attention to the highly important work which the Birmingham Jewish Refugee Committee was doing under the chairmanship of Mrs H. Silverstone, and to the Wheeley's Road Hostel for Refugees, a generous gesture of Julius Leek and family. He suggested that the Congregation Charities Sub-Committee be enlisted to raise funds for the hostel.

On 14 May 1939, Mr E.P. Hollander moved that a levy be raised on seat rentals for the relief of refugees in Birmingham. He suggested it should be about 25%, and that other Congregations be approached to take similar action. He pointed out that the Refugee Committee in Birmingham had undergone considerable financial and legal obligations as follows:

- (i) There were 500 refugees in Birmingham.
- (ii) 170 refugees had been brought to Birmingham by the direct efforts of the Committee.
- (iii) It was the duty of the Community to look after refugees in their time of need.
- (iv) The requirements of the Committee amounted to £2,500 p.a., but they had only a few hundred pounds.
- (v) He had arranged for 60-70 children to be brought to Birmingham and had £1,000 in form of guarantee.
- (vi) He had succeeded in placing 35 children in private houses, but was again finding monetary difficulties.

Three methods of raising money were to be put to the Representative Council, viz.

- (i) Levy on seatholders.
- (ii) Weekly or monthly contributions.
- (iii) a lump sum donation.[8]

The next reference to the refugee problem was devoted to their accommodation during the High Festivals. There was not room for them at Singers Hill Synagogue, in fact there were insufficient seats even for members; so the Central Synagogue was to be asked to accommodate them at their religious services. If that failed, they could hold their Divine Service in the Hebrew School. [9]

The AGM held on 19 May 1940 reported that much activity had taken place in the Community in connection with the succour and relief of refugees. Prof. Brodetsky, President of the Board of Deputies, and Mr M. Sieff, had been to Birmingham and outlined the position of World Jewry, and appealed to the Community to participate in the Government's offer of pound for pound for helping refugees. Mr O. Deutsch hoped that Birmingham would do its share.

He also referred to the Hostel for Refugee Boys, which had recently opened at Elpis Lodge, 117 Gough Road, under the auspices of the Representative Council. The Hostel was made possible by the members of the Birmingham and Coventry Christadelphian Ecclesias, who had purchased the premises and were providing the necessary funds for its upkeep and maintenance. The Council passed a vote of thanks and gratitude for this extraordinarily generous gesture. [10]

No further reference is made to the refugees until September 1944. This took the form of a long report of a meeting of the Representative Council presented by Mr Ivan Shortt (President 1943-1955). It referred to the Hostel for Orthodox Children in Aldridge. The Hostel had been donated, but it was dilapidated and inadequate. £3,000 had been spent on the building and a further £1,500 per annum would be required to keep it going. Rabbi Reuben Rabinowitz of the Central Synagogue had made a passionate appeal for support but this was rejected on the grounds that there were other Orthodox hostels available with established overheads which could easily dispose of (sic) the boys. Mr Shortt concluded by stating, "Here is a case where the Representative Council by firmly dealing with the matter has been instrumental in putting an end to what was a great dis-service to the boys themselves and had saved the Community needless expenditure of money and energy."

At the same meeting of the Representative Council, an appeal received from London for support of the Jewish Fund for Soviet Russia was rejected. [11]

There are only two more relevant entries. On 22 April 1945, Miss R. Simmons, Secretary of the Refugee Club, asked for a special thanksgiving service for refugees on the first Sunday following VE Day. They hoped to invite a Rabbi from the Continent. [12] The last entry concerns this service. Miss R. Simmons thanked the Congregation for the use of the Synagogue. 450 people had been present and £24 was collected. Half of this sum was sent to the Lord Mayor's Victory Fund and the other half to the Central British Fund for Jewish Relief and Rehabilitation abroad. [13]

The relationship between hosts and guests in the Birmingham Jewish Community was mixed. It must be stressed that many young people were happily placed in Birmingham families. Lisa M's remarks are typical: "I shared all their joys and sorrows. They even tried to arrange a *shidduch* (Yiddish — match) for me, and when I found a husband on my own, they took us both under their wing and set us on the right path."

The recollections of some of the adult refugees were more ambivalent. One after another spoke of the cool reception accorded them by the members of Singers Hill. This Synagogue was under the learned leadership of the Revd Dr Abraham Cohen and the English character of the congregation reflected his personality. The refugees, many of whom had only the slightest acquaintance with the English language when they arrived, felt excluded.

The majority of the established members were children and grandchildren of the previous wave of immigrants from Eastern Europe. Perhaps they feared the new influx would give rise to anti-semitism, which might threaten their own comparatively recent acceptance. The remainder were thoroughly anglicised and proud to trace their ancestry in this country — or even in this city — for a century or more. Among them were many who gave devoted service to the refugee cause, but some resented the foreigners, or were indifferent. The refugees saw them at best as patronising. "I seemed to have to say 'thank you' to these English ladies and gentlemen all the time."

Sometimes they countered the rebuffs they received with a show of independence. "We didn't want their friendship", said one lady about the members of Singers Hill, "we had our own circle which we preferred." Some were inclined to look down on the outlook of their hosts, judging it too materialistic, caring little for music or the arts, and indeed many of the newcomers were better educated, both in religious and secular matters. Much of this was dismissed by the local Jewish Community as "typical German arrogance".

In many cases it seemed the Christians, especially the Quakers and Christadelphians, understood the psychology and strain of the persecuted minorities better than their co-religionists. Ernest Aris and his brothers, Ruth Shire and Lia Lesser, were among many who were brought up in Christian houses. There was no attempt at conversion, more often anxiety that the foster-children should cling to their own faith. "My family went to church each Sunday, but whenever possible they took me to synagogue in London." Frank Reinach was helped by the Student Christian Movement, Ruth Price by the Adult School Union, and the sisters, Helga Loeb and Iolanthe Fox, by the Quaker Cadburys. Ruth Simmons recalls the help and co-operation from people of various religious faiths, serving together on the Birmingham Council for Refugees. It was a time of coming together, Quakers, Christadelphians, Protestants, Catholics and Jews combining forces in an emergency.

Many of the refugees who came to England had belonged to the strong Liberal Jewish movement in Germany. Nevertheless, despite their sensitivity to the chilly atmosphere, a large number of those who wished to attend a synagogue went to Singers Hill. Here at least the services, which were mainly in Hebrew, were familiar. The Liberal services in Germany, though liberal in thought, were based on traditional Hebrew Liturgy. In England at that time the Liberal Jewish prayer-book included a great deal of English philosophical literature and was nearly all in the English language. After the war, the position changed; a more traditional prayer-book was compiled in the 1960s and many more former refugees, now anglicised, became strong supporters of the Liberal (now the Progressive) Synagogue.

But as far as the Jewish religious establishment was concerned, with notable exceptions, it was left to the Central Synagogue (the *Beth Hamedresh*) to show true warmth towards the newcomers. The "Central" in any case had always been more attuned to the needs of the Orthodox Continental Jews. Fischel Grossman, a young man from Galicia, employed near Handsworth as a farm-worker, attended Singers Hill on three consecutive Sabbaths, believing it to be the only synagogue in Birmingham. "Nobody bothered about me; I felt lonely and isolated. Then I was told about the Central. I was overwhelmed with kindness and the *Shammas* (beadle) took me home for a Sabbath meal."

In the larger communities, the Jewish refugees of the 1930s appear to have had considerable influence on the development of communal life. In Birmingham they increased the numbers, but do not seem to have changed the character of the comparatively small community. One can say with certainty that the Orthodox wing, as represented by the Central Synagogue, was strengthened by the influx. The Prais family, the Grossmans, the Mendelsohns, Bergmans, Spiers and Slymovics added a vigorous dimension to the Orthodox Community. However some of the potential leaders emigrated to Israel, leaving the Birmingham Jewish Community the poorer for it.

Gradually, the newcomers were absorbed into the congregations whose religious philosophy suited them best, Orthodox, "Middle of the Road" or Progressive. But for some time their social life remained centred in the Refugee Club and each others' houses, where they celebrated weddings and birthdays with poems in the old Continental style.

In 1952, the Revd Chaim Pearl, then Chief Minister at Singers Hill, together with Dr Robert Singer, started a local B'nai B'rith. This flourished, its membership deriving equally from the established Jewish Community and former refugees, and led to the foundation of a Birmingham Hillel House hostel for students.

Those who had served in the Pioneer Corps and other branches of the Services during the war, formed a deep attachment to Ajex, the Jewish Ex-Servicemen's Club. In such ways, the newcomers gradually became integrated into the Birmingham Jewish Community.

References

1. Minutes of the Birmingham Hebrew Congregation 26 March 1933. No. 10621
2. ibid. 23 April 1933 No. 10624
3. ibid. 16 May 1933 No. 10631

4. ibid. 16 May 1933 No. 10632
5. ibid. 30 July 1933 No. 10643
6. ibid. 5 April 1936 No. 10784
7. ibid. 30 October 1938 No. 10897
8. ibid. 14 May 1939 No. 10912
9. ibid. 23 July 1939 No. 10913
10. ibid. 19 May 1940
11. ibid. 4 September 1944 No. 77
12. ibid. 23 April 1945
13. ibid. 14 June 1945

Unfortunately the Minutes of the Central Synagogue for this period were destroyed, along with the building, by bombing. The Representative Council minutes only exist as far back as 1950. The Minutes of the Liberal (Progressive) Synagogue were unavailable.

16

The Survivors

As World War II drew to a close, CBF (The Central British Fund for Jewish Relief and Rehabilitation), which had been instrumental in rescuing so many thousands from Central Europe before the war, was now forced to turn its attention to the survivors of the concentration camps. The Fund undertook responsibility for seven hundred and thirty-two children, bringing them to this country and dealing with their rehabilitation, care and maintenance.

Many of the young people were in a terrible condition, in need of medical and psychiatric care. Amongst them was thirteen year old Magda Bloom, who arrived in England in the autumn of 1945, having spent the previous year in Auschwitz and Belsen. To this day she bears her camp number tattooed on her arm.

Her childhood in Hungary had been happy. Her parents were landowners and she was brought up on the family farm. Here she and her brother lived in idyllic surroundings. As the wine-harvest approached they regularly visited their grandmother, who owned vineyards with cellars running underground for storing the famous Tokai wine. Here they would join in pressing the grapes, gathering peaches and walnuts, and before they returned home, would watch the peasants dance to gypsy music in celebration of the harvest festival.

In 1944, Magda's father, who had been serving in the Hungarian army and had in the past been decorated for conspicuous bravery, was sent with his fellow Jewish soldiers to a labour camp. Their rifles were taken away and they were ordered to pick up mines in front of the German army. Before long they heard he was dead. Magda, her mother and brother were driven from their farm, first into a ghetto, and thence by cattle truck to Auschwitz. On her thirteenth birthday, Magda's brother perished in the gas-chambers.

The war was now reaching its final stages. Magda and her mother spent the worst weeks of the freezing winter of 1944/1945 being shunted back and forth in cattle trucks to an unknown destination, which turned out to be the concentration camp of Belsen. All the time in the background was the noise of gunfire and falling bombs.

On 14 April 1945, Belsen was liberated by the British. But Magda hardly cared. The previous night her mother had died, and as the British tanks rolled down the street she had been taken from the barracks. "People were dying everywhere. There were carpets of dead people. In our barracks, which had held a thousand people, there were forty left. We were human skeletons, covered with sores, infested with lice and typhus, wandering around like zombies ..."

Many people died of typhus and dysentery after the liberation, but after a time life began to settle down to a kind of convalescence. In Belsen Magda and her mother had been befriended by a violinist in one of the orchestras formed by the prisoners. Another good-hearted young woman, who spoke several languages and now acted as interpreter for UNRRA (United Nations Relief and Rehabilitation Administration) also felt sympathy for the Hungarian girl. Together they took her under their wing and moved Magda into the UNRRA building, formerly the comfortable headquarters of the SS officers. "Time stood still that summer. We did nothing but recuperate. Food was our main concern." Magda now only wanted to go home, but there was no home to go to. Everybody put forward good advice about starting a new life, and she was offered transport to America, Israel or England. But there was no-one to welcome her in any of these countries. Eventually, because Marta, her friend, was going to England, she opted to accompany her.

Now that the decision had been made, week followed frustrating week of delay. At last in October 1945 they left for the airport of Celle, *en route* for London. Excitement ran high. There were eighty-two children on the 'plane, all singing, "We don't know where we're going, but we're going out of the hell of the camps".

Magda Bloom (centre) taking her first cup of tea in England, 1945.

Wintershill Hall, a large old house near Winchester, had been taken over for the children from Belsen. To Magda and her friend it was fairyland. It was a mild autumn. The trees were still green and there were roses everywhere. Inside it had all been beautifully fitted up with bunk beds and fresh linen. Marta slept above her in the top bunk. Magda had arrived wearing an old SS jacket. "After the liberation everybody raided the clothing-stores, everything we had was full of lice." But now fresh, pretty clothes awaited their choice, "second-hand, but to us they were splendid ... We had some basic English lessons, but for the rest we just revelled in being free." They took long walks through the gardens and into the woods; pocket money was given to them so that they could go shopping in Winchester. "Everybody made a fuss of us, there were photographs in the newspapers; I danced a *csárdás*[1] for the newsreels and a young man picked me a rose."

Nevertheless Magda often felt depressed. She missed her mother and her future was uncertain. Wintershill was only a temporary resting place, and many of the children, including Marta, were going to a hostel in London.

Magda meanwhile had been offered a home in Birmingham with an orthodox Jewish family. She was alarmed at the prospect, but allowed herself to be persuaded to try it for a fortnight. She travelled alone to London. "A crowd of British soldiers got on the train. I sat scared, with my little wooden box I had brought from Belsen on my knee. They offered me chewing gum and tried to get me to talk. I hid behind a newspaper but it was upside down! When we got to London one of the soldiers stayed with me until my name was called over the loudspeaker and someone from Bloomsbury House collected me.

"A jolly plump lady, wearing a fur coat, was waiting for me in the office smoking a cigarette. She was quite unlike the formidable person I'd imagined. She gave me a bag of apples and we set out for Birmingham. It was Friday night, and when we arrived the table was set out for dinner, shining silver and glass and candles. I couldn't speak. I hadn't seen anything like it since I'd left my home. I couldn't help feeling that perhaps after all I had come at last to the right place at the right time". Mr and Mrs Joshua Hesselberg adopted Magda and sent her to the Edgbaston High School. She gradually acclimatised to the English way of life. But some things remained a mystery. "I was surprised at the tricks the girls played on the teachers; it was so different from the discipline of school in Hungary. I was in a dilemma. I didn't want to be naughty, but I didn't want to be different. Nevertheless it was a very happy time for me."

Magda afterwards trained at the elegant gown-shop "Millicent" in New Street. Everybody was attracted by the "Little French Girl" as she was known, and she was greatly in demand by the dowagers, descending in their chauffeur-driven limousines. She had a good eye for colour, and they would insist on her help in choosing the all-important accessories to their outfits.

She later married David Bloom, a member of a long-established Birmingham Jewish family; they had first met kissing under the mistletoe, another inexplicable English custom.

Magda lost her family, but has now established one of her own. Her son is a solicitor, practising in Birmingham; her daughter is married and lives in Israel. Magda is now the proud grandmother of two *sabra*[2] grandchildren. She had always determined she would work in some way to express her gratitude for her good fortune. After her marriage she founded the Kinnereth Ladies' Group of the Women's International Zionist Organisation and she now is Life President of the Birmingham branch. From time to time she visits local schools and groups to talk about her experiences. Like all survivors she is anxious these shall never be forgotten.

Magda Bloom with the wooden box she brought with her from Belsen, 1988.

Kitty Hart and Mindu Hornick, like Magda Bloom, were children of the concentration camps. Kitty Hart has documented her ordeal in her two well-known books *I am Alive* (1961) and *Return to Auschwitz* (1981). She has also made television programmes.

Mindu Hornick owes her life to a Yiddish-speaking Polish guard who was waiting for the cattle trucks to unload their victims at Auschwitz.

"Two doors faced us as we came down the ramp. The guard asked my mother how old we were. She told him my sister and I and a friend were just thirteen.

" 'Say you're all eighteen', he hissed at us. 'And go ahead. Leave your mother. But for God's sake go now', and he pushed us through the right hand door."

Mindu Hornick never saw her mother and brothers again. "We were made to queue up naked for clothes for hours on end ... they threw us rags ... we ate from a trough on our hands and knees, until we were pushed aside ..."

After a time she was sent to Bremen to work on munitions in an underground bunker, twisting the tops on to grenades.

"The SS officers were laughing to see how their great army depended on little girls ... As the war ended we were put on another train, we believed to freedom. But the Americans, thinking it was booby-trapped, blew it up ... I looked around me and saw little corpses ... There were just two hundred and thirty survivors from five hundred of us."

The Red Cross brought Mindu Hornick to England where she was reunited with her uncles, who had fought in the British army.[3]

The Oppenheimer Children, originally from Berlin, were saved by their mother's foresight. "In 1936 she was expecting a baby", said Paul Oppenheimer, "and she was determined to have it in England. In due course our sister Eva was born in London. We wanted to stay there, but my father couldn't get a work permit for England. He managed to find work in Holland and we followed him."

In the spring of 1940 the Germans steam-rollered across Holland and Belgium. "It was obvious that sooner or later we Jews would be sent to concentration camps. For months we had our bags packed for the emergency, but we lived very quietly and it was June 1943 before we were sent to Westerbork, a transit camp on the Dutch-German border.

"At first it was a bit like a holiday camp. Our quarters were very cramped but food was adequate and we never felt in danger of our lives. The guards were Dutch, but the camp was run by Jews. Father was separated from us but we three children were left with our mother. I was fourteen years old, my brother Rudolf was twelve and Eva was seven.

"In February 1944 the Nazis began regular transports from Westerbork into Germany by cattle trains. Sixty people at a time were shoved into a single truck, furnished only with two buckets, one filled with water for drinking, the other for a lavatory. But we were lucky. Because my sister had been born in London we were classed as political prisoners and given 'privilege passports'. These enabled us to travel on ordinary trains with people who had visas for the United States or Palestine. Even the Nazis wished to keep up appearances and it was thought that we might be exchanged for German prisoners of war.

"Our destination was Belsen. Again as 'privileged persons' we were housed in a small sectioned-off area. I never saw the whole camp. Now it was every man for himself. People didn't make friends, just formed relationships for self-protection. Families stuck together. Food was terribly scarce, mostly bread, which was given out each day. Those who collected it might get a few extra crumbs, but it was solitary confinement for anyone caught scrounging more than their fair share.

"The day started with roll-call. We could be left standing for hours if the numbers didn't tally. Sometimes we had showers, but we were scared they might be gas-chambers. Some people worked in the crematoria so we knew what was going on. I didn't have to work, but I had no schooling either, just stayed with the very young and the very old.

"Then came rumours that things were going badly for the Germans. Bombers kept screaming overhead. Gassings and mass executions ceased, but people were dying of starvation and disease. Our main occupation was searching our clothes for lice.

"My brother and I had been separated from our parents, who were in hospital. We heard our mother had died of starvation, but had no idea what had happened to our sister. On 1 April 1945 we left Belsen to the sound of approaching guns and marched to the railway station. We moved east, by night, passing through burnt-out cities. By day we would get out and dig the fields. The Germans always buried potatoes near the railway lines and we burnt the benches in the carriages to cook them. Sometimes, though, we had to eat grass, and when people tried to run away German marksmen shot them down. But the journey gave us hope; we knew that our time was coming. Once an American 'plane attacked us and we got out and watched. Now even the German guards were becoming less fanatical.

"Towards the middle of April we passed through Berlin and saw the terrible devastation. But the Germans kept moving us on, still hoping, I think, to exchange us for prisoners of war.

"We were on that train for two and a half weeks, when our liberation came as a surprise. One evening we were sleeping, waiting to be moved on as usual, but nothing happened. Next morning our German guards had gone, there were just a few Russians around. My brother, who was a first-rate scavenger, went into the nearby village and came back with potatoes, greens, strawberries and milk. The Germans had ceased to worry about us, they were just terrified of the Russians.

"Now once again it was every man for himself. We ransacked everywhere around, 'liberating' bicycles to extend our range. We plundered a cheese factory and came back with a bag full of tubes of cheese. Many people died now from the sudden change of diet. I myself was in a bad shape and finally went down with typhus.

"When I left hospital, the Russians took my brother and me to Leipzig in the American Zone. Here, by the most extraordinary coincidence, we bumped into our sister Eva. She had left Belsen on the train in a group of orphans, but we didn't remember seeing her.

"We were all taken to Holland and contact was made with an uncle in London, who came to help us. Eva, as a British citizen, was able to return with him immediately, but Rudolf and I were still German citizens according to Dutch law. We had a final horrible experience of being put into a camp with German SS men. Eventually we were cleared and in November 1945 we crossed the Channel to England and a new life."

Günter Faerber lived with his parents in a small town in Upper Silesia, Poland, three miles from the German frontier. They ran an outfitting shop and were fairly prosperous. At the time of the invasion of Poland, in 1939, Gunter was eleven years old.

The family fled to Cracow, but once the German occupation was complete, they returned home. "The business was confiscated and my father was sent away with all the other male Jews to a labour camp in Russia.

He made his escape by walking back to Poland to the town of Bendzin, where we managed to join him. Altogether in those three years we moved seven times, each time to smaller premises. My parents turned all their savings to gold coins, which were deposited with one of their former employees for safe-keeping. From time to time she would receive a message, 'bring me some peppermints'. We sold the coins, one or two at a time, on the black market and so we managed to survive.

My grandmother had, all this time, been running an agency for Swiss lace, over the border in Germany. In 1942 lorry loads of 'buses, full of old women, came to our railway station. I saw her in the queue waiting for the train; I was the only one in the family able to say good-bye to her."

In 1942 Bendzin was turned into a ghetto.

"For months people had been going away and not a single postcard arrived to say where they had gone. The Germans kept inventing new ways of getting rid of the Jews a few hundred at a time. When at last only 10,000 out of the original 25,000-strong Jewish population were left, we were requested — they were always very polite — to report on a football pitch outside the town, men, women and children. We stood there from eight o'clock in the morning, surrounded by German soldiers with machine guns. In the afternoon, the Gestapo men came and sorted us into groups, the strong, the crippled, the elderly and the children. The old and sick were deported, but my family were among those left together and sent back to the ghetto.

"Now we were really frightened. Everyone made hiding places in their homes, in the cellars, or by building double walls. I made a hole in the garden, hiding it under a lot of old furniture. One morning the Gestapo surrounded the ghetto, to flush out anyone they could find.

"They did this frequently, recruiting Yiddish-speaking Ukranians who were quite ruthless. They would call out 'the Germans have gone', in Yiddish, and the unsuspecting Jews would come out. This time all my family hid, but after a time no one seemed to be coming to our flat, so I ran out and was caught."

Günter Faerber was sent with twenty-two other youngsters to a labour camp in Upper Silesia administered from Auschwitz. Here, deep in the forests, a huge factory was being extended for making petrol and other synthetic products out of the Silesian coal. "The forest was being cleared for building and it was my task to clean the soil off the newly uprooted trees."

The works covered sixteen square miles and were served by thousands of prisoners of war, each in their separate camps, British, French, Ukranian and Russian, besides Frenchmen recruited from Occupied France, and German civilians.

"We got up at three o'clock in the morning — four in winter — and stood outside a couple of hours waiting for roll-call. At six o'clock we'd be marched off to the works, and we came back to the camp at six in the evening. We twenty-two youngsters were all housed in one room of a barracks. It had radiators but seldom any heat, except sometimes after midnight, because all the steam generated went to keeping the German quarters warm. We would put our wet clothes on the radiators at night and, generally, they'd be just as wet next morning.

The Faerber's family business in Poland, 1928.

"Things improved a bit after a time, when we were taken over by the SS from Auschwitz. After tattooing us all, they built de-lousing cubicles, and we had showers and striped camp clothes, clean each week. But every month or so they would visit the hospital and remove the very sick — they wouldn't let anyone die in peace.

Concentration Camp money.

"Our rations were half a small black loaf daily, one ounce each of margarine and jam and a bowl of some sort of soup. We usually ate all this in the evening when it was handed out. If you saved it, as often as not it was pinched."

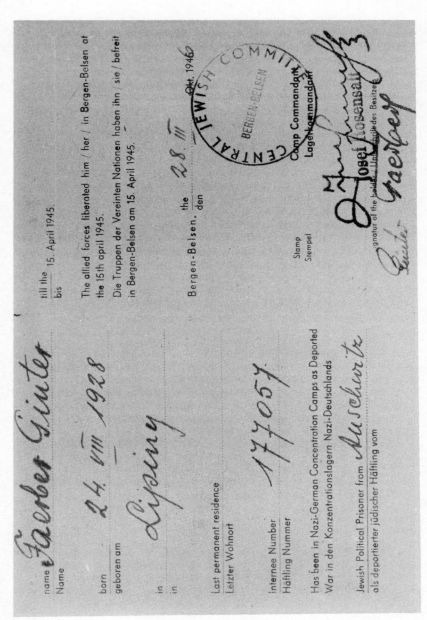

Günter Faerber's certificate of liberation, 1946.

The black bread became camp currency and Günter Faerber's wits were sharpened by captivity. "After a time I was put on to more important work like road-building. Then I was allocated to a German engineering firm. All sorts of civilians were now working at the factory, welders, pipe-fitters, painters and plumbers. We weren't supposed to speak to people from the other camps, but one day a British prisoner of war asked me if I could get him a frying pan. A friendly German made me one and I sold it to the prisoner of war for cigarette ends. Now the German civilians couldn't get paint, but one of the prisoners in the paint factory got me some and I gave him the cigarette ends in exchange. Then I sold the paint to a civilian for good German bread. The British prisoners were never short of food; they had plenty in their Red Cross parcels, but they hated the black bread which was their ration, as it was ours. So I exchanged the good bread for a lot of black bread, and for a time at least I wasn't hungry.

"It was January 1945 when we heard the Russian guns advancing. I had an accident which probably saved my life. Outside the barracks was a pit which took the outflow from the central heating. We would take buckets and collect hot water for washing. I slipped into the pit, badly scalded my leg and was taken to hospital. Meanwhile, the camp was evacuated and everyone marched deep into Germany. Nearly half the prisoners died. We patients were left to our own devices and after a week the Russians liberated us.

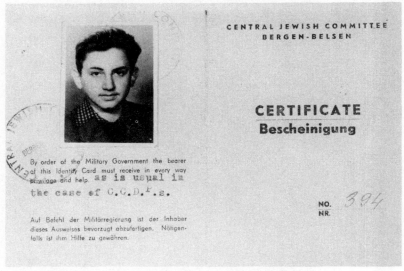

Günter Faerber's identity card as a displaced person, 1945/46.

"I was taken to a Russian Army Hospital in Poland, and stayed there several months. I had arranged with my parents that if we survived we would meet at a certain town in Germany where I had a cousin who was married to a non-Jew. I found his flat and heard what had happened in the ghetto where my family lived. The Gestapo had surrounded the place and kept it covered for four or five weeks until everybody was starved out. I never found out what happened to my parents. They had brought me up to say my prayers at night and I continued all that time, but when I found how my parents had gone, I stopped.

"I stayed with my cousin nearly six months in the hope that somebody would turn up. My father, after all, was an able-bodied man and might have worked." Finally, still only seventeen years old, Günter Faerber made his way to the Displaced Persons' Camp at Bergen-Belsen, where they traced an uncle who had emigrated to England before the war. For a time he lived with him and his family in London, but when volunteers were being recruited in 1948 to fight for the newly-established State of Israel, he joined Hagana (the Israeli army). "I felt it my duty. Israel is essential to us Jews. If a Hitler were to arise now, we would have somewhere to go."

Günter Faerber in Israel, 1948.

He had every intention of living on a kibbutz after demobilisation, but his experience of England had given him a taste for independence and he returned. Eventually, he was offered work with good prospects in the scrap-metal industry and settled in Birmingham.

On 18 May 1944, Lola Maté of Hungary, her husband, her two children, Sara aged ten years and Josef aged eight, her mother and her grandmother boarded a train which, unbeknown to them, was to take them to Auschwitz. She immediately received an intimation of the brutal treatment that she was to experience for many months to come. Her grandmother was very small and had difficulty climbing into the high cattle truck. She was assisted by a sharp kick upwards from an SS guard.

The two thousand Jewish inhabitants of the town of Nagykanizsa and the surrounding villages were squeezed on to that train. "While we were still in Hungary, it was given out that doctors, veterinary surgeons and architects might leave the train to help make up the shortages caused by the war." The family decided that Lola's husband, an architect, and her uncle, who was a veterinary surgeon, should go; they might be in a better position to help if they remained in their professional work.

22 May happened to be Josef's birthday. He had asked for a *tallith* (Hebrew — praying shawl) for his present and had stowed it in his rucksack. "Shall I put it on today?" he said the day before. "No, I'll keep it for my proper birthday, tomorrow." It was never to be.

At last they arrived at their bleak destination. "No grass, no trees, no birds, just a horrible smell from thick blackish fumes which made the atmosphere heavy." Still the travellers did not realise what the smoke signified.

"On dismounting from the train, we were straightaway divided into two queues. I was sent to the right with the younger, stronger people. The weak, the pregnant women, the older people and the children were hustled to the left. We did not know it, but they went straight to the gas chambers. I think Dr Mengeles was there, picking out twins for his experimental research.

"Our group of three hundred women were taken to long low huts to sleep. There were no beds and no covers and you could scarcely sit up. For lavatories there was a long double line of fifty holes in the ground. No toilet paper. I think that was the thing I missed most of all.

"Our hair was cut and our clothes were taken from us. We were each given a grey cotton dress and a sort of combination undergarment. I was handed a pair of men's boots, but no socks. One woman was so fat, nothing could be found to fit her. She was taken away and we never saw her again. Besides the clothes, we each received a tin plate and a spoon. We had nothing else of our own.

" 'But where are the children?', people kept asking. For a time the Kapos, who were the privileged Polish and Polish-Jewish women who did the work of the camp, put us off. On the third day one of them burst out. 'You stupid fools! Can't you see the smoke? That's where your children are.' Yet still we hoped. After all, the SS guards had children too.

"Friday evening came, the eve of the Jewish Sabbath. If ever I did any good thing in my life, it was at this moment. As a teacher in a Jewish school, I knew all the hymns and at the top of my voice I started to sing *Le-cho Dowdi*, the song which welcomes the Sabbath as a bride. This calmed everyone down a bit and then—it seemed a miracle—somebody lit a candle and we passed it from hand to hand. We did this every Friday afterwards.

"Where had the candle come from? We possessed nothing. Some women were put to work in 'Canada'. I can't think where the Germans got the name, perhaps because Canada is a rich country. The contents of all our luggage had to be sorted and sent into Germany to help the war effort. There were great mounds of jewellery, shoes, false teeth, everything. Anybody caught stealing was punished by an appalling beating-up, but people did take things and that was where the candle came from.

"Every morning at 4.30 came the counting. We were driven out of the huts by the Kapos and the SS women soldiers who ran up and down shouting at the Kapos 'get on with it'. We stood in the cold for two hours and it was so dark you could see the stars. This counting took place every morning and evening. I don't know why. There was nowhere to escape.

Sara Kertesz. Josef Kertesz.

Lola Maté's children by her first marriage who both perished in Auschwitz in 1944.

"We went back to our huts for breakfast of ersatz black coffee, a piece of black bread and a tiny cube of margarine. After work we queued again for potato soup. We'd drink the liquid and mash the potato with a bit of margarine, if we'd managed to save any. I can still hear the rattle of the tin spoons against the dishes. We were always hungry.

"A favourite camp word was 'organise'. Some people managed to organise a little extra for themselves. If you worked in the kitchens you might—at great risk—conceal a carrot or a bit of raw potato. I myself managed to organise a notebook and pencil, in which we wrote down poems from memory.

"One girl with a fine voice (the Germans always called her the 'opera singer') entertained the officers on a Saturday night. They sent special clothes for her to wear for the performance and gave her good food. Often she'd hide things in her knickers or stockings for the younger girls amongst us. They were always the hungriest. Many people criticised her, but I don't blame her. She ensured her own survival and helped others to survive."

After six weeks in Auschwitz Lola Maté was moved to a munitions factory in Germany. Six months later she was sent to Essen to clean up the station and airport after Allied bombing. The attack on the Ruhr was now at its height and on one occasion the prisoners themselves were machine-gunned after a horrific raid. "Two hundred and fifty people were killed, and afterwards we had to clean up, picking up severed heads and limbs."

By the end of March, it was obvious that the war was coming to an end. The Nazi camp leader was never separated from a small suitcase in which he kept a labourer's outfit, ready for a sudden escape. "It was like a voice from heaven for us to realise that even the Germans knew they were near defeat."

Eventually the prisoners were marched out of their camp, moving by night and shut up in barns by day. "All at once we stopped. The German guards disappeared. We were just a band of Jewish women on our own."

At Gelsenkirchen the Burgermeister billeted them on the local population. "There was plenty of food, in fact several people fell ill and some died from the unaccustomed richness of the milk and butter." Quite suddenly they were told by the Burgermeister to assemble at the station. Lola Maté had 'organised' a long coat and a skirt, but was still wearing her camp boots!

With the help of the American-Jewish Joint Distribution Committee they travelled by train to Austria. "We passed Dresden in ruins, nothing but walls and chimneys standing. As we entered the Russian Zone, we had to change trains. The Russians hadn't seen women for years, and tried to rape the younger ones in the corridors. We were very frightened.

"On 1 June we reached Budapest and straightaway started to make enquiries for our relatives. My mother's two brothers were alive. They had been helped by Raoul Wallenberg[4], who had obtained false passports for them, so that they passed as Swedish citizens. My brother had been shot fighting in Russia, but his life was saved by a wad of letters and photographs in his breast pocket.

"My sister had been working in the north of Germany. On the last day of the war, they were pushed out to sea in a boat loaded with explosives. Eight people managed to swim to safety. The rest, including my sister, were killed in the explosion or drowned.

"My husband followed me to Auschwitz not long after I'd left. He'd heard I was still alive and was convinced we'd be all right. He was one of those who always came out on top. Even in Auschwitz he had a special job and tried hard to help everybody."

By the end of January 1945, the Germans had decided to get every able-bodied prisoner out of Auschwitz and blow up the place with its horrifying evidence. But the Russians and the Americans came in so quickly, they had only time to destroy the crematorium.

"Everybody who could walk was marched out at night. Two of my husband's friends, ill in hospital, were left behind. They thought they were going to die, but the Russians cared for them and they were sent back to Hungary.

"Within half-an-hour of leaving the camp, the prisoners were told to stop and dig a large pit in the ground. Then they were shot and thrown into it. Half of them were still alive.

"Why did the Germans have to kill my husband and sister in the last moments of the war? Were they so full of hate?"

Budapest had been liberated by the Russians on 4 April. Thousands had been killed in the house-to-house fighting and all the bridges were down. Lola Maté returned to Nagykanizsa on 8 June. Nothing remained but an empty house, despite the fact that there had been no fighting in the town. She managed to locate the furniture from her children's bedroom, but when she went to enquire, the "owner" swore at her, and nearly pushed her over.

All the Jewish houses had been stripped. Lola Maté went to work in the Jewish Communal Offices. Here the incoming mail for the missing families was collected. One day a postcard arrived from a prisoner of war in Russia. "I shall soon be home", it read, "kiss the children for me." The writer was a friend of Lola Maté's childhood and she knew his beautiful young wife and their children had perished in Auschwitz.

Lola Maté with her second husband in England, 1964.

Lola and the prisoner of war came together and were married. After the uprising of 1956 they fled to England with their two daughters and settled in Birmingham.

"But how is it I can still smile, and cook chicken soup and have children?"

The passage to freedom was not easy. Mrs A., a former refugee, was moved to tears at the recollection of a young relative, a boy of twelve, who had spent much of his childhood with his parents in Belsen. His mother had died in the camp, his father of typhoid after liberation. "The boy was pushed around France and Belgium, but finally a permit was obtained for him to join some cousins in Argentina." Mrs A. met him at Newhaven to take him to the boat. But it had been damaged in a collision in a fog, and Mrs A. returned with the lad to her home in Birmingham to await its repair. "I bought him his first pair of shoes. He'd never had any of his own, and he couldn't stop looking at them. He would never eat with us, always by himself, huge meals. He'd have to lie down afterwards ... He would have liked to stay, but he had no permit for England."

Others received less understanding. "If you come to live with us, you must never speak of your experiences." This was the condition laid down to one former inmate of the concentration camps.

The survivors of the Holocaust who have settled in Birmingham, all appear to have been remarkably successful in the lives which have so fortuitously been spared to them. But as Mindu Hornick concluded, "The shadow of the Holocaust never leaves one. It is one's burden for life."

References and notes

1. *csárdás.* Hungarian national dance.
2. *sabra.* Native-born Israeli (Hebrew)
3. *Birmingham Evening Mail,* 5 August 1987.
4. Raoul Wallenberg. (1912–). Swedish diplomat who issued protective documents to several thousand Hungarian Jews, thereby preventing their deportation. He disappeared in 1946 and was said to have died in a Russian labour camp the following year.

17

Restitution and Compensation – Weidergutmachung

The German word *Wiedergutmachung* literally translated means "making good again". The words which normally replace it in English refer separately to the restoration of confiscated or stolen property and a form of damages for suffering and notional losses — unfulfilled expectations. "All the money in the world can never compensate for the fear, insecurity, the loss of parents and relatives ..." writes Else Schott.

In a paper delivered to the Jewish Historical Society of England in June 1979, Joan Stiebel explained how the machinery for making claims in respect of persecution and loss came to be set up: "Even before the end of the war, the possibility of eventually reclaiming property misappropriated by the Nazis, and claims for suffering, was exercising the minds of a number of lawyers, themselves refugees. It was realised that many victims would not be able to afford to engage individual lawyers, and to meet this difficulty the United Restitution Organisation was established in London in 1948, with the Central British Fund for World Jewish Relief providing the first working capital. In the event, this body was successful in recovering very substantial amounts.

"Two organisations, the Jewish Restitution Successor Organisation and the Jewish Trust Corporation were established to reclaim the heirless and communal forfeited property in the American and British Zones of Germany. The CBF took a leading role in the Jewish Trust Corporation which recovered DM160,500,000, of which almost a quarter — DM28,000,000 — was made available in this country for the benefit of former refugees."

A proportion of this money was used by CBF to set up homes for aged refugees in London and Manchester, a block of flatlets and a home for mental after-care, which are run with the assistance of the Association of Jewish Refugees. The old age homes continue to fulfil a very real need for people who, no matter how well they integrated into their adopted country in their middle years, still find comfort in old age in the companionship of those with similar backgrounds and experience. In addition, through the work of the Association for Jewish Refugees and the Central British Fund, some of the money recovered as "unclaimed funds of Nazi victims" was used to help individual refugees in this country as well as new generations of Jewish refugees elsewhere. Organisations in Israel also benefited and were thereby enabled to provide a home and a new life for the destitute survivors of the Nazi holocaust. In this country, too, unclaimed money contributed to the setting up of "Self-Aid for Refugees". This is a small organisation offering help, advice and limited financial assistance. Its annual fund-raising concert at the Queen Elizabeth Hall, London, has become a notable social event.

Inevitably in an operation as vast and complex as that undertaken by the various bodies attempting to establish and reclaim the losses suffered by the millions of victims of Nazism over a period of more than fifteen years, there were many inequalities and undoubted injustices. Communication was a problem in the late 1940s and 1950s. Refugees living in areas away from principal Jewish communities were often unaware of the work of the aid organisation and either failed to learn about the claim procedures or heard about them too late.

Professor John Grenville asks: "What happened to the property that should have gone to the children?"

During his researches into the Jews of Hamburg, Professor Grenville found that his great-uncle, a lawyer, had had a villa on the Alster. This had been confiscated by the Nazis together with other property. His great-uncle had been killed.

He explained: "The claims had to be made by 1953/54; otherwise, the property became part of a general agreement whereby equivalent monies could be sent to Israel ... No effort of any kind was made to trace the children. I tried to trace my uncle's property many years later. It appeared it had been placed in a Jewish Trust organisation for a short time. Then it was sold. All these children, from babes-in-arms, were deprived of their property. They weren't even old enough to know about it. Only some of the older people reclaimed their property.

"All property taken from the Jews was carefully recorded — it only had to be looked up.

In the light of these remarks, an attempt has been made to establish the extent to which the people interviewed for the purpose of this history were aware of the possibilities of making claims, how much detailed knowledge they had of the types of claims which might be considered and to what extent their claims were successful. According to a former officer of the Association of Jewish Refugees, the main source of information was the monthly newsheet "AJR Information" which, he claims, directly or indirectly reached the majority of prospective claimants. Gradually, over some twenty years from the end of hostilities in 1945, certain standard procedures emerged and standard amounts of compensation were laid down to apply to the vast majority of claimants.

Else Schott told us: "I found out about restitution from the AJR. I didn't want to apply at first. Later I took a German solicitor through AJR. The first payment was far more than I expected. AJR kept drawing attention to restitution. Most people got their information through it. Some people didn't put in early enough but they kept on extending the time limit."

Of the people interviewed, where information regarding restitution was available, a high proportion of those who came as children or young adults bringing with them no more than the permitted single suitcase, said that the only compensation they received was a single payment in respect of loss of education and, where applicable, a lump sum for loss of parents. This is borne out in some general comments on restitution made by Mr Henry Warner:

"The provisions made by the German Government were very extensive. Yet only part of the refugees benefited, and even among these there were great differences: some may have received small once-only payments, others substantial lump sums and life pensions. It was necessary to produce documentation to substantiate claims. Statements had to be made under oath, where documents were insufficient or missing, to be confirmed by further statements from relatives or former friends, possibly living in other countries. In most cases specialist lawyers had to be employed to advance claims. Many refugees, particularly the younger ones uncertain about their entitlements, did not have the necessary background information on which to base their claims, or did not consider it worth the effort to get involved."

Henry Warner goes on: "To those who did receive more than minor amounts, restitution payments could be of major assistance in the struggle to establish themselves and their families in Britain. Such payments bought badly needed clothing, household equipment and furniture in the first place. They financed family holidays and in several cases provided the deposit for a first house" (first, that is, since their flight from an established home) ... He continues: "For people with ill health or for old age pensioners, the regular pension payments from Germany help to put the jam on the bread and butter of life in retirement."

These views are confirmed by the experience recorded by Else Schott: "We needed the money; we were still living in furnished rooms. I wanted my own place, even if it was orange boxes. The landlord had raised our rent because the rooms looked so good and we kept the garden so nicely. So we were glad to get into a place of our own. It made an enormous difference. We could have holidays twice a year comfortably."

Among a small number of former refugees, there is a different view. They make a stand in principle against applying for or accepting money in compensation for their loss of families and possessions. In their eyes such payments are "blood money". They are, however, a very small minority and their anger at the idea of being offered compensation is more than matched by the disgust of those who have been unable to get what they feel is theirs by right, merely because their homes were the wrong side of a border. A story on the lines ... "Father had a good business, a limited company, but it was in East Berlin so he got no pension. I just got a small amount for interrupted education."

Ruth Price reported that the applications she made were long and complicated, continuing over many years with not much at the end of it. Questions were asked which she was unable to answer — first by a lawyer in London and then by somebody in New York. She eventually got some payment for loss of her mother and another in respect of household possessions and jewellery. She applied for an orphan's pension but owing to a mix-up the deadline had expired. She felt she had fallen between two stools, not qualifying for an orphan's pension and, as she had been too young to have worked in Germany, she did not qualify for a retirement pension either.

In sharp contrast is the story of a couple who came over in the early 1930s. They brought with them all their movable possessions and by the outbreak of war in 1939 were reasonably established both in work and in a small house of their own. After the war, the husband, by then in business on his own account, received full compensation for loss of earnings resulting from his emigration, a First World War Pension and the German National Insurance Pension of which his widow continues to receive 60%.

The difference in the degree of success and in the speed of obtaining compensation often lay in whether or not there was a personal contact in the former place of residence. Those refugees who knew a lawyer or other influential person still living in Germany, who could verify their story of forced sale or confiscation, were able in many cases to obtain full restitution through the German courts long before the international rules on *Wiedergutmachung* were laid down. It also helped if people were able to make a personal visit to Germany to meet the lawyers and officials there — a recourse usually beyond the means of those who had lost everything in 1938/9 and who, in the late 1940s, were still struggling to make a living in rented accommodation.

Berta Strauss came to this country from Bavaria in 1934. Her father owned a large and prosperous textile business in the small town of Weiden where, she told us, everyone knew everyone else and he was well respected. After the Kristallnacht her father was taken first to Dachau and then to prison in Munich where he was made to sign papers making over his business to a German firm in Weiden.

"In 1948 my father started to prepare for restitution. He began by writing to Weiden where everybody knew the circumstances. There was a firm of solicitors who were very Catholic, very opposed to the Hitler regime. My father wrote to them and asked if there would be any ways and means of obtaining compensation for his property for which he had not received any money. The solicitors, a father and two sons, wrote that they would do their best to get him some compensation. They were very successful because the house was still standing — it was a very big house and each room was let to a family. The business was still a going concern.

"In 1949 we, the Strauss family and my father, went to Weiden, saw Mr Pfleger, the solicitor, and he took down all the details and started working on reparations. Of course, Germany at that time was in a very poor state and things to do with reparations only developed very slowly. I think it was in 1950 he got his first money award.

"Then he was told by someone that he was supposed to get a lump sum. Then somebody — I forget who but all the Jews got together to compare their experiences — somebody said 'don't take a lump sum, ask them to give you the money in instalments'. Really everything was very much in flux. There were no hard and fast rules. The whole thing was very confused, but from these early beginnings developed the business of reparations.

"We got some compensation for loss of education — each of us, myself and my two sisters. It was my first possession of money in England at the time."

Berta Strauss continues:

"My husband was a different case altogether. He came to England with a job to go to. He didn't have any compensation until very much later: I think in the 1960s or 1970s when the laws for reparation were already very sophisticated. He was told one could get reparation for loss of retirement pension. As he had been employed by a firm in Halle on the Saale in 1931/2, he had contributed to their pension scheme. The firm folded up and he went back to university in Karlsruhe. He heard that he might be entitled to restitution for loss of pension if he had stayed in Germany.

"He wrote to a lawyer in Berlin who told him it sounded a very plausible case though the place where he had worked was now behind the Iron Curtain. He would be entitled to it if he could prove that there was a pension scheme. We couldn't find any proof and the people in Halle said that without proof they wouldn't, of course, recognise it — which was fair and we accepted it. Then, when I did my *Pesach* (Passover) spring cleaning, I found a letter from his former boss saying he was sorry that my husband was going to leave. That was the necessary document. He sent it to Berlin and the man in charge sent it to Halle and within four weeks he had the pension which is still working and I am in the lucky position that I now get from Germany 60% of the pension to which he was entitled and for which I am grateful."

Former refugees from Czechoslovakia faced a long and arduous process in claiming restitution: Gerda Solomon explained:

"My father did eventually get compensation for loss of the house, loss of the factory and loss of livelihood. It was not easy and it took years. I remember he had to get documentation which was very difficult because everything had been burnt by the Gestapo. There were no relations alive to verify anything. He had to write to the Czech Government and a Czech lawyer in London. There was a problem of language because he did not speak Czech: in the Sudeten part of Czechoslovakia where we came from everyone spoke German. My father had to go to London, I remember, and he had to swear affidavits because there was no-one to verify the claim.

"My father was disappointed at how little he got. After all the hard work and all that he had lost, it was a drop in the ocean. Had we been Germans it would have been much easier and the sum would have been far greater. All the same it made a difference to my parents: when we came over we had 15/- (75p) and a suitcase and we were living in a Czech hostel all during the war, so whatever it was it had to be better than that.

"I did not get anything for loss of education because I was too young and had not really started school. In later years we tried to get something because a new rule came out but I reckon it would have cost us more in solicitors' fees than we would ever have got so we did not pursue it."

For those who came from Austria compensation was also slow and relatively difficult to come by. Gina Gerson, who came over as a young girl without her parents, applied reluctantly in 1957. She was persuaded and helped to do so by the United Restitution Organisation in London. She says she received a pittance in 1958 and was much upset at "being granted so much for each month of my parents' incarceration". Under recent new legislation (1980s) people from Austria have been able to apply for a pension: Gina Gerson says she was turned down "for incomprehensible reasons". She continues: "I am convinced this whole belated change of heart by the Austrian Government is a big con trick and publicity exercise following the Waldheim outcry. To my knowledge nobody who has recently applied has been granted a pension." This is an understandable view from one still feeling a deep sense of loss of family and childhood. However, for the record, it is important to say that at least one person in the group interviewed is now receiving a pension from Austria after paying in a nominal lump sum in much the same way as was asked of some applicants to Germany.

There is some evidence to suggest that the amount of compensation and the ease with which it was obtained depended not only on where people came from but also where they settled. Again, however, many factors have to be taken into consideration, not least among them being access to advice and help from appropriately informed lawyers.

Geoffrey (Günter) Faerber spent four years in a concentration camp between the ages of 12 and 16. He said:

"I applied for restitution while I was in England before I left for Israel in 1948 — I think the first little bit came in 1960-63 ... I received no compensation for loss of education because I was a Polish citizen. I had no education after my first five years, whereas my wife who had a full English education received money (for loss of education in Germany) — a paradox.

"I was only accepted as being entitled to restitution because I was registered in Berlin. I got money for being in a concentration camp and for loss of parents. No pension. A lump sum — altogether £4,000 over 15 years. Camp money backdated to 3 September 1939. Two years later for loss of parents, not family. A few years later for furniture — nothing for my father's business because it was Polish.

"I went back to Poland in 1963 and met the employees in my father's business. Marta, the woman who had hidden the gold coins my father kept for us to live on, had gone to Germany. I went to Germany a year or two later and she gave me a full report in front of a solicitor of everything that had gone — though she did not know the actual amounts. Although the Germans took our possessions away, because it was in Poland I got nothing.

"As the law stands only people who were persecuted from 1937 can claim. I was not persecuted until 1939. The Israelis had a different arrangement and Israelis who had lived in Poland did better than people who claimed from Great Britain, France and other countries."

In the final analysis, how well or badly any individual came off in the scale of reparations is impossible to assess objectively. So many factors played a part. To some securing their claim was perhaps part of a duty to establish the fact of the loss and bereavement they had suffered:

Else Schott: "I did go back to pursue claims on my father's estate and I kept wondering who had pushed my father into the gas oven."

Ilse Lewen: "I personally had no feelings either way. I knew we were entitled to have that money ... it just came and I put it in the bank. My cousins in Israel who had it for the same reason — loss of education and loss of parents — wouldn't touch it; they said it's blood money. They put it into the kibbutz and opened a library in memory of both their parents.''

Money cannot ''make good again'' the destruction of families or compensate for years of imprisonment and suffering in concentration camps. However, for the survivors the compensation they received meant, in many cases, the difference between being just survivors and becoming once again the providers they had been in the past: providers for their families, for the community in which they live and, in a wider sense, providers of income and employment to the country of their adoption.

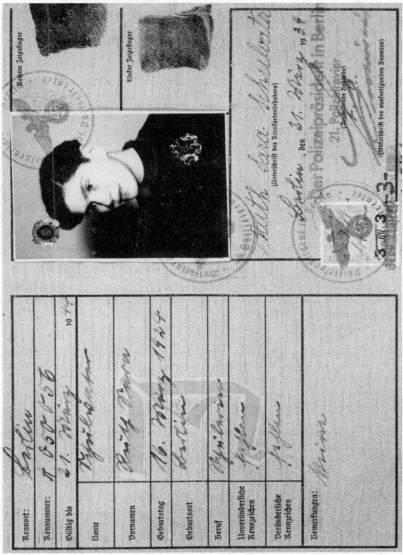

Details of passport belonging to Ruth Price (neé Schulvater). March 1939.

N.B. By German law, every Jewish woman had to take the name of Sara and every man the name of Israel. (See the illustration on page 95.)

18

The Next Generation

Despite their growing integration into the industrial and academic life of the city, and into the local Jewish community, the middle aged and elderly refugees remained socially much apart. Typical were the bridge circles of the Continental ladies, while their husbands gathered together to play Skat.[1] It was to take another generation to break down the barriers.

Twelve people of the next generation were interviewed, all of them British born, one or both of whose parents were refugees from the Nazis. This number does not include younger people, now approaching the end of their schooldays. Their parents had come here as young children, and particularly in the cases where only one parent was born abroad, their children seemed barely aware of their foreign origin. They appeared surprised to be questioned and had little to say.

Those in their twenties and thirties were more articulate, but they cannot be considered representative. They all came from homes where the parents had stabilised themselves in their new country and succeeded in their careers. Their children were forging ahead likewise.

There must be many others who did not come forward for interview. Many have left Birmingham, some for Israel. Others must have been assimilated into the general community and lost to Jewish life.

There were also the sad cases whose stories remain untold, except perhaps to doctors and social workers. Among these were the children of ill-considered marriages undertaken to obtain British nationality, or simply to combat loneliness, resulting sometimes in unhappiness and even mental disorders for both parents and children. These children are the victims of the Nazis, no less than those who perished in Europe.

Yet quite apart from such extreme examples, most of the people interviewed, born into stable families and accustomed from their earliest years to the English way of life, complained of feelings of insecurity. "My father's experiences ... (in a concentration camp) ... made me aware of the precariousness of Jewish life. I'm always conscious of what can happen from day to day. I've never had the urge to buy property like many of my friends who begin to think about buying a flat as soon as they leave university. I'd rather be free to get away whenever I like. For this reason

I support Ajex[2] and I'm active as a member of the Board of Deputies[3] defence against aggressive tactics."

Of the twelve people interviewed, three claimed to feel wholly English, six English and Jewish in equal proportion, two more Jewish than English. One young woman, who had married and settled in Israel, said she had felt Jewish in England and English in Israel! After five years and the birth of two children, however, she was beginning to feel Israeli. Another young woman, both of whose parents came from the Continent, received an unpleasant shock on this subject. "I had always considered myself English. One day an acquaintance pointed out to my husband, 'we've both married German girls'. So although I saw myself as very English, others obviously did not." Many felt that they were "different". "I never felt I belonged anywhere properly. My home was different, the food was different and my parents' attitude to life was different, even from the English-born parents of my Jewish friends."

The use of the German language was an added factor in the feeling of "difference" and the consciousness of roots lying elsewhere. Where both parents were refugees they spoke German between themselves "especially when we weren't supposed to understand" They seldom spoke German to the children once they had started school, and if they did the children answered in English. Only one boy regretted that he had not been brought up to be bilingual. Several studied German at school. "I practised with my grandmother, but not with my parents." The daughter of a committed member of the Christian Church, who had suffered because three of her grandparents were Jewish, hopes to train as a minister of the United Reformed Church after she has finished her degree course. Her dissertation for her final examination is to be a study of the attitude of the German Protestant Church to anti-semitism between 1933 and 1945. "She is linking her career with her family history", remarked her father, "so there is an influence that seems to be preserved in the next generation as well."

All but two of the people interviewed had been brought up in the Jewish tradition, although they varied greatly in degrees of orthodoxy. One young man, now a Reform student-rabbi, had always been interested in Jewish matters and saw the synagogue as his second home. A young doctor affirmed, "I could never lightly throw aside the beliefs so many, including my grandparents, had died for." A third, married and in his thirties, felt that he now identified more closely with his Jewish heritage than the secular culture in which he had been reared. "I have gravitated to a fast-growing Jewish community on the outskirts of London. It's very different from Birmingham where we are very few in number and it's easy to become assimilated with the majority culture. I find I am becoming more orthodox." By contrast, to another young man his Judaism "was only a background feeling. It doesn't affect me. I can't quite get away, but it's not relevant."

Without exception, all felt a strong affinity to Israel, "the means by which the Jews can avoid the disadvantages from which our parents suffered … a lot of misery could have been avoided if the Jews had had a homeland." They did not all wish to live there, often practical realities made this impossible. Yet one girl felt guilty about her comfortable English lifestyle. Perhaps Israel needed her more. The young woman, who has made *Aliyah* (emigrated to Israel), explained, "I was influenced by *Habonim* (a youth movement with strong Zionist affiliations) but my family background was the main thing. Only in Israel can I live a normal life in a normal society. Here I can stand up for myself."

Even those with only tenuous connections with their Jewish background felt the pull. A young sailor on leave after months in a submarine wanted a holiday "somewhere in the sunshine. I just happened to choose Israel. Somehow I found myself at Yad Vashem (the memorial to the Holocaust) and I felt all that my father and his parents had suffered."

Even more poignant was the visit of the young doctor, whose mother's family had been completely wiped out. "I felt Yad Vashem was the proper place to pay homage to my grandparents. I got the archivists to put on a search, but they couldn't find out exactly which camp they had died in. But they had some record of them and the whole experience became very real and close, not just something you read about. Then I went to the Memorial with its Everlasting Light and the names of the dead in all the camps. I said *Kaddish* (prayer in memory of the dead).

"I really felt I was communicating with my grandparents. The next time I went to Israel I was able to take my wife and introduce her to them. I told them about all that had happened since my last visit."

The student-rabbi took an unusual view. "I value the State of Israel, but my roots subconsciously go back to Central Europe, so I find my links with Europe stronger than with Israel. Having no access to my parents' childhood, I feel I've been robbed, something is missing. I have a sense of living in an 'after life'. Everything in the former life was golden, times were better ... Since I've been working in the United States especially, I feel completely British and Jewish, yet at the same time European in my love of nature, the arts, walking. This is the England of the refugee community and this is what I completely identify with. Perhaps this is my way of coming to terms with my parents' experience."

The children's attitude to the German people was ambivalent, and in some cases less tolerant than that of their parents. One distrusted even young people of his own generation, although he admitted it was irrational. With regard to their parents' or grandparents' contemporaries, all found it impossible not to speculate on what they had been doing under the Nazi regime. None wished in any way to be identified with Germany. "When people remark on my name, I always have to make it quite clear it is a German-Jewish name. I don't want to be taken for a German and I would never want to visit Germany, Austria or Hungary." Only the student-rabbi harked back nostalgically to the Germany of happier times, "the Germany of the 1920s in which my parents grew up. It's a love-hate relationship. I can't help being moved by the German national anthem and when I see a film about Germany at this period, I hate the dialogue, yet the setting, the furniture and the food seem familiar and I think I could have lived there."

His sister, likewise, "did not feel repulsed. A great deal of good came out of Germany and German culture had a great influence on our home."

Common to every child of refugee origin was the stress, sometimes almost obsessive, laid on education, a common enough attitude where parents are anxious that their children should have advantages they themselves lacked. "My parents weren't interested in non-academic matters.

They frowned on discos. They introduced us to all sorts of new ideas, theatres, visits abroad, but the importance of education was the be-all and end-all. They pushed me and I got further than I would have done." Her brother had been expected to follow the family tradition of medicine, but he found he was academically unsuitable. He changed course and achieved great success. Nevertheless he felt a sense of guilt that he had not taken up the career expected of him and he felt that his parents should have encouraged him in other directions.

Some of the children felt that they had lacked practical advice on their careers, because of their parents' unfamiliarity with English ways and with the English educational system. "They felt all that mattered was that I should get to university, but the subjects I studied did not lead to employment and I had to retrain." The son of a concentration camp prisoner felt quite otherwise. "My father's experience gave me a lot of practical knowledge. In fact I think I have benefited in having a wider outlook than most people. Both my Jewish and my non-Jewish friends showed little interest in what went on outside Birmingham. I always wanted to know about current events. In that way I was different. I was more worldly."

In most homes, the experience of the parents was discussed quite openly. "They talked about the past at every mealtime", claimed one daughter, to the astonishment of her parents, and even her brother. He, on the contrary, felt the day to day details had been rather glossed over. "I used to feel apprehension about what had really happened. I had dreadful imaginings." By contrast, to a student reading history at university, his father's past was "purely academic. His story wasn't hidden, it was just not talked about".

Another father managed to speak of his formative years in a concentration camp in a comparatively light-hearted way, stressing the amusing incidents and omitting the terrible punishments he received. The children grew up to respect his courage and resolution which had been so cruelly fostered by hardship. Generally parents and children appeared to have very close relationships. "I admire my mother. I often think of her leaving home at the age of sixteen to go to a strange school in a strange country. It makes me realise how lucky I am to have freedom of speech and freedom to practise my Judaism."

Where the story was particularly tragic, the children felt instinctively that it was better not to ask about the "bad times", but as they grew up their parents took them increasingly into their confidence.

"My parents are very tolerant of all religions ... they have influenced me to appreciate other people's beliefs." A sympathetic understanding for minorities seems to have been passed on by all parents to the children, although one person admitted to feeling prejudiced against those who came to England for purely economic reasons, and not because of persecution. "In the 1950s and 1960s the doors were open — but not to the Jews in the 1930s who were in danger of losing their lives."

"One of the great difficulties of trying to understand the Holocaust is how a whole race of people can be condemned, not for anything they did, but for what they were. It's easy in this country to pick out anyone with a dark skin; these are the people who are suffering at the moment. Nowadays, especially with the second and third generations, Jews blend in with the general population." Yet, as the young doctor pointed out, there is danger here. "People who are otherwise well educated are astonishingly ignorant about Jews. My colleagues are often amazed when I tell them I'm a Jew, just because I seem so normal. I don't blame them. It's the system."

Nobody seemed to have experienced any serious anti-semitism. "But there's a good deal on the campus", said a student, "thinly veiled as anti-Zionism ... I am continually alarmed by the lack of understanding and knowledge of what happened in Germany in the thirties, although it is the most significant point of modern history. Now Jews are being accused of collaborating with the Nazis, or we are being told, 'it didn't happen'. We must make sure everybody knows exactly what did happen, so that it will never occur again."

"I always know the children of refugees", concluded the student-rabbi. "There's a kind of bond. We're all over-achievers. There's a constant struggle to reach the goal for which our parents survived. I'm always searching why I was allowed to live, while others died. Yet as survivors we have an optimistic outlook on life, a sense of hopefulness. Survival leads me to see a rebirth after such a terrible tragedy. Perhaps if we work hard for it we can have 'the golden time' again."

Notes

1. Skat. A three handed card game popular in Germany.
2. Ajex – The Association of Jewish Ex-Servicemen.
3. The Board of Deputies of British Jews developed from an inter-synagogal committee of 1760. It includes delegates from all synagogues and Jewish organisations and is regarded as an Anglo-Jewish parliament.

19

Conclusion

In the early 1950s, CBF was on the point of being disbanded, its task apparently fulfilled.[1] Those fortunate enough to have escaped from the Nazis had mostly settled down and rebuilt their lives. As for the indigenous Jewish Community, the war years, the experience of dealing with the victims of Hitler and, above all, the knowledge of the Holocaust, had produced a more compassionate understanding. Added to this, the establishment of the State of Israel brought a sense of security and pride to the Diaspora, encouraging a more outward-looking attitude.

But before the winding-up process was completed, the Russian invasion of Hungary in 1956 resulted in some 1,800 Jewish refugees arriving in this country to be followed (almost immediately) as a consequence of the Suez crisis by an approximately similar number of Jews from Egypt. Many of these needed assistance and an appeal was launched. The Jewish Community as a whole hastened to welcome all the new arrivals and ease them as quickly as possible into their strange environment.

The refugees from Egypt in 1956 differed in every way from those of the 1930s. The latter had either suffered themselves, or seen their relatives and friends attacked, beaten up and persecuted. This horror had reacted on their health and emotions, leaving their nerves raw and sensitive. The newcomers from Egypt, on the other hand, once they had adjusted to the cold climate, the loss of their homes and, in some cases, of their possessions, quickly settled, and many, especially the businessmen, were soon making a real contribution to the community at large.

The case of the refugees from Hungary was rather different. "I received a call from the CBF Head Office asking me to investigate the condition of some Jewish refugees in a reception centre for Hungarians in Hednesford in Staffordshire", said Ruth Simmons. She found them in wretched plight, subject to harrassment by non-Jewish Hungarians.

The Russian invasion had been followed by a general uprising and among those fleeing for genuine reasons were many undesirables who had taken advantage of the free-for-all to scramble across the frontier in search of a better way of life. The small Jewish group had almost all been victims of the German invasion of Hungary in 1944. They had been in concentration camps, where some had seen their parents and children perish.

As survivors, they had been endeavouring to rebuild their lives, often with new partners, and now they were forced to uproot themselves again, this time to escape from the Russians. It was essential to get them away from the Reception Centre as soon as possible and this Ruth Simmons was able to do, with the assistance of the CBF and local friends.

Ruth Simmons with her husband Ernst Wolf and her son Jonathan, 1970.

In 1968, a number of young Czechs, mostly students at the University of Prague, had come, under the relatively liberal regime of Prime Minister Dubjek, to spend a summer vacation in Britain. Suddenly they received messages from their parents telling them that the Russians had overthrown their government and warning them not to return home. Again, CBF arranged the necessary permits with the Home Office and negotiated the continuation of their studies. A number of them came to Birmingham, where they were enabled to complete their professional training.

In the 1970s, with the rise of the Ayatollah Khomeini, pressure began to increase on the Jews of Iran. Communities which had been settled for centuries found themselves in acute danger. CBF help again enabled some Iranian students to complete their courses at the University of Birmingham and, in some cases, rescue their families.

Nor has the story of the refugees from Nazi Europe reached its end. The psychological trauma runs deep, even if overlaid by the humdrum activity of everyday life in a free country. In some cases old age has re-opened painful wounds. An elderly lady, happily settled in this city for over forty years, happened to live near the scene of the Handsworth Riots of 1985. She cried out in terror that the Nazis had returned and could not be re-assured. Such cases need special care. A National Centre for the Psycho-Social Support for Survivors of the Holocaust has been set up recently in Israel with the help of a grant from CBF. CBF are also assisting in the establishment of a Jewish Mental Health Centre in London. These will be able to offer survivors the help they require.[2]

Many hands have been linked in this long work of rescue. Throughout, CBF has been in the forefront, guided locally for the past half-century by Ruth Simmons, who, in her turn, has received the unfailing support of her husband, Ernest Wolf. Not content with her work for refugees, she has been for many years Secretary to the Midland Council for the Preparatory Training of the Disabled, for which in 1978 she was appointed MBE.

There must be hundreds of people who owe their lives, or the quality of their lives, to the courage and tenacity of Ruth Simmons.

References

1. Joseph H. Oscar. *Forty years on. A short history of CBF. 1933-1973.*
2. *Jewish Chronicle* 26 June 1987.

REFUGEES IN BIRMINGHAM

Jewish refugee children from Vienna and Berlin being entertained to tea at the Jewish Communal Hall, Ellis Street, after their arrival in Birmingham yesterday.

Refugee children being entertained to tea in Birmingham (*Birmingham Mail*, 30 December 1938)

A party of Jewish children who were expelled from Germany and have been living in a neutral zone on the German-Polish frontier, arrived in London yesterday. They are seen disembarking from the ss. Warszawa.

Jewish children arriving in London (*The Times*, 16 February 1939)

20

Postscript

The following letter arrived just as *Survivors* was going to press. The recipient, Ellen Ehrlich, formerly of Königsburg, East Prussia, was forced to leave her High School in 1938 when she was thirteen years old. Although her parents were fortunate enough to escape to England just before the war, she and her brother suffered much hardship.

Nearly fifty years later she received an invitation to attend a class reunion at her German school. She refused. "I was very angry that the writer did not say a word about what had happened to me, or even indicate that she was pleased I was alive."

After some weeks she received the letter, given below*, from one of her classmates. Despite some ominous undertones it seems to show a growing compassion and desire to do something to amend the past.

22 December 1987

Dear Ellen

I doubt if you can remember me. We were together in a class in Königsberg at one time; thin, fair and short hair, squinting a little, with a rather flat nose caused in an accident — in other words not a pretty girl. I was, therefore, rather lonely and was always pleased when you and I walked together on the way to and from school. I liked you very much.

You did not return to school suddenly. I comprehended only gradually what tragic events must have happened to you. I learned about the whole extent of the persecution of the Jews only after the war, as probably most people here. It distresses me still that all this could occur and I, who was a witness of those times and the Hitler-madness, could also not understand that many people deny the holocaust really happened.

I heard from Greta who traced your address as a result of much effort, that you are apprehensive about a class reunion. I can understand this but I would like to let you know what took place here as far as you are concerned. Ilsa — also tall and thin at the time — read an extract from your letter and found some fine, fitting words regarding your decision (not to come to the reunion) and all of us accepted it in thoughtful silence. I think you ought to know that we are not indifferent to you and we would have liked to have you in our midst, even though you were amongst us only a short time.

There is, of course, a great difference when one is forced to leave one's home when one has started the war or, like you, been driven towards mass murder. You ought to know that anti-semitism still exists in some circles. It is understandable that you do not want to expose yourself to it, dear Ellen.

I experienced a little of the Nazi power when the Gestapo searched our home as my mother took an interest in anthroposophy and in the Christian-Gemeinschaft, both of which were banned. They came to confiscate books, but that is relatively harmless.

Dear Ellen, I wish you a happy and peaceful New Year and send you fond greetings.

Yours Anna

This is not the only communication of this sort sent recently to the Birmingham Jewish History Research Group. Some students from the University of Heidelberg have requested copies of our tapes, and a history teacher from the Rheinland has asked for details of our researches so that he "may teach his pupils the truth".

* To preserve anonymity, names in this letter have been changed.

Refugee Contributors

Werner ABRAHAMS — Germany
Henry ARON — Born Poland, husband of Lily
Lily ARON — Berlin, née SOBERSKY, died 1987
Ernst ARIS — East Prussia
Joachim AUERBACH — Berlin
Lucy BENEDIKT — Austria
Louise BERGMAN — Germany, née FREUDENBERGER
Magda BLOOM — Hungary, née FIXLER, by adoption HESSELBERG
Bernard BORKON — East Prussia
Paul DAVID — Czechoslovakia
André DRUCKER — Austria, died 1987
Martin DEUTSCHKRON — Berlin, died 1982
Anneliese EISNER — Berlin, née ROSENGERG
Ellen EHRLICH — East Prussia, née RAWRAWAY
W.E. — Austria
Elli FAERBER — Berlin, née SPIELMAN, wife of Geoffrey
Geoffrey FAERBER — Poland, né Günter FAERBER
Henry FINKE — East Prussia, né Heinz FINKE
Iolanthe FOX — Austria, née KLEINER, sister of Helga LOEB
Henry FREELAND — Germany né Heinz FRIEDLANDER died 1986
Helen FREELAND — Germany, née SANDERS, wife of Henry
Emmy GOLDING — Germany, née KAUFMANN
Harry GOLDMAN — Germany
Susan GOLOMBOK — Hungary, née HEIMLER
Rudi HART — Germany, né HERTZ
Nellie HEWSPEAR — Austria, née SCHONFELD
Peter HEGEDUS — Hungary
Gina GERSON — Austria, née Regina BAUER, wife of Frank
Frank GERSON — Germany, né Franz Gerson
John GRENVILLE — Germany, né Hans-Jürgen GUHRAUER
Fischel GROSSMAN — Galicia
Joe HIRTENSTEIN — Czechoslovakia
Mindu HORNICK — Hungary, née KLEIN
Hilde HUNT — Austria, née POLITZER
Renate JACOBS — Germany, née GERSON, sister of Frank Gerson
Herman KAY — Austria, born Poland, né KIRSCHENBAUM
KATE KOBER — Germany, née SILBERBERG
Berthold KORNHAUSER — Berlin, husband of Stella, brother of Gerhardt
Stella KORNHAUSER — Austria, née LUSTIG
Gerhardt KORNHAUSER — Berlin, husband of Blanca
Blanca KORNHAUSER — Austria, née ADLER
Henry KRONHEIM — Germany, né Heinz KRONHEIM
Ilse LEWEN — Germany
L.H. — East Prussia
L.V. — East Prussia
Liana LESSER — Czechoslovakia, née BLUM
Henrietta LEYTON — Austria, née SPITZER, later Hetty PEDHAZUR
Sophie LÉVI — Germany, died 1978
Frank LINDEN — Germany , né Franz LINDENSTEIN, husband of Herta
Herta LINDEN — Germany, née AUFHAUSER
Irma LINDENSTEIN — Germany, née MAYER, mother of Frank, widow of Louis
Ernst LITTHAUER — Berlin

Helga LOEB — Austria, née KLEINER, sister of Iolanthe FOX
Relly MARX — Germany
Lola MATE — Hungary, née VAGDA, (first married name KERTESZ)
Gerda MENDELSOHN — Germany, née STRAUSS
Lotte MUNTZ — Germany, née KANTER, wife of Walter, died 1984
Walter MUNTZ — Germany
W.N. — Austria
Berta PRAIS — Germany, born Poland, née KAUFFMANN
Samuel PRAIS — Germany born Poland, husband of Berta
Ruth PRICE — Berlin, née SCHULVATER
Frank REINACH — Germany, né Franz Reinach, died 1985
Ilse REINSTEIN — Czechoslavikia, née SONNENSCHEIN
Emil RICH — Austria, né REICH, died 1987
Kurt ROSE — Berlin, né ROSENBERG
Margarete RUBENSTEIN — Austria, née KORNFELD, died 1987
Gerhard SALINGER — Berlin, husband of Hilde, died 1986
Hilde SALINGER — Berlin, née MOOS
Sonja SHINDLER — Czechoslovakia, née ECKSTEIN, wife of Kenneth
Kenneth SHINDLER — Berlin, né SCHINDLER
Else SCHOTT — Germany, née ISAAKSOHN, mother of Walter
Walter SCHOTT — Germany
Heinz SHIRE — Germany, né SCHEYER, husband of Ruth
Ruth SHIRE — Germnay, née COHEN
EMMI SIMSON — Germany, née BLEIER
Charlotte SINGER — Germany, née BODLANDER
Gerda SOLOMON — Czecholslovakia, née LOEBL
Manuel SPIELMAN — Poland, father of Elli FAERBER
Walter STRANZ — Berlin
Ruth S. — Berlin
Berta STRAUSS — Germany née STERZELBACH, wife of Kossi
Kossi STRAUSS — Germany, cousin of Gerda MENDELSOHN, died 1984
Henry WARNER — Berlin, né WOHLAUER, husband of Ursula
Ursula WARNER — Berlin, née DROPLOWITZ
Eric WEISS — Germany
Joseph WINROOPE — Poland
Ernst WOLF — Germany
A.X. — Germany

211

Bibliography

Bentwich N. *I Understand the Risks* (1950)
Bentwich N. *They Found Refuge* (1956)
Essinger A. *Bunce Court School* 1933-1943
Gershon K. *We Came as Children* (1966)
Gilbert M. *The Holocaust* (1986)
Levine H. *Scrapbook**
Sharf A. *The British Press and Jews under Nazi Rule* (1964)
Sherman A.J. *Island Refuge* (1973)
Spielman M. *The Stricken Tree — Memoirs* (Unpublished)*
Steven A. *The Dispossessed* (1975)
Wasserstein B. *Britain and the Jews of Europe. 1939-1945* (1971)

Birmingham Council for Refugees. *Five Year Survey. 1939-1944*
Bloomsbury House. *The Care of German and Austrian Refugees* August 1942
Elpis Lodge Scrapbook 1940-1948
Refugee Children's Movement Limited. *Annual Reports 1939-1942*
Minutes of Singers Hill Synagogue 1933-1939
Minutes of the Birmingham Refugee Club 1939-1943

Birmingham Post*
Birmingham Mail*
Jewish Chronicle*
AJR Information (Journal of the Association of Jewish Refugees)

Further secondary sources are noted individually in the references to the relevant chapters.

* Available in the Local Studies Department, Birmingham Central Library

Index

213

214